£4.99

CW00501647

THE JESUS PHENOMENON

How did it originate?
What is the hidden secret?

Greg Rigby

Strategic Book Publishing and Rights Co.

Strategic Book Publishing and Rights Co., LLC
USA I Singapore

For information about special discounts for bulk purchases, please contact Strategic Book Publishing and Rights Co. Special Sales, at bookorder@sbpra.net.

ISBN: 978-1-68181-323-3

Book Design: Suzanne Kelly

DEDICATION

This book is dedicated to all those in search of truth.

*Special thanks to Frank Fletcher and Sarah
who helped me, and to Robert Seaton
for starting me on the path.*

TABLE OF CONTENTS

Greg Rigby

INTRODUCTION

The results of our previous research were published in *The God Secret* where we showed how the mysteries of the Egyptian religion had grown out of interpretations from the links that were imaginatively formulated between the stars that revolve around the northern pole position. In the Egyptian tradition, these stars were known as *the imperishable stars* or *the stars that never set.*

The analysis was conclusive and we were able to show that the ancient Egyptian mysteries had been carried through into many aspects of Christianity and in large part, were duplicated in the Book of Revelation.

At the end of the book, we confidently proclaimed that Christianity had grown out of the old Egyptian Religion that had been violently suppressed and condemned by the Hebrew hierarchy since the time of Moses and that it could well have emanated from an underground minority who wished to resurrect the old beliefs in a more up-to-date form. We went even further and stated that as there is no tangible proof that anyone named Jesus Christ actually existed and that the entire story of Jesus may be an elaborate fiction.

In this book, we would like to take another look at this broad brush elimination of the Jesus Christ figure and examine (with some scepticism) the possibility that there was an individual that the Christ story was based on.

Logic tells us that an incarnate Almighty God, who controls the power to create everything in the Universe including each individual life, would be able to see all things including the future. At the stage in time when the Judeo/Christian God is said to have chosen one infinitesimally small planet from all the billions of planets in the Universe, and condemned the forebears of humanity to be banished from the Garden of Eden, the implications of such actions would have already been clear to him/her/it.

Despite that, sometime later Christians tell us that God sent His 'son' in human guise to be murdered by humans in reparation for the sins of disobedience attributed to Adam and Eve and to thus get the Human Race get off the hook.

He/it had given humanity free will but because we hadn't used it the way that He/it found appropriate, He/it had decided to intervene to save us from ourselves.

This God sounds like a being who is altruistic on the one hand but self centred and selfish on the other. He/it is projected as a being full of infinite love but His/its actions betray ultimate violence and punishment to all who are not subservient to His/its will.

Why would such an infinitely aware God interrupt the pattern of normal evolution with an altruistic gesture that would help save humanity from its inherited condemnation and create a route to eternal salvation, oftentimes prosecuted by violence? Why did the race of people into which the 'saviour' of humanity was born reject him? More importantly, why did such an all-knowing deity chose this route from the infinite number of possibilities available? Why did God need the gesture?

If this God entity exists, is He/it as fallible as us humans and does He/it suffer from anger, loneliness and pride as the scriptures would have us believe? Or, is the story as illogical as it sounds and without any real foundation?

A long time ago, the service manager of a well known car dealership proclaimed, "There's always some truth in every story." This was a man who met people in the early days of motor cars when there were manual chokes, manual window winders and the car owner needed to insert a key to unlock the door. One customer, who complained that her car cut out after several miles, was asked to drive it by this Service Manager and he discovered that she pulled out the manual choke and used it as a place to hang her handbag. Small wonder that the car did not function correctly. This Service Manager's story stuck with the author and since then his proclamation has been one of the principals that have guided all our research into the mysteries that surround the foundations of organised religion. Because of this, and despite the obvious illogicality of the Christ story, we believe that it is likely that there is some truth in the story. Two thousand years ago something must have happened that was the basis for Christianity and for the deeply persuasive nature of the doctrine it continues to propose.

In ancient times, communication was slow. The stories about and beliefs of those with great influence were incorporated into monuments for everyone to see and read. Centres of learning and official record keepers kept accounts on scrolls or they were sometimes written in stone. Most stories, however, were passed from person to person and suffered all the problems of distortion inherent in such a method. With regard to the Christians, a large number of documents were written after the time of Christ, many based on hearsay. More than three hundred years after the so-called life of Jesus, Emperor Constantine congregated a group of bishops (so called) in Nicaea, and any distortion problem was attacked by assembling one group of documents into a single text, which has become known as the New Testament and which incorporates what have become known as the Canonical Gospels. Some of the writings circulating at the time were omitted and came to be known as the Apocryphal or Gnostic gospels. The New Testament was then described as the Holy Word of God so that no one would dream of questioning it, never mind altering it and at the time of its publication, it was accompanied by a creed that every believer was invited to repeat on a regular basis.

> I believe in one God, the Father almighty, maker of heaven and earth, of all things visible and invisible.
> I believe in one Lord Jesus Christ, the Only Begotten Son of God, born of the Father before all ages. God from God, Light from Light, true God from true God, begotten, not made, consubstantial with the Father; through him, all things were made. For us men and for our salva-

tion he came down from heaven, and by the Holy Spirit was incarnate of the Virgin Mary and became man.

For our sake he was crucified under Pontius Pilate, he suffered death and was buried, and rose again on the third day in accordance with the Scriptures. He ascended into heaven and is seated at the right hand of the Father. He will come again in glory to judge the living and the dead and his kingdom will have no end.

I believe in the Holy Spirit, the Lord, the giver of life, who proceeds from the Father and the Son, who with the Father and the Son is adored and glorified, who has spoken through the prophets.

I believe in one, holy, catholic and apostolic Church. I confess one Baptism for the forgiveness of sins and I look forward to the resurrection of the dead and the life of the world to come. Amen.

This move to consolidate the faith was accompanied by the repetitive incantation of the creed by priests and by the inculcation of stories into canticles, ballads and poems that have been reproduced by monks, priests and bards over the centuries.

We will attempt to examine the evidence and investigate the various possibilities to help us find a realistic basis for the Jesus Christ story and for the existence of the personality that is portrayed in the New Testament Gospels and this person's claim to the title Son of God. The possibility that a real person existed around whom the legend was woven will be examined. In doing so, we will attempt to attribute a legitimate basis for his universally proclaimed divine inheritance.

CHAPTER 1

The Written Evidence

Several places need to be examined for evidence of Jesus Christ. These include The New Testament, the Talmud, any Roman records or bibliographies and the Nag Hammadi and/or Dead Sea Scrolls. In addition, we will look for other historical references that may have been passed down through time that could have been created and formed at that time and which have retained their original integrity.

The Canonical Gospels

It is generally accepted by historians, that the Jesus stories were written variously between 50 CE and 100 CE and that they were written in Greek. Up until that time it is claimed that there was an oral tradition that was either folkloric[1] or rabbinic in nature[2]. This would indicate that persons able to write in Greek were the authors, which would probably exclude the kind of simple folk described in the Gospels as the apostles. There is dispute amongst Christian scholars, who may take a biased perspective, and historians as to whether the Gospels are accurate descriptions of the life of Jesus or alternatively whether they are simply testimonies of faith written many years after the years they describe.

It is generally agreed that the nativity, the baptism of Christ and the crucifixion are all based on a strongly proclaimed oral tradition. These events are central to the claim that Jesus Christ was divine and they are outlined, with variations, in three of the

---

1 *History of the Synoptic Tradition*, Rudolf Bultmann
2 *The Reliability of the Gospel Tradition*, Birger Gerhardsson

1

four canonical or synoptic gospels. No evidence, other than that recounted in these gospels can be found of these events.

There are at least fifty-eight known gospels or apocrypha, which were believed to have been written in the first and second centuries CE or later, all of which are based on oral tradition. The current biblical cannon incorporating the Gospels of Matthew, Mark, Luke and John were recognised by the Church under Pope Innocent I in the fifth century CE. This followed their previous recognition by the Council of Nicea in 325 CE and the Council of Rome in 382 CE.

The Council of Nicea was convened by the Emperor Constantine who invited 1800 bishops although only 250 and 300 bishops actually attended. The principal purpose of the council was to resolve the disagreement between the Church of Alexandria and the Arians concerning the nature of the Son in relationship to the Father.

The council was in favour of the Alexandrian point of view that both the Son and the Father had no beginning. The Arians believed that the Son had a beginning, and because of this belief, they were declared heretics.

The Gospel attributed to John established Jesus as Logos: "In the beginning was the Word, and the Word was with God, and the Word was God." This proclamation provides a direct connection to ancient Egyptian beliefs, which connection is further exposed in the Book of Revelation, a work that is also attributed by some to the same author, John. An in-depth investigation of this work might help us unravel the significance of these claims.

In none of the four Gospels is there a single claim about any event that can be separately confirmed. Even significant historic claims such as the slaughter of the innocents are not recorded elsewhere.

If we examine the actions of politicians and church leaders today, we can see that their conduct and proclamations are designed to further their own particular view of how things should be and to persuade others to see the legitimacy of their cause, no matter how spurious or lamentable. Such political thought and manoeuvring would have been equally visible at the beginning of the Christian era. By the time that the four Canonical Gospels became legitimised and all other possible versions had been sidelined or rejected, the church was a formidable power base. Is it a co-incidence that the Synoptic Gospels, those of Matthew Mark and Luke, include a passage where Peter proclaims Jesus as the Messiah and Jesus in turn declares Peter, who had based himself in Rome, to be the rock' on which he will build his church? The Gospels are short documents that purport to be documentaries of Jesus Christ's life and teachings. It may even be significant that these pronouncements, which helped secure the Church's headquarters in Rome (rather than Alexandria, which was competing with Rome as the centre of the emerging Christian theology) and its leader's infallible link to God Almighty, is made in three of the four documents.

A more in-depth analysis of the way the Canonical Gospels contribute to the unravelling the mystery of Jesus Christ is made in Chapter 10.

Against Heresies

In the second century, a bishop named Irenaeus wrote a four-volume treatise entitled *Refutation and Overthrow of Gnosis, falsely so called*. This learned person was born in Smyrna (now Izmir in Turkey) in 130 CE and is known to have spent time in Lyons and Rome. His book, written circa 180 CE is useful because it tells us of all the things that early Christian theologians identified as a threat to their religious formulations and beliefs.

At this same time, Clement of Alexandria (150-215 CE) was teaching that men had mistakenly believed the Sun, the Moon and the other heavenly bodies to be gods. He was alluding to the influence of ancient Egyptian beliefs but his proposition had little effect on his most prominent student Origen (185–254 AD) who wrote:

> *Do you not see that the dragon fought with the angels, and when he was hard pressed he was thrown*

down from heaven? As he fell he drew with him a third of the stars. It is likely that these stars were divine powers which had revolted with him, and they were borne down with the dragon, as Isaiah said, How the morning star fell from Heaven which perpetuated the same claim.

At this time, Alexandria and Rome were competing to be the rightful hub of the Christian movement. The Alexandrian philosophy was akin to and leant heavily on the Greek philosophies that had been taught by Pythagoras and Plato, where the soul comes from the heavens and returns there at death. Origen in particular studied astronomy and sought to explain early Church teachings in the context of a heaven full of stars. He included Hellenistic (ancient Greek) theories on the life and nature of stars into his cosmology. For this he was eventually condemned as a heretic by Rome but he was successful in incorporating traditional theories about the stars into biblical theology.

The ethos of the Roman school is best exemplified by *The Refutation of all Heresies* a treatise published in ten parts by Hippolytus (170—235 CE), and which was almost contemporaneous with that of Irenaeus, of whom he was a disciple. It catalogues the pagan beliefs and thirty-three Gnostic Christian systems deemed heretical, making it a major source of information on early opponents of Catholic orthodoxy and/or philosophies that the Roman Church believed were threatening. Some of these philosophies/theologies had existed for many centuries prior to the time of Hippolytus and the publication of *The Refutation of all Heresies* was the first move by "The Church" to condemn any and all teachings or beliefs that were different to its own. It must also be argued that one immediate purpose was to eliminate the influence of Alexandria. The value to us of this treatise, is that it explains clearly and unambiguously the popular beliefs of the time.

Amongst its compendious pages it mentions two subjects that are of interest. In particular it outlines the belief that "The Beast" and "The Dragon" and even Jesus (the logos) are amongst the northern polar constellation of Aratus, Lyre, Canis, Corona,

Ursa Minor and Ursa Major and gives guidance as to where exactly they were thought to be found. In particular, it describes Ursa Major as the symbol of Heaven, the one by which we are regenerated and which fights against "The Beast" on our behalf.

Along with the references to Ursa Major in The Book of the Dead, this is the most direct and unambiguous link between the key players in the Book of Revelation and the northern constellations. It tells us that this belief was prominent at the time and that Hippolytus found it necessary to include it amongst those things it was important to condemn. Taking a broad view, these emanations from Alexandria are a perpetuation of the basis of the Egyptian pantheon and show clearly that there was conflict between Alexandria and Rome regarding the core structure of Christian belief. An analysis of these beliefs and their relevance to our investigation is expanded in chapter 14.

The Epistles

There is no doubt that the work and writing of Saul of Tarsus had significant effect on the establishment of the Church. Saul was his name in Hebrew but his Roman name was Paul, which is the name we have come to know him by.

He had a pessimistic mood which was the result of an illness that affected his body and his mind. He speaks of it as "a thorn in the flesh," and as a heavy stroke by "a messenger of Satan"[3] which often caused him to realize his utter helplessness, and which made him an object of pity and horror[4]. It was most likely epilepsy, called by the Greeks "the holy disease," which created a frame of mind that may have greatly impressed his target Gentile audience.

Paul had no contact with Jesus but claimed to have had a vision of the resurrected Christ. There is no indication in Paul's writings or arguments that he had received the rabbinical training ascribed to him by many Christian writers. His quotations from Scripture, which are all taken from the Greek version, show

3 2 Cor. Xii. 7
4 Gal. 4:13

little familiarity with the original Hebrew text. It is claimed by Jewish sources that the Hellenistic literature, such as the Book of Wisdom and other Apocrypha, as well as Philo were the sole sources for his eschatological and theological system.

Whatever the truth of it, Paul influenced the early Church and called on beliefs that had been carried from Egypt and Greece to elicit the support of Gentiles. He claimed that God's Messiah would put an end to the age of evil and would initiate a new age of righteousness. In Antioch, Paul reviewed Israelite history from the life of the Hebrews in Egypt to King David. In what was a duplication of ancient Egyptian theology, he taught that the Resurrection' brought the promise of salvation to believers. Paul wrote that, when Christ returned those already dead but who died while believing in Christ (as the saviour of humankind) would be brought back to life, while those still alive would be "caught up in the clouds together with them to meet the Lord in the air"[5]. Perhaps Paul's most revealing comment proclaims Jesus as the new Adam, who restored through obedience what Adam lost through disobedience.[6] This is a direct link to the creation story, which had been founded in the secrets of the ancients and which pre-dated the Christian area by over three thousand years.[7] It is also significant that the person known as Adam in Judeo/Christian theology was the first man on earth and therefore he must have been the first . For that reason he and Eve must have represented the same personalities as Osiris and Isis from the Egyptian tradition.The letters which are the Epistles, contain no direct evidence of the existence of Jesus Christ and only wishful assertions about his divine status. A more in-depth analysis, including letters that do not form part of the New Testament, is detailed in Chapter 13.

The Book of Revelation

There are fourteen mentions of Jesus in this text:

---

5 1 Thess. 4:14-18
6 (Romans 5:19, NIV). In 1 Corinthians 15:22
7 *The God Secret*, Greg Rigby

- A revelation of Jesus anointed (1:1)
- (John, who confirmed) the testimony of Jesus anointed (1:2)
- Jesus anointed, the martyr, the faithful one, first born of the dead and the ruler of the kings of the earth. (1:5)
- Kingdom and endurance of Jesus and the testimony of Jesus (1:9)
- And it (the dragon) went away to make war with (the ones) having the testimony of Jesus (12:17)
- Here the endurance of the saints is the ones keeping the commandments of God and the faith of Jesus (14:12)
- And I saw the woman drunk from the blood of the saints and from the blood of the witnesses of Jesus (17:6)
- A fellow slave of thee I am and of the brothers of thee, the ones having the witness of Jesus to the one God worship actual testimony of Jesus is the spirit of the prophecy. (19:10)
- . . .the souls of the ones beheaded because of the testimony of Jesus (20:4)
- I, Jesus, sent the angel of me (22:16)
- Yes, I am coming quickly. Amen. Come, O Lord Jesus (22.20)
- The grace of the Lord Jesus with you all (22.21)

None of these give direct evidence of the actual existence of Jesus and whilst they make indirect claims that Jesus was the teacher of a personal testimony or belief they also claim (1:5) that Jesus was 'ruler of the kings of the earth' and 'first born of the dead'. This implies a direct link to Adam and Osiris, which creates another connection to the theological traditions of ancient Egypt.

One topic condemned in *The Refutation of all Heresies* that is of interest to us in the context of our understanding of the Book of Revelation is Numerology, Isopsephia or Gematria. Interestingly, the condemnation of this subject had the effect of giving it credibility. Why condemn something that has no meaning and is no threat?

Greg Rigby

The arcane science of numerology involved the allocation of a numerical value to each letter of the alphabet and a numerical value to each word, it being the sum of the letters in the word. The table of Greek and Hebrew values for each letter of the alphabet is included in the appendix 1. The Greeks used a sophisticated system, which they called Isopsephia and by the fifth century BCE every Greek God's name was formulated according to isopsephic principles. It was in common Greek usage by the time of the Hellenisation of Palestine and Egypt in the second century BCE at which time it was introduced (in its final form) into Hebrew, probably simultaneous with the introduction of Square Hebrew.

We can be reasonably sure that Isopsephia was used in the formulation of the Book of Revelation. This is shown by an extrapolation from the discovery of David Parker, professor of New Testament Textual Criticism and Palaeography at the University of Birmingham in England. He has been using modern technology to scour some four hundred thousand bits of papyri which were originally discovered in 1895 at a dump outside the ancient Egyptian city of Oxyrhynchus. Many of the sections have been damaged and discoloured, but a modern imaging process is shedding new light on the sacred text of the Book of Revelation. Interestingly, analysis of one piece of papyrus shows that 616 was the original number of the beast.

The papyrus in the spotlight (Fig 1) is believed to originate circa 300 CE and is probably about one hundred years before any other version known. The find is significant because the previously common version of the Book of Revelation created an interesting play on the numbers associated with these particular words.

Below is the numerical value of each of the final words of Revelation 13, 18 in normal versions of the text.

And	the	number	of it/him	six hundred	sixty	six
31	70	430	1171	446	514	65

8

Fig 1 The ancient Greek papyrus

If the last three numbers (446, 514 and 65) are replaced by 666 (the number itself, rather than the words) then the total of the phrase becomes:

And	the	number	of it/him	six hundred sixty six	
31	70	430	1171	666	= 2368

The sum of this phrase is equal to 2368 and this number (2368) is the Isopsephia (numerical value) of the genitive of the words Jesus Christ. The complete verse 18 would then read (in equivalent terms)

Here the wisdom/knowledge is. The (one) having mind/ insight/intention let him count the number of the beast. The actual number of man is of Jesus Christ.

9

The new (old) version: And the number of it/him 616', would mean that this play on the words no longer exists and that the numerical total of the words in the phrase would be 2318. This number (2318) using Isopsephia, is equal in value to three phrases in the Book of Revelation:

"and he shall be to me a son"
"and he cried (out) from the glory/splendour of him"
"because of the word /computation / assertion/ proportion of the proof"

With 616 inserted (instead of 666), verse 18 would then read (in equivalent terms):

Here the wisdom/knowledge is. The (one) having mind/insight/intention let him count; the number of the beast a number in fact (of) man is, because of the computation of the evidence/proof.

It would appear therefore that whoever changed the number of The Beast' from 616 to 666 did so to hide this embedded message from the scrutiny of anyone versed in the science of Isopsephia and to lead them falsely to the name of Jesus Christ. The change itself is evidence of the very thing that the perpetrators were trying to hide, that the document was compiled using Isopsephia or numerology to incorporate hidden and perhaps sacred messages. It also shows that the document was designed to promote Jesus Christ and his esoteric associations.

The spreading of the Jesus message, whether orally or via mystical texts such as the Book of Revelation would have been the first Century equivalent to the promotion of Harry Potter. The difference was that in those times, people believed in a vengeful God that lived in the heavens and that (in the absence of scientific evidence to the contrary) the stories concerning God in his various forms and guises were all true. For over three thousand years, such theology had been sold to unsuspecting peoples and the ground was fertile to the acceptance of variations to the ancient theme, particularly those that reinforced the fundamentals.

If there was a person who came to known as Jesus Christ, we will need to uncover the ways in which this person's existence was promoted to achieve this.

The Talmud and other Jewish writings

Most scholars believe that the Talmud references to Jesus are quite late (hundreds of years after the time referred to) and give no historically reliable information about the teachings or actions of Jesus during his life.

Several Talmudic sources include passages which identify a "son of Pandera" (*"ben Pandera"* in Hebrew), which are believed to be references to Jesus. A few of the references explicitly name Jesus ("Yeshu") as the "son of Pandera": these explicit connections are found in the Tosefta, the Qohelet Rabbah, and the Jerusalem Talmud, but not in the Babylonian Talmud. In the Jerusalem Talmud the name "Jesus" ("Yeshu") is found only in a marginal gloss in some manuscripts.

The texts include several spellings for the father's name (Pandera, Panthera, Pandira, Pantiri, or Pantera) which are probably the same individual. In some of the texts, the father produced a son with a woman named Mary (*Miriam* in Hebrew). They claim that this Miriam was not married to Pandera, and was committing adultery and, by implication, Jesus was a bastard child. Some of the texts claim that Mary's husband's name was Stada.

Peter Schäfer states that there can be no doubt that the narrative of the execution of Jesus in the Talmud refers to Jesus of Nazareth, but claims that the rabbinic literature in question are from a later Amoraic period and may have drawn on the Christian gospels. He concludes that they were most likely written as responses to them.

The most prominent Romano-Jewish historian was Josephus Flavius, born CE 37. He wrote late in the first century and included two passages in his manuscripts that mention Jesus:

In the *Testemonium Flavium*[8], he writes:

---

8 Book 18, Chapter 3:3 of the Antiquities

Now there was about this time Jesus, a wise man, if it be lawful to call him a man; for he was a doer of wonderful works, a teacher of such men as receive the truth with pleasure. He drew over to him both many of the Jews and many of the Gentiles. He was [the] Christ. And when Pilate, at the suggestion of the principal men amongst us, had condemned him to the cross, those that loved him at the first did not forsake him; for he appeared to them alive again the third day; as the divine prophets had foretold these and ten thousand other wonderful things concerning him. And the tribe of Christians, so named from him, are not extinct at this day.

In the *Antiquities*, he states:

Festus was now dead, and Albinus was but upon the road; so he (Ananus) assembled the Sanhedrim of judges, and brought before them the brother of Jesus, who was called Christ, whose name was James, and some others, [or, some of his companions]; and when he had formed an accusation against them as breakers of the law, he delivered them to be stoned: but as for those who seemed the most equitable of the citizens, and such as were the most uneasy at the breach of the laws, they disliked what was done; they also sent to the king [Agrippa], desiring him to send to Ananus that he should act so no more, for that what he had already done was not to be justified; nay, some of them went also to meet Albinus, as he was upon his journey from Alexandria, and informed him that it was not lawful for Ananus to assemble a Sanhedrim without his consent.

The first of these references may be discounted since it is believed to have been to have been a forged inclusion by Christians. The latter reference is believed to be authentic but may be discounted on the basis that Josephus wrote about many people who were named Jesus, Yeshua or Joshua. On the other hand, it might possibly relate to the person on which the Christian religion was based. If this is case, we need to ask ourselves why Josephus was directing his readers towards James and did not include a more in-depth reference to the Christ person and to the actions it is elsewhere claimed that he performed.

If it does relate to the Jesus Christ we are investigating, this passing reference would seem to indicate that the person had only passing significance at the time that this was written.

Roman records

No contemporary Roman records mention Jesus Christ:

> *The failure to chronicle Jesus Christ in authentic history books was not because of poor Jewish or Roman record keeping. It was quite the opposite, for with care and diligence, all noteworthy Jewish historical events were accurately recorded on papyrus scrolls, goatskin or sheepskin, not just in Judea and Galilee, but also in neighbouring Syria and Asia Minor.[9]*

The only records mentioning Jesus were made almost a century later but may have value in the computation of a body of evidence.

Cobelius Tacitus's work called the *Annals* (written circa 116 CE) is important to Christianity because it is considered by many Christians to confirm the historicity of Jesus. Book 15:44 designates Christ as a person who was executed by Pontius Pilot during Tiberius' reign. He wrote:

> *Consequently, to get rid of the report, Nero fastened the guilt and inflicted the most exquisite tortures on a class hated for their abominations, called Christians by the populace. Christus, from whom the name had its origin, suffered the extreme penalty during the reign of Tiberius at the hands of one of our procurators, Pontius Pilatus,*

---

9 *The man who sold Jesus to the world; Andrew Hillhouse*

and a most mischievous superstition, thus checked for the moment, again broke out not only in Judæa, the first source of the evil, but even in Rome, where all things hideous and shameful from every part of the world find their centre and become popular. Accordingly, an arrest was first made of all who pleaded guilty; then, upon their information, an immense multitude was convicted, not so much of the crime of firing the city, as of hatred against mankind.

This text would seem to confirm that there were those in Rome who had been made aware of the execution of a trouble-maker in Palestine named Christ. Other records were made. One was made by Gaius Suetonius Tranquillas, who was chief secretary of the Emperor Hadrian (117-139 CE) which read:

Because the Jews of Rome caused continuous distur-bances at the instigation of Chrestus, Claudius expelled them from the city.
After the great fire of Rome punishments were also inflicted in the Christians, a sect professing a new and mischievous religious belief.

Another was made by Pliny the Younger, Roman Gover-nor of Bithinia in Asia Minor around 112CE who wrote, "The Christians were in the habit of meeting on a certain fixed day before it was light, where they sang in alternative verses a hymn to Christ as to a God . . . ."

All these mentions of Christ and Christians occur in retrospect and whilst they indicate that a Christian movement was in existence, they offer only circumstantial proof of its origin and of the life and death of Jesus Christ. Despite that, some scholars quote Tacitus (above) as proof of one of the three indisputable historical events portrayed in the Gospels; the birth, baptism and execution of Jesus.

The Scrolls

The Dead Sea or Qumran Scrolls were a collection of 981 different texts discovered in eleven caves along the northwest shore of the Dead Sea between the years 1947 and 1956. They were most likely written by the Essenes and/or Zadokites during the period from about 200 BCE to 68 CE.

The first reference to the Essenes is by the Roman writer Pliny the Elder (died c. 79 CE) in his *Natural History*. A little later Josephus gave a detailed account of the Essenes in *The Jewish War* (c. 75 CE), with a shorter description in *Antiquities of the Jews* (c. 94 CE) and *The Life of Flavius Josephus* (c. 97 CE). Claiming firsthand knowledge, he lists the *Essenoi* as one of the three sects of Jewish philosophy alongside the Pharisees and the Sadducees. He relates the same information concerning piety, celibacy, the absence of personal property and of money, the belief in communality and commitment to a strict observance of Sabbath. He further adds that the Essenes ritually immersed in water every morning, ate together after prayer, devoted themselves to charity and benevolence, forbade the expression of anger, studied the books of the elders, preserved secrets, and were very mindful of the names of the angels kept in their sacred writings.

Although the Qumran community existed during the time of the ministry of Jesus, none of the Scrolls refer to Him, nor do they mention any of his followers described in the New Testament. More detailed analysis is included in Chapter 12.

The Nag Hammadi scrolls were discovered in anciently constructed caves in Upper Egypt in 1945. They incorporate what have become known as the Gnostic Gospels and speak of a living Jesus who preaches illusion and enlightenment not of sin and repentance like the Jesus in the New Testament.

Some sayings in this collection criticize common Christian beliefs, such as the virgin birth or the bodily resurrection, as naïve misunderstandings. Bound together with them is the Apocryphon (literally, "secret book") of John, which opens with an offer to reveal "the mysteries [and the] things hidden in silence" which Jesus taught to his disciple John.[10] This book reads like a Science Fiction soap opera spun around Adam and

---

10 *The Gnostic Gospels* by Elaine Pagels

Eve in the Garden of Eden. Since we know that the Adam and Eve story is based on one written in the stars as the northern pole position moved through the heavens[8] one can only assume that these texts were another attempt to link Jesus to the ancient Egyptian Mysteries. A more in-depth analysis of these connections will be made in later chapters.

Ballads and/or religious myths and traditions

Nothing in the New Testament tells us the actual date of Christ's birth. What pointers there are, such as the shepherds watching their flocks, would seem to indicate that it was not December.

The date of December 25 was chosen in the third century to coincide with festivals honouring the birth date of prominent Pagan gods. In particular, it coincided with *natalis solis invicti* (the Roman "birth of the unconquered sun"), and the birthday of Mithras, the Iranian "Sun of Righteousness" whose worship was popular with Roman soldiers.

The date of December 25 followed an established tradition. Plutarch and Diogenes claimed that Zoroaster as he appeared in the Old *Avestan Gathas* originated prior to 6000 BCE (albeit that recent scholars suggest dates that vary between 1800 and 600 BCE). He was born of a virgin and "immaculate conception by a ray of divine reason." He was baptized in a river. In his youth, he astounded wise men with his wisdom and was later tempted in the wilderness by the devil. He began his ministry at age thirty. Zoroaster was baptized with water, fire and "holy wind." He cast out demons and restored the sight to a blind man. He taught about heaven and hell, and revealed mysteries, including resurrection, judgment, salvation and the apocalypse. He had a sacred cup or grail. He was slain. His religion had a Eucharist. He was the "Word made flesh," and is expected to return in a second coming.

The personality most similar to Jesus was the Greek God Dionysus, worshipped as early as 1500 BCE. He was reputedly born of a virgin on December 25 and, as the Holy Child, was placed in a manger. He performed miracles, rode in a triumphal procession on an ass and was considered to be a sacred king. Like Christ, he was killed and eaten in a Eucharistic ritual. Dionysus rose from the dead on March 25. He was the God of the Vine, and turned water into wine. He was called King of Kings and was considered the Only Begotten Son, Saviour, Redeemer, Sin Bearer, Anointed One, and the Alpha and Omega. Is it possible that some of these Dionysian attributes were grafted onto the story of Jesus?

The Greek Pantheon included Attis, whose cult began around 1250 BCE. Like Dionysus, Attis was born on December 25 of a virgin. He was considered the Saviour who was slain for the salvation of mankind. His body as bread was eaten by his worshippers. He was both the Divine Son and the Father. On "Black Friday," he was crucified on a tree, from which his holy blood ran down to redeem the earth. He descended into the underworld and after three days, he was resurrected.

The Egyptian pantheon includes Gods Osiris and Horus who have accredited to them elements that are included in the story of Jesus Christ:

Osiris was the first god-king and was therefore the same person as Adam. This person came to earth because the position of his picture in the stars changed over time from one that rotated around the pole position and was always visible to one where the figure touched earth. The key parts of the Osiris story that are similar to key parts of the Christ story are those concerning his persecution and torture, his murder and his resurrection.

Horus was the son of Osiris. Like Jesus, he is claimed to have been conceived of a virgin. Both Jesus and Horus were the "only begotten son" of a god (either Osiris or Yahweh). Horus's foster father was called Jo-Seph, and Jesus' foster father was Joseph and both foster fathers were of royal descent. Both Jesus and Horus had their coming announced to their mother by an angel and Horus's birth was heralded by the star Sirius (the morning star) while Jesus had his birth heralded by a star in the East (the sun rises in the East). Ancient Egyptians celebrated the birth of Horus on December 21 (the Winter Solstice) while Christians celebrate the birth of Jesus on December 25. After the birth of Horus, Herut tried to have Horus murdered. After the birth of Jesus, Herod tried to have Jesus murdered. To hide from Herut, one of the gods tells Isis, "Come, thou goddess Isis, hide thyself with thy child." To hide from Herod, an angel tells Joseph to "arise and take the young child and his other and flee into Egypt.Both Horus and Jesus were baptized in a river at age thirty. Horus was baptized by Anup the Baptizer while Jesus was baptized by John the Baptist. Both Anup and John were later beheaded. Both have disciples, walked on water, cast out demons, healed the sick, and restored sight to the blind. Both of them were crucified next to two thieves and were resurrected after three days.

Horus is known as KRST, the anointed one. Jesus was known as the Christ (which also means "anointed one"). Both Jesus and Horus have been called the good shepherd, the lamb of God, the bread of life, the son of man and the Word.

In summary, none of these coincidences to traditional mythologies tell us whether the person of Jesus Christ existed. What they do suggest, is that the personality that did exist (assuming that he did) was probably embellished and that stories were attributed to him to associate him with the qualities and traditions of God figures that would have been known to those living in Israel and its surrounds at the time.

As we have already seen, the mythology of Attis, Osiris and Horus included their resurrection. Other examples of Gods who were resurrected include the ancient Near Eastern, Greek, and Norse deities Baal, Melqart, Adonis, Ashmun and Tammuz.

The cult of Baal was prominent in the fourteenth century BCE and Semitic races celebrated resurrection as a part of the Canaanite fertility rituals. **Melqart**, whose name means "king of the city" was the patron god of the Phoenician city of Tyre and one of the major gods of the Phoenician and Punic pantheons. He was also known as Baal Sur (Lord of Tyre) and was identified with Herakles (Hercules) since at least the sixth century BCE. During an annual ritual, the god "died" (perhaps in a fire) and was awakened or resuscitated, perhaps through a sacred marriage (*hierosgamos*) with the goddess Astarte.

The name Adonis derives from Semitic origin and is a variation of the Phoenician *Adon* meaning "Lord." The name Adonis also bears striking resemblance to *Adonai,* one of the names used to refer to Yahweh, the singular God of the ancient Israelites. Adonis became an avid hunter, and ended up being killed by a wild boar during the hunt. Aphrodite, his wife mourned feverishly, pleading to Zeus for the renewed life of her lover. Zeus was swayed by Aphrodite's pleas, and eventually resurrected Adonis.

According to Damascius, Eshmun was the eighth son of Sydyk, whence his name, and the chief of the Cabeiri. Whereas they were dwarfish and misshapen, he was a youth of most beautiful appearance, truly worthy of admiration. Like Adonis, he was fond of hunting in the woods that clothe the flanks of Lebanon, and there he was seen by Astronoë, the Phoenician goddess, the mother of the gods (who sounds similar to Astarte), who hounded him to such an extent that to escape her he was driven to the desperate resource of self-emasculation. Upon this the goddess, greatly grieved, called him Paean, and by means of quickening warmth brought him back to life, and changed him from a man into a god, which he thenceforth remained. The Phoenicians called him Esmun, the eighth, but the Greeks worshipped him as Asclepius, the god of healing, who gave life and health to mankind.[11]

Tammuz (Damuzu) was thought by some to be the same person as Adonis. He is reputed to rise from the dead annually and, after half a year, descend to the Netherworld' for the other half. He is mentioned in the Old Testament:

> *"Then he brought me to the door of the gate of the Lord's house which was toward the north; and, behold, there sat women weeping for Tammuz. Then said he unto to me, 'Hast thou seen this, O son of man? turn thee yet*

---

11 George Stanley Faber, *The Origin of Pagan Idolatry Ascertained from Historical Testimony and Circumstantial Evidence*, vol. 2 (London: 1816), 262.

again, and thou shalt see greater abominations than these. "[12]

Like the tradition of December 25 and the virgin birth, we see that the resurrection of a god king was a deeply established concept at the beginnings of the Christian era.

Some authors and historians have suggested that the end December tradition was centred on the time of the Winter Solstice.

It was at this time that new life started as the sun commencing its new emergence and that resurrection' occurred around the time of the Spring Equinox, which was the point at which light fully conquered darkness and the Sun took complete dominance of the heavens.

There are more recent stories and traditions, which are thought to have been linked to ancient religious beliefs and whose traditions may hide some clues.

The Grail story and the Tarot (for instance) contain the common elements of the cup, the spear or rod, the sword and the pentacle/pentagram or stone. These four elements are closely linked to the ancient mysteries; they appear in the New Testament as the cup of the Eucharist and the spear of Longinus but are linked more intricately to Christ and Christianity through the Book of Revelation.[8]

The ancient mysteries emanate from patterns created in and around the seven stars that are at the centre of the constellation of Ursa Major, when this constellation had control of the northern pole position in the early part of the third millennium BCE. In this cosmology, the pentagram was held in the cup of the constellation, represented by the shape of Nut the mother of God and this shape was therefore the sacred shape of the Son of God (Ra) and the Mother Goddess.

It is possible therefore to create an obtuse link between the mystical claims concerning Jesus as portrayed in The Book of Revelation to the ancient mysteries of Egypt and its related cos-

---

12 Ezekiel 8:14-15

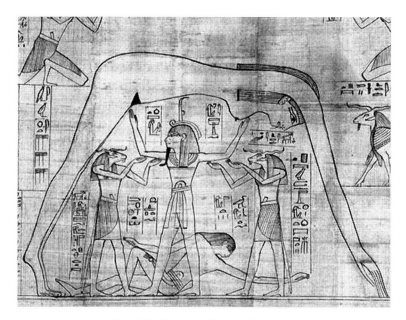

Fig 2 Nut as mother of heaven

mology. Despite this, none of the intriguing links provides tangible proof of Jesus's existence and only point to a compendium of intended ambiguity and associated intrigue.

Perhaps when we examine the manifest desire to perpetuate the ancient mysteries and beliefs in the Christ story we will find clues to the existence of the personality around which the stories were re-presented.

Another personality that appears in compendious documents and legends is that of Satan or the devil. This personality who had many names comes from an ancient source, and because of that, the idea of an evil being in conflict with God was well establish in the Egyptian pantheon. Plutarch, speaking of his own days[13], says, *"The power of Typhon, although dimmed and crushed, is still in its last agonies and convulsions. The Egyptians occasionally humiliate and insult him at certain festivals. They nevertheless propitiate and soothe him by means of certain sacrifices."*

---

13 On Isis and Osiris, Chapter XXX; Plutarch

Greg Rigby

**Fig 3 The pentagram traced round the face of Osiris
as depicted on the walls of the Tomb of Senedjem;
Servant in the place of Truth**

In some instances, this being was portrayed as a threatening dragon. A concept that is long standing and which is based on the conflict between the star constellations Bootes, Ursa Major and Ursa Minor and the constellation Draco for their possession of the Pole position (the place at the centre of the heavens around which everything rotates).

The name Satan is a Hebrew word that means adversary. In the God Secret,[8] we show clearly that the picture of Satan can be obtained by joining stars in the Ursa Major constellation. This picture can be seen at night when the pentagram inside the constellation of Ursa Major has rotated through 180° Because of that the shape represents the opposite of God, whose hidden configuration in the constellation, when the constellation has rotated 180° around the pole position and it is hidden by the Suns brightness in the day. The stories told by Egyptian and Hebrew priests over the years reinforced the idea that Satan was a real personality who was in conflict with both God and man. The fact that this personality is picked up in the Gospels[14] is a clear indication of the degree to which this tradition was main-

---

14 Matthew 4:1-11, Mark 1:12-13, Luke 4:1-13

tained and that Hebrew belief influenced the writers. The stories in the Gospels concerning Jesus being spoken to and tempted by Satan are an indication of how real this tradition had become. It is also a good early indication of the human predisposition to blame someone or something else for the way we as individuals see things. To attribute such human frailty to God incarnate is a blasphemous insult at worst or an acceptance that the personality being written about was in fact human and not divine at best.

In summary, the written evidence for Jesus Christ's existence is limited and is confined to claims of the effect of his existence rather than proof of his existence. There seems to consensus amongst historians, particularly biased Christian historians, that the birth, baptism and execution of Jesus Christ did in fact take place. Some elements of these events as reported are mysterious in themselves, and may give us a starting point for further investigation. Additionally, the reports of Christ that do exist seem to incorporate connections to ancient beliefs that are inherent and fundamental to the Ancient Mysteries, as they were believed and practised in Egypt. This too suggests a route worthy of further examination.

CHAPTER 2

The Hebrew Connection to the Egyptian Pantheon/Mysteries

Important Canaanite populations first appeared in Northern Egypt towards the end of the twelfth dynasty (circa 1800 BCE), and between that time and 1720 BCE they formed an independent realm in the eastern Nile Delta. The Canaanite rulers of the Delta regrouped during the fourteenth dynasty and coexisted with the Egyptians during the thirteenth dynasty, based in _Itjtawy_. The power of the thirteenth and fourteenth Theban dynasties progressively waned, and circa 1650 BCE Egypt was invaded by the Hyksos, a Semitic people including some Hurrians and Hittites who formed their own Egyptian dynasty, the fifteenth dynasty, and created their own northern power base in the city of Avaris.

Eventually Seqenenre, Tao Kamose and Ahmose defeated the Hyksos in battle and expelled Khamudi, their last king, circa 1550 BCE.

As both Hyksos and Hebrews were Semitic groups who were immigrants into Egypt from Canaan and beyond, and because the earliest Israeli and Egyptian historians tell us so, the Hyksos have been confused with the Hebrews. The name Hyksos was used by the Egyptian historian Manetho (300 BCE), who, according to the Jewish historian Flavius Josephus (first century BCE), translated the word as "king shepherds" or "captive shepherds." Josephus himself wished to demonstrate the great antiquity of the Jews and thus identified the Hyksos with the Hebrews of the Bible.

There is no doubt that there was an intermingling of Hyksos and Hebrews. The Old Testament tells us that Joseph stood

24

before Pharaoh as an interpreter of dreams,[15] and it seems likely that this was a Hyksos Monarch who ceded a choice parcel of land to Joseph's family.[16] Josephus cites Manetho's history, which associated the Israelites with the Hyksos:

> *After the conclusion of the treaty, they left with their families and chattels, not fewer than two hundred and forty thousand people, and crossed the desert into Syria. Fearing the Assyrians, who dominated over Asia at that time, they built a city in the country which we now call Judea. It was large enough to contain this great number of men and was called Jerusalem.*[17]

Many modern scholars see problems with Manetho's combining of the expulsion of the Hyksos and the biblical narrative. Manetho lived many centuries after these events took place, and his reading of events may well have been inaccurate. Most historians believe that Ahmose's defeat of the Hyksos occurred centuries before the traditional date of the Exodus. In addition, the basic premise of the Hyksos and Exodus histories differ: the Hyksos were expelled rulers of Egypt, not slaves, and they were forced out, not pursued. If Manetho was correct, the Hebrews would have been included among the rulers of Egypt—an idea that we will return to.

An alternative explanation might solve these differing views: the Hyksos kings and pretenders were expelled by Ahmose. After the Hyksos were defeated by this pharaoh, some Hyksos people probably remained in Egypt, perhaps as a subjugated class. This is upheld by the fact that the Egyptian Queen Hatshepsut recorded the banishment of a group of Asiatics from Avaris, the former Hyksos, capital many years later (1489—1469 BCE). During this time, they probably mingled with the many other Semitic peoples occupying parts of Northern Egypt. This being

---

15 Genesis 41:14-37
16 Genesis 47: 6
17 Josephus, *Against Apion*, 1.73.7, quoting Manetho's *Aegytiaca*

the case, there would have been two minor Hyksos expulsions, the one by Ahmose and the one by Hatshepsut followed by the Exodus of the Old Testament many years later.

There is considerable debate concerning the actual date of the Hebrew Exodus. We are told that the Hebrews spent 430 years in Egypt.[18] If this is correct, we would need to know the date of the first settlement in order to compute the date of departure. If the settlement occurred between 1800 and 1720 BCE, this would date the Exodus to somewhere between 1370 and 1310 BCE. The rulers of the eighteenth dynasty were:

- Nebpehtire Ahmose I—1550-1525 BCE
- Djeserkare Amenhotep I—1541-1520
- Aakheperkare Thutmose I—1520-1492
- Aakheperkare Thutmose II—1492-1479
- <u>Menkheperre Thutmose III</u>—1479-1425
- Maatkare Hatshepsut, a rare female ruler—1473-1458
- Aakheperrure Amenhotep II—1425-1400
- Menkheperure Thutmose IV—1400-1390
- Nebmaatre Amenhotep III—1390-1352
- Neferkheperure-waenre   Amenhotep   IV Akhenaten—1352-1334
- Ankhkheperure Smenkhkare (co-regent and successor of Akhenaten. The identity of this individual is uncertain and disputed. Usually believed to be either a son or son-in-law of Akhenaten but sometimes identified as Akhenaten's wife Nefertiti. Other scholars distinguish two individuals between Akhenaten and Tutankhamun, namely Smenkhkare, who is then seen as male, and a female ruler, who is then most often identified as Akhenaten's eldest daughter Meritaten)—1334-1333
- Nebkheperure Tutankhaten/Tutankhamun—1333-1324
- Kheperkheperure Ay—1324-1320
- Djeserkheperure-setpenre Horemheb—1320-1292

---

18 Exodus 12:40

This fits well with the contentious claim that Moses, the person who led the Israelites out of Egypt, was the unorthodox pharaoh Akhenaten who conveniently disappeared from history after his attempt to have the Egyptian religion amended. His crime was to change the Egyptian pantheon from a series of gods or aspects of god with different names and to limit the act of worship so that it was directed at/to one single God, the God Aton. Whilst the detail changes, this too fits with the Old Testament tradition, that Moses prosecuted the theological concept of one god.

Since antiquity, many writers have tried to associate Moses with Akhenaton including Manetho, who claimed that the founder of monotheism, whom he called Osarsiph, assumed the name Moses, and led his followers out of Egypt in Amenhotep's reign. The spectre of Akhenaton was also transformed into Moses by writers such as Lysimachus, Tacitus and Strabo. Agreeing with this school of thought was Sigmund Freud,[19] who described himself as thinking the unthinkable, and more recent authors such as Donald B Redford and Ahmed Osman.

The name Moses means "son of" or "born of/from" and because of that, it was a common epithet, particularly to those in high positions. The name Mose was normally attached to a named suffix as with the name Ahmose, which meant son of Ah.

Use of Moses on its own would have been abnormal. It possibly could have been used where the suffix (the father) was assumed. If this were the case, the father would need to have been well known and might confirm the speculation that Moses was the son of the pharaoh.

Whatever the timing and the true pedigree of Moses, it is certain that the Hebrews/Israelites left Egypt and were in all likelihood pursued by the enemies of Moses. The number of people involved is the subject of debate, depending on the way the original Hebrew text is interpreted. Calculations vary from 100,000 to 600,000 and up to as many as two and a half million. This higher figure would approximate half the total population

---

19 *Moses and Monotheism* (New York: Knopf, 1939)

of Egypt, which makes it extremely unlikely. Whatever the true numbers, it is clear from the claims made in the book of Exodus that there were disagreements between Moses and the bulk of the migrants accompanying him:

> *When the people saw that Moses delayed to come down from the mountain, the people gathered themselves together to Aaron, and said to him, "Up, make us gods, who shall go before us; as for this Moses, the man who brought us up out of the land of Egypt, we do not know what has become of him." And Aaron said to them, "Take off the rings of gold which are in the ears of your wives, your sons, and your daughters, and bring them to me." So all the people took off the rings of gold which were in their ears, and brought them to Aaron. And he received the gold at their hand, and fashioned it with a graving tool, and made a molten calf; and they said, "These are your gods, O Israel, who brought you up out of the land of Egypt!" When Aaron saw this, he built an altar before it; and Aaron made proclamation and said, "Tomorrow shall be a feast to the Lord." And they rose up early on the morrow, and offered burnt offerings and brought peace offerings; and the people sat down to eat and drink, and rose up to play.[20]*

The peoples making up the Exodus were descendants of those who had lived in Egypt for over 400 years. They had been born in Egypt and intermarried with Egyptians. It is not surprising therefore that a sizeable number of them had adopted the religion of Egypt and worshipped the many traditional gods of their adopted land. According to the verses in Exodus, even Moses's trusted advisor and lieutenant, Aaron, (who is described in Exodus as the brother of Moses) was a follower of the Egyptian pantheon and was happy to facilitate worship of the golden calf. Hathor, who was among the oldest of Egyptian deities,

---

20 Exodus 32:1-6

was often depicted as a cow, a cow goddess, a sky goddess and a tree goddess. She was the mother to the pharaoh and earlier mother to the universe. She was undoubtedly the golden calf of the Bible, and was the goddess of love and music. The calf as displayed in Thebes contains the same angles of a regular pentagram displayed in the traditional picture of Nut (Figure 2 above).

Fig 4 The Calf displayed in Thebes

Moses was the principal proselytiser of the new religion based on the veneration of a single god, and on his reappearance from the mountain, we are told:

> *And when Moses saw that the people had broken*
> *loose (for Aaron had let them break loose, to their shame*

29

among their enemies), then Moses stood in the gate of the camp, and said, "Who is on the Lord's side? Come to me." And all the sons of Levi gathered themselves together to him. And he said to them, "Thus says the Lord God of Israel, 'Put every man his sword on his side, and go to and fro from gate to gate throughout the camp, and slay every man his brother, and every man his companion, and every man his neighbour.'" And the sons of Levi did according to the word of Moses; and there fell of the people that day about three thousand men. And Moses said, "Today you have ordained yourselves for the service of the Lord, each one at the cost of his son and of his brother, that he may bestow a blessing upon you this day."[21]

Given Moses's instructions, it is surprising that only three thousand people were put to the sword. This might be an indication that the group was smaller than some religious historians have claimed. When read together, the two passages tell us:

- The group travelled in fear, and the new religion was prosecuted with force
- Women were spared

These actions might encourage the following conclusions:

- There was a deeply felt love of the old religion, so much so that people gave up their wealth to help create a calf of gold.
- The old religion was sent underground by Moses's actions
- Any women secretly holding on to the old religion were free to pass it discreetly to their children.

This being the case, we can assume that any rejection of the Egyptian pantheon was made by the leaders of the Semitic

---

21 Exodus 32:25-29

group leaving Egypt for Israel and that this rejection did not necessarily mirror the views of the ordinary people. If we go back in the Book of Exodus to a time prior to the flight, we are told that as part of his forceful negotiation, Moses called a series of plagues onto Egypt, the last of which involved the slaughter of the first-born:

> *So Moses said, "This is what the* Lord *says: 'About midnight I will go throughout Egypt. Every firstborn son in Egypt will die, from the firstborn son of Pharaoh, who sits on the throne, to the firstborn son of the female slave, who is at her hand mill, and all the firstborn of the cattle as well. There will be loud wailing throughout Egypt—worse than there has ever been or ever will be again.* [7] *But among the Israelites not a dog will bark at any person or animal.' Then you will know that the* Lord *makes a distinction between Egypt and Israel All these officials of yours will come to me, bowing down before me and saying, 'Go, you and all the people who follow you!' After that I will leave." Then Moses, hot with anger, left Pharaoh.*[22]

This excerpt makes it clear that the members of the Israeli hierarchy were violent in the prosecution of their demands, but it gives no information about the views of those they represent. Interestingly, the phraseology is such that Moses could have been talking about himself in the third person (as royals do) when he used the epithet Lord.

Later descriptions of these events have been sanitised. Stephen in the Acts of the Apostles tells us the following:

> *"This is the Moses who told the Israelites, 'God will raise up for you a prophet like me from your own peo-*

---

22 Exodus 11:4-8

ple.' He was in the assembly in the wilderness, with the angel who spoke to him on Mount Sinai, and with our ancestors; and he received living words to pass on to us.

"But our ancestors refused to obey him. Instead, they rejected him and in their hearts turned back to Egypt. They told Aaron, 'Make us gods who will go before us. As for this fellow Moses who led us out of Egypt—we don't know what has happened to him!' That was the time they made an idol in the form of a calf. They brought sacrifices to it and revelled in what their own hands had made. But God turned away from them and gave them over to the worship of the sun, moon and stars. This agrees with what is written in the book of the prophets:

"'Did you bring me sacrifices and offerings forty years in the wilderness, people of Israel? You have taken up the tabernacle of Molek and the star of your god Rephan, the idols you made to worship. Therefore I will send you into exile' beyond Babylon."[23]

The above quotations make it clear that the aspects of the Egyptian religion that were brought out of Egypt, and which were violently repressed, were those relating to worship of the sun, moon and stars. We do not know where Stephen obtained his information other than from Exodus 20 and from Amos 5:26, which states, *"You carried along the statues of the god Sikkuth/ Moloch as your king and the star Chiun/Kiyyun, the gods you made for yourselves."*

What we do know is that he spoke of things that his audience was aware of: The God Moloch went by many names including Ba'al, Apis and Milcom, and was widely worshipped in Egypt among the Canaanites (the people occupying the land which is now Northern Egypt) who considered him a fertility deity and one of the most important gods in the pantheon.

As a Semitic common noun *baal* (Hebrew *ba al*) meant "owner" or "lord." The tabernacle of Molech is more difficult

---

23 Acts 7:37-43

to identify, but in the context of sun, moon and stars it may well represent the shape of the tabernacle (Fig. 5) and the shrine which in turn holds the pentagram or star as identified in *The God Secret*.[8]

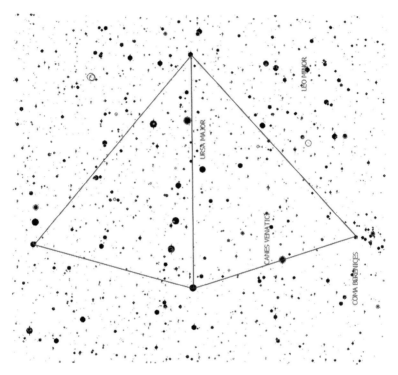

Fig 5 The tabernacle that surrounds the seven stars of Ursa Major, which holds the shrine

In the earliest of times, the tabernacle held the shrine, and over time, these titles replaced one another so that the tabernacle became the innermost sanctuary. This means that an altar or stand shaped like the inverted cup of Ursa Major could have been referred to as the shrine.

If this analysis is correct, the star of your God Rephan will relate to the five-pointed star that was synonymous with the Egyptian god Osiris and with the earthly god kings that followed him.

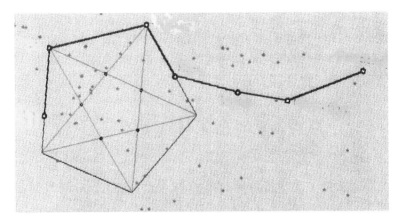

Fig 6 The figure of Ursa Major, its cup and the five-pointed star as duplicated on the ground in Northern Europe

In Israel, the five-pointed star was changed to a six-pointed star in medieval times and was officially adopted by the First Zionist Conference in 1897. This new shape has become known as the Seal of Solomon and the Star of David. The instigator of this change and the date when it happened is unknown. The appellation does not mean that the two symbols of Solomon and David were six-pointed. In fact, the little evidence that exists points to the contrary and that the Seal of Solomon was a pentacle.

There was no history of a six-pointed star in Egypt. The only pre-historical references relate to occasional finds in Babylon and a find in the shrine that opens out from the palace at Mallia (constructed circa 1900 BCE).[24] All references to a six-pointed star linked to Israel appear to commence in recent history. If there was any change in ancient times, it is possible that it came from the transposition of the triangle that made one of the sides of the heavenly pyramid.

There was a close and enduring link between Egypt and the Canaanite peoples. The little evidence we have suggests that despite early deadly pressure from Moses, this link was not demolished at the time of the Exodus. Such a supposition was

---

24 *Yavneh* page 83 footnote by Raz Kletter, Wolfgang Zwickel and Irit Ziffer.

confirmed at the highest level when *Solomon "became allied to Pharaoh, king of Egypt by marriage, and took Pharaoh's daughter, and brought her into the city of David, until he had made an end of building his own house, and the house of the Lord, and the wall of Jerusalem round about."*[25]

These links continued until the time of Jesus. Concerning the impending slaughter of the innocents, the Gospel of Matthew tells us:

> *And when they were departed, behold, the angel of the Lord appeareth to Joseph in a dream, saying, Arise, and take the young child and his mother, and flee into Egypt, and be thou there until I bring thee word: for Herod will seek the young child to destroy him. When he arose, he took the young child and his mother by night, and departed into Egypt: And was there until the death of Herod: that it might be fulfilled which was spoken of the Lord by the prophet, saying, Out of Egypt have I called my son.*[26]

> Then again, briefly: *"But when Herod was dead, behold, an angel of the Lord appeareth in a dream to Joseph in Egypt."*[27]

Such links with Egypt as a place of safety is not surprising as there was a large Jewish community exiled in Egypt at the time of Jesus: "The presence of a large number of Jews, attracted by special advantages offered by Alexander and renewed by Ptolemy 1, when the city was in its infancy, admitted the worship of Jehovah. An Aramaic papyrus[28] tells us that this worship was not, however, entirely new to Egypt, for a large colony of Jews had settled under Darius in the immediate neighbourhood of the

---

25 1 Kings 3:1
26 Matthew 2:13-15
27 Matthew 2:19
28 Sachau, Aranaische Papyrus und Ostraka aud Elephantine, Leipzig 1911; Sayce and Crowley, Aramaic Papyri 1906

first cataract and had built a temple there, apparently becoming prosperous and having established an important colony."[29]

Another important link between Israel and Egypt was in the actual name of Israel. El was used by the Canaanites as the name of the chief God of their pantheon. The Ugaritic texts, the major extra-biblical source on Canaanite religion, describes El as a grandfatherly figure who was revered by the Canaanites as the father of the gods, the father of humans, and the Lord of Heaven. Major decisions considered by the other Gods in the pantheon had to be approved by El. The word comes from a root word meaning might, strength, power. In Scripture, the primary meanings of this root are god (pagan or false god) and God (the true God of Israel).

Re, also spelled Ra, or Pra, in ancient Egyptian religion, was god of the sun and the creator god. He was believed to travel across the sky in his solar bark and, during the night, to make his passage in another bark through the underworld, where, in order to be born again for the new day, he had to vanquish the evil serpent Apopis (Apepi). As one of the creator gods, he rose from the ocean of chaos on the primeval hill, creating himself and then in turn engendering eight other gods.

Originally, most solar gods were in the form of a falcon and were assimilated to Horus. By the fourth dynasty (2575—2465 BCE), however, Ra had risen to his leading position. Syncretism were formed between Re and other gods, producing such names as Re-Harakhty, Amon-Re, Sebek-Re and Khnum-Re.

Aspects of other gods influenced Re; for instance, his falcon-headed appearance as Re-Harakhty originated through association with Horus. From the fourth dynasty, kings held the title "Son of Re," and "Re" later became part of the throne name they adopted at accession. As the father of Ma'at, Re was the ultimate source of right and justice in the cosmos. At Thebes, by the late eleventh dynasty (circa 1980 BCE), Re was associated with Amon as Amon-Ra, who was for more than a millennium

29 Philip David Scott Moncrief, *Paganism and Christianity in Egypt 1913*

the principal god of the pantheon, the "king of the gods," and the patron of kings.

Is- (ισ-) is a prefix meaning equal', literally "divine-power synchronized." The prefix ισ figures prominently in Greek words pertaining to politics, mathematics, and knowledge.

Thus, the word Is-ra-el meant El (and) Ra; divine power synchronised, or El (and) Ra equal. This etymology indicates that the originators of the State of Israel recognised the divine power of the principal Egyptian and Canaanite deities.

In summary therefore, the ancient culture of Egypt was inculcated into those that left to live in Israel. Additionally, as we have demonstrated, because of constant migrations and inter-communication between the two neighbours, the immediate pre-Christian era was a time when there was a deep respect in Israel for the beliefs and traditions of Egypt.

CHAPTER 3

The Ancient Mysteries and Their Connections to Christianity

The links between the ancient Egyptian Mysteries and the Christian polemic is most obviously created via the Book of Revelation. This book uses mystical language to weave a story around the seven stars of Ursa Major. It mentions the seven stars five times, and the text makes it clear that this group of stars somehow embraces a throne and four living creatures (a calf, an eagle, a lion and the face of a man) and the names of God in Egyptian, Greek and Hebrew, as well as a series of other shapes such as the lamb, the sickle, the Alpha and the Omega and the tabernacle.

With only a small amount of research all of these figures can be easily located in the vicinity of the Ursa Major constellation.[30]

The author of The Book of Revelation tells us that he is John and it has been assumed by students of theology that he was John of Patmos. He claims he had a vision in which Jesus relayed information to him: *I Jesus . . . am the star bright the (one) of morning*[31] *. . . and I will give to him (the father) the star, the (one) of morning.*[32] *And from Jesus anointed, the witness the (one) faithful, the firstborn of the dead, and the ruler of the kings of the earth . . . .*[33]

Crucial to our analysis is a correct interpretation of the morning star. Some authors have claimed that it refers to Venus,

---

30 *The God Secret,* Greg Rigby
31 Revelation 2:16
32 Revelation 2:28
33 Revelation 1:5

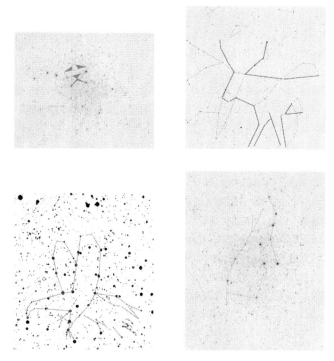

Fig 7 The four living creatures contained in the constellation of Ursa Major

Sothis or Sirius. Others claim that it was Horus[34]. These claims indicate that the connection is likely to be with Egypt as the pyramid texts tell us:

> *The sky will weep for you and the earth shake for you, the Moorer will scream for you and the great Mooring Post cry out for you, feet stomp for you and arms wave for you, as you go forth to the sky as <u>a star, the morning god</u>. Pepi has come to you, his father has come to you, Geb.[35]*

34 *Ancient Egypt, The Light of the World*, Gerald Massey
35 *Recitation 526, Writings from the Ancient World, The Ancient Egyptian Pyramid Texts,* James P Allen

Greg Rigby

O Osiris Pepi, Nut your mother, spreads herself above you, She conceals you from evil, Nut protects you from evil, You the greatest of her children . . . . [36]

These lines make it clear, that the most esoteric meaning of the term 'morning star' was as a reference to Osiris. He was the star in the body of Nut (Ursa Major) that was to accompany/ferry the sun across the sky following its rising.

The second reference in the Book of Revelation above refers to Jesus as the firstborn of the dead and the ruler of the kings of the earth. These designations also place Jesus as Osiris, since it is likely that the firstborn of the dead was the first man on earth. The ancient tradition was that the first person on earth was also the first God king. If this explanation is valid, Osiris would have been the firstborn in the Egyptian pantheon, the one whom all the pharaohs were descended from.

An alternative explanation might be that the definition the first-born of the dead referred to Osiris role as God of the afterlife. The Book of the Dead is a compendium of spells and prayers that are extracted from Ancient Egyptian tombs and funereal texts. They tell us: *"Osiris was the god of the underworld and was the god that made a peaceful afterlife possible."* [37]

The second title, ruler of the kings of the earth, completes the picture since this identifies the person as the first king and father of the kings of the earth (the pharaohs) and must therefore be Osiris: *"Osiris became (known as) the great Ancestor-god of Egypt, and was a reincarnation of his great-grandfather."* [38]

This picture of Osiris is best confirmed by the opening hymn in the Book of the Dead:

Homage to thee, Osiris, Lord of eternity, King of the Gods, whose names are manifold, whose forms are holy, thou being of hidden form in the temples, whose Ka is

---

36 *Uterance 446, Pyramid text in the pyramid of Pep1,* Jimmy Dunn
37 *Prefix to The Egyptian Book of the Dead* translated by E A Wallis Budge
38 *The Story of Creation,* E A Wallis Budge

*holy. Thou art the governor of Tattu (Busiris), and also
the mighty one in Sekhem (Letopolis). Thou art the Lord
to whom praises are ascribed in the nome of Ati, thou
art the Prince of divine food in Anu. Thou art the Lord
who is commemorated in Maati, the Hidden Soul, the
Lord of Qerrt (Elephantine), the Ruler supreme in White
Wall (Memphis). Thou art the Soul of Ra, his own body,
and hast thy place of rest in Henensu (Herakleopolis).
Thou art the beneficent one, and art praised in Nart.
Thou makest thy soul to be raised up. Thou art the Lord
of the Great House in Khemenu (Hermopolis). Thou art
the mighty one of victories in Shas-hetep, the Lord of
eternity, the Governor of Abydos. The path of his throne
is in Ta-tcheser (a part of Abydos). Thy name is established in the mouths of men. Thou art the substance of
Two Lands (Egypt). Thou art Tem, the feeder of Kau
(Doubles), the Governor of the Companies of the gods.
Thou art the beneficent Spirit among the spirits. The
god of the Celestial Ocean (Nu) draweth from thee his
waters. Thou sendest forth the north wind at eventide,
and breath from thy nostrils to the satisfaction of thy
heart. Thy heart reneweth its youth, thou producest the
. . . . The stars in the celestial heights are obedient unto
thee, and the great doors of the sky open themselves
before thee. Thou art he to whom praises are ascribed
in the southern heaven, and thanks are given for thee in
the northern heaven. The imperishable stars are under
thy supervision, and the stars which never set are thy
thrones. Offerings appear before thee at the decree of
Keb. The Companies of the Gods praise thee, and the
gods of the Tuat (Other World) smell the earth in paying homage to thee. The uttermost parts of the earth
bow before thee, and the limits of the skies entreat thee
with supplications when they see thee. The holy ones are
overcome before thee, and all Egypt offereth thanksgiving unto thee when it meeteth Thy Majesty. Thou art a
shining Spirit-Body, the governor of Spirit-Bodies; per-*

*manent is thy rank, established is thy rule. Thou art the
well-doing Sekhem (Power) of the Company of the Gods,
gracious is thy face, and beloved by him that seeth it. Thy
fear is set in all the lands by reason of thy perfect love,
and they cry out to thy name making it the first of names,
and all people make offerings to thee. Thou art the lord
who art commemorated in heaven and upon earth. Many
are the cries which are made to thee at the Uak festival,
and with one heart and voice Egypt raiseth cries of joy
to thee.*[39]

So here we have it: the descriptions of Jesus in the Book of
Revelation give us a direct link to Osiris and, if this is what is
intended, they must designate Jesus as the five-pointed star in
the heavens and the reincarnation of the first god king, Osiris.

The Book of the Dead makes it clear that heaven, the place
where all the various aspects of God are is in the vicinity of the
Constellation of Ursa Major. This is confirmed by the famous
astrological zodiac on the ceiling of the temple at Dendera, which
shows the thigh (Ursa Major) at its centre. This is not surprising
since the pole position (the place in the sky around which everything appears to revolve) was located in and around Ursa Major
during the period when the Egyptian pantheon evolved.

The following quote from the Egyptian Book of the Dead
gives us clear and unequivocal proof that Ursa Major, the constellation of the Great Bear, was thought by the Egyptians to be
the home of the royal court:

*Here I am; I have come to you that you may drive out
all the evil which is on me just as you did for those seven
spirits who are in the suite of the Lord of Sepa, whose
places Anubis made ready on the day of 'Come thence'.*
*Who are they? As for those gods the Lords of Jus-
tice, they are Seth and Isdes, Lord of the West. As for the
tribunal which is behind OsirisImsety, Hapy, Duamutef,*

39 *Papyrus of Ani; The Book of the Dead*, E A Wallis Budge

Fig 8 The ceiling at Dendera

and Qebehsenuef, it is these who are <u>behind the Great Bear in the Northern sky</u>. . . . O Re . . . may you save me from that <u>god whose shape is secret</u>, whose eyebrows are the arms of the balance, on the night of the reckoning of the robbers.

Who is he? He is Sheshmu, he is the mutilator of Osiris.

Otherwise said: He is Apep, he has only one head which bears righteousness.

Otherwise said: He is Horushe has two heads, one bearing right and one bearing wrong; he gives wrong to whoever does it and right to whoever comes with it.

Otherwise said: He is Horus the Great pre-eminent in Letopolis.

Greg Rigby

> *Otherwise said: He is Thoth*
> *Otherwise said: He is Nefertum, son of Bastet. These*
> *are the tribunal who take action against the enemies of*
> *the Lord of All.*[40]

This gives us clear and unequivocal proof that Ursa Major, the constellation of the Great Bear, was thought by the Egyptians to be the home of the Royal Court. This royal court appears to consist of three key personalities or aspects with other less significant gods or aspects of the same god in support:

- Osiris, the god contained within Bear in the northern sky
- Re or Ra who has the power to protect the supplicant against the power of the Gods
- The God whose "shape is secret," the Lord of All who is the mutilator of Osiris. This God could either be the invisible God who is associated with the pole position (around which Ursa Major rotated at that time) in the northern sky or the God described in the Book of the Dead whose eyes are in the position of the wings of Isis and whose shape (to the onlooker) changes as it rotates around the pole position each day.

The goddess Isis, who is described as both the wife and sister of Osiris, is located in the same place, and her wings overlie the eyes of God.

> *"Beneficent in command and word was Isis the woman of magical spells, the advocate of her brother. She sought him (Osiris) untiringly, she wandered round and round about this earth in sorrow, and she alighted not without finding him. She made light with her feathers, she created air with her wings, and she uttered the death wail for her brother. (Who had been killed and been dismembered by Seth)."*[41]

---

40 *Spell 17, Book of the Dead*, R O Faulkner
41 *The Papyrus of Ani, Book of the Dead*, E A Wallis Budge

44

A separate entry tells that the eyes of God are located in the position of the wings of Isis:

> *As for the plumes on his head, it means that Isis and Nephthys (another version of Isis) went and put themselves on his head when they were the Two Kites, and they were firm on his head. Otherwise said: They are the two great and mighty uraei (winged serpents), which are on the brow of his father Atum. Otherwise said: The Plumes on his head are his eyes.*[42]

Fig 9 The winged figure of Isis

These extracts correspond well with one of the most provocative statements in the Book of Revelation:

> *And were given to the woman the two wings of the eagle the (one) great in order that she might (fly) to the desert to the place of her where she is nourished there a right place/time and right places/times and half of right place/time/proportion/circumstance of/from a face of the serpent.*[43]

The Book of the Dead quotations imply that the plumes, which are the wings of Isis, are the eyes of God. The locations of the eyes of God are the extensions on either side of the four

---

42 *Spell 17, Book of the Dead*, R O Faulkner
43 Revelation 12:14

principal stars of Ursa Major. This means that the wings of Isis should be similarly positioned, thus placing the head and torso of Isis over the four central stars of the constellation.

Fig 10 The wings of Isis in the same location as the Eyes of God (inset)

In this coincidence of shapes, one aspect of Isis (and therefore God) overlies the eyes of God. By implication therefore, it overlies the face of God. This location of Isis is one of the clearest visual insights into the concept of differing names and aspects of one and the same God, a view that is a confirmation of spell 17, above.

Apart from the identities and locations of the three God personalities, there is a coincidence between the Book of the Dead and the Book of Revelation, which leads us to the undeniable conclusion that these texts refer on the one hand to Jesus and on the other to Osiris, and they are both talking about aspects of the same personality. This conclusion is confirmation of two additional similarities between the Jesus and the Osiris stories that we previously noted. The first was that they had the same birthday and the second that they were both murdered and resurrected.

Yet more direct references to Jesus in the Bible, which can be cross-referenced to Osiris, describe Jesus as someone who will judge the living and the dead:

> *He commanded us to preach to the people and to testify that he is the one whom God appointed as judge of the living and the dead.[44]*

> *I charge/testify before God and Jesus Christ who shall judge the living and the dead and by his appearing and his kingdom.[45]*

In relation to similar claims made for the Osiris, we are told,

> *(So) thou sittest upon the throne of Osiris, thy sceptre in thy hand, thou commandest the living.[46]*

> *In the Pyramid Texts, the rapid growth of individualized ethics and Osiris' assumption of the role of judge of the dead are not yet discernible, although the king is truly Osiris.[47]*

> *When Osiris comes back to life, however, he never returns to the land of the living, but remains in the underworld, The Duat, where he rules as King of Eternity and supreme judge of the dead.[48]*

> *When the dusk is in your sight, you wardens of Osiris, do not restrain my soul or hold back my shade;*

---

44 Acts 10:42
45 2 Timothy 4:1
46 Utterance 213; 134b Pyramid texts translated by A B Mercer
47 *Escaping Osiris*, Wim van den Dungen
48 *The Egyptian Book of the Dead*, Commentary by Dr Ogden Goelet

open a way for my soul and my shade; that it may see the Great God within the shrine on the day of examining souls.[49]

This similarity of description and qualities between Jesus and Osiris seems to imply that to find an explanation for the Jesus story, we should perhaps look closer at the Osiris inheritance and in particular the way it might have existed at the time of Jesus Christ.

At this stage, you (the reader) may be tempted to believe that this all sounds like mumbo jumbo. How could an examination of the Osiris tradition give us an understanding of the existence of a person named Jesus, born from humble parents in a small town in Palestine? How was this person chosen as the one who would be called Messiah and Son of God?

We propose that the answer to these questions must be somehow related to Jesus's anonymity or that it is contained in a direct link between Jesus and Egypt and Egypt's ancient beliefs.

If it is the former, as has been claimed by the Church over the centuries, then there is no rational explanation. It is "a question of faith" that Jesus was chosen by God incarnate to be born as a man, to die and to rise again. This appeal to faith is not new and has been used by the Christian hierarchy to discourage those who want to research the origins of the Jesus story.

If, on the other hand, linking Jesus with the Osiris personality is real and was intended, the only logical explanation to such connections stretch the limits of credulity and would certainly create dissonance amongst Christian believers.

The only hypothesis that would fit the facts is that Jesus was thought to be a vessel of the Egyptian royal blood and a direct descendant Osiris.

At first announcement, such a hypothesis would seem to be utterly incredible. However, if such a link to the pharaonic bloodline can be shown to have been the case, the claims made

---

49 *Spell 92, Book of the Dead*, R O Faulkner

by recent authors[50] and popularised by the movie *The Da Vinci Code* would assume a new and more impelling significance.

To investigate such a hypothesis for a direct link from the pharaonic bloodline to an actual person named Jesus Christ, we will need to analyse all the available facts concerning the following:

- The pharaonic bloodline, its progression and inheritance and the views of its incumbents and those commanded by its presence
- The Egyptian kings/queens and the state and perception of the royal bloodline at the time of Jesus's birth
- The annunciation and the birth of Jesus
- The baptism of Jesus
- The death of Jesus
- The people who grew the myth and their motivations
- What has happened since the time of Jesus

As with all historical analysis, the findings will produce only circumstantial evidence. Writings from the time were interpretations of facts and beliefs as transcribed by their authors. In the case of the Egyptians mysteries and beliefs, we are helped by the existence of significant and lasting monuments and texts, which were constructed at the time that the beliefs were existent. Because of this, we will assume therefore that the information we retrieve and use was based on the actual beliefs of the priests and pharaohs of the time.

Everyone has the right to believe whatever they wish, unless the expression their beliefs are judged by the rest of humanity (or by those making the rules) to be evil or inappropriate. The teachings by the Church that Christians must have faith in the Bible and the claim that the Bible is a sacred text that has been given by God have been believed by the faithful for centuries.

---

50 *The Holy Blood and the Holy Grail* by Richard Leigh, Michael Baigent, and Henry Lincoln

Greg Rigby

As science expands our awareness of the Universe and the origins of life, these tenants of Christian belief and their origins must be open to rational examination.

If the story of Jesus Christ is not about a divine being, given today's interpretation of what that that means, then the trust that the faithful has maintained in the Gospel and its teachings will have been misplaced. The blood that has been shed in the defence of the doctrine of Christianity will have all been for nothing.

For all of these reasons, and (if we can) in order to shed some light on the truth, it is essential that we investigate this mystery further and attempt to find an answer.

CHAPTER 4

The Royal Bloodline

The divinity of the pharaoh was an essential element in his claim to legitimacy:

- "Scholars were long ago familiar with doctrines of the king's two bodies, earthly and divine (Lanny Bell 1985) and of his divine birth and succession."[51]
- "The conception of the ideal king—divine descent, warrior prowess, reverence towards the gods, and wealth coupled with generosity towards his subjects—fits well into both Egyptian and Hellenistic ideology (Samuel 1993:181)."[52]

This divinity of the pharaoh was most easily claimed by having a manifest physical link back to Osiris, the first god-king, a link that was established via lineage and genealogy. For this reason, we first need to discuss the validity of the pharaonic bloodline.

The list of pharaohs from the first known incumbent is detailed in Appendix 2. The bulk of this list came from work by Manetho, who was an Egyptian priest from Heliopolis. Under the patronage of Ptolemy I, he compiled an Egyptian history, titled *Aegyptika*. It was written in Greek and finished circa 271 BCE. Manetho attempted to describe Egyptian history from its inception and rule by Cronos and Osiris to Alexander the Great. His original work was lost, and all we now have are extracted

---

51 *The Last Pharaohs*, J B Manning
52 *Ibid*

from short transcripts and summaries created by Christian historians in later centuries. A few different translations of Manetho's work exist:

- Josephus Flavius, from the first century CE
- Sextus Julius Africanus, third century CE
- Eusebius of Cesarea, third/fourth century CE
- George Syncellos (a Byzantine historian) from the eighth century CE

Mistakes made in translation, and by scribes making copies, reduce the value of *Aegyptiaca* as an historical document. Most of the dates simply don't match. However, Manetho is the basis for most of the chronologies and naming conventions for Egyptian pharaohs. His king list is often referenced by Egyptologists, some of who claim that there seems to have been some political hay made by exaggerating the reigns of some of the kings and by minimizing others. Significantly, Manetho traced the kings back to pre-dynastic period when Egypt was ruled by gods and demi-gods. He lists Cronos, Osiris and Typhon as the first gods who held sway in Egypt and Orus as the first demi-god.

The entire concept of dynasty comes from Manetho, who categorised the kings in reasonably logical groups by location or family or other identifying feature. The Manetho list is supplemented by the incorporation of kings from the Turin list, the Palermo stone and the Abydos Kings list which is inscribed on the walls of the temple of Seti.

The Turin kings list is also known as the Turin Royal Canon. It is an Egyptian hieratic papyrus thought to date from the reign of Pharaoh Ramses II, now in the Museo Egizio (Egyptian Museum) in Turin, which gives details of eighteen kings reigning in the ninth and tenth dynasties. In this papyrus, the God kings in the pre-dynastic period are listed and include Osiris, Horus, Thoth and Ma'at.

The Palermo stone, often known as the Royal Annals is an important primary source. It originates from the end of the fifth dynasty (twenty-fifth century BCE). The stone annotates mythical pre-dynastic kings of Egypt followed by pharaohs from the first five dynasties. Each pharaoh had up to five names, which were chosen to represent the individual's personality, their devotion or affiliation to a particular god:

- A Horus name
- A Nebty name (attaching the person to a name of the goddess)
- Golden falcon name
- Formal name
- Informal name (the name most often referred to)

A description of the stone and its contents is eminently described in the works of Cedric Leonard:

Since ancient kings often had more than one name, phonetic agreement between the Palermo Stone and other king-lists is not really necessary. Most Egyptologists seem to be reasonably sure of the top line containing the names of the god-kings, even though it is obvious that most of the glyphs are badly worn. Regardless, I am offering alternate readings in certain instances to point out the possibility of actual phonetic agreement.

Although portions of nine of the original ten god-king's names are in evidence, only seven of the names are complete. The first two king's names are almost entirely missing, as well as the last one of the ten (reading from right to left). The remainder of the top line containing demi-god kings (the left portion) is broken away. Each name is contained within a "box" (not really a cartouche) made of horizontal and vertical lines. The names are very simple—usually indicated by two glyphs each (three in some cases). Directly below each king's name and attached to the "cartouche" (box) is the hieroglyphic determinative for god-king.

I believe a few of the glyphs merit an alternate reading from that which has been provided by the experts.

53

Immediately below is a photo of the top line of hiero-glyphs, which may be compared with my reconstruction (farther below) of the names.

The first name is completely broken away, and only a piece of the second name shows on the Palermo Stone (far right). The first complete name (the third king) seems to read "Ska." Egyptian spellings being as fluid as they are with the passage of time, this could later have become the Shuor Su of the Turin Canon. Next (reading to the left), I believe the strangely slanted oval-shaped glyph (thought to be an H) is in reality a very worn side of the goose "Seb," (its legs and head no longer visible). The glyph below it seems to be a reclining animal of some sort, but it's very faint and nearly impossible to be read with any assurance. The goose by itself can be read "Seb." The third complete name starts with a very small glyph that is nearly unreadable. Egyptologists have taken it to be the common glyph (a loaf) for T, but it could possibly be a not so common glyph (a small loop) for S. The next glyph, a reed (Y), is not very clear either. The bird glyph looks like a chick (U); but should it be a swallow (WR) it would read SYWR: I think it possible that this name is "Ausar," the Egyptian name for the god Osiris. The fourth "cartouche" from the right has two very wide "rectangular" shaped glyphs. The experts see the top one as a rope glyph and the bottom one as a rect-angle, but they are damaged and I believe the reverse to be just as possible (I don't have the stone itself to look at). The rope represents a T or TH, and the rectangle an S or SH. They have, therefore read it TSH; reverse this sequence, and it reads SHT, or the god-king Set.

At the top of the next cartouche is a rather long, thin line, which Egyptologists assume to be a wavy line, the letter N. From what I can see, this is impossible: it looks straight, not wavy. It appears to be one of the uncommon versions of the letter H (a club). Below this is a very obscure glyph, which could well be the swallow glyph,

54

UR or WR. Therefore, I read this as Hwr (Egyptian for Horus).[53]

One of the key aspects of the Egyptian religion was that every king could be traced back to Osiris. This way they could claim to be god kings or Sons of God. For this to happen, the bloodline would have needed to be unbroken from Ra and Osiris; the Palermo stone attempts to show that this is the case up to the end of the fifth dynasty: *"From the beginning pharaohs were considered gods—the embodiment of Horus while living and living on as Osiris after death."*[54]

The traditional lineage of the pharaohs from the fifth dynasty was descent from Ra, who once ruled Egypt. All pharaohs were descended from Ra and a mortal mother. Pharaohs were always titled Son of Ra.[55]

The Abydos King List, also known as the Abydos Table, is a list of the names of seventy-six kings of Ancient Egypt, found on a wall of the Temple of Seti I at Abydos. It consists of three rows of thirty-eight cartouches (borders enclosing the name of a king) in each row. The upper two rows contain names of the kings, while the third row merely repeats Seti I's throne name and praenomen. Besides providing the order of the Old Kingdom kings, it is the sole source to date of the names of many of the kings of the seventh and eighth dynasties, so the list is valued greatly for that reason. This list omits the names of many earlier pharaohs who were apparently considered illegitimate—such as Akhenaten, Hatshepsut, Smenkhkare, Tutankhamen and Ay.

When tracing through the list of kings from the first recorded king up until the end of the Ptolemaic dynasty, several aspects become obvious:

- To ensure that the bloodline is intact and sacred, it is oftentimes passed via daughters as well as sons. On

---

53 *The Palermo Stone*, R Cedric Leonard
54 *Mercer Dictionary of the Bible*, Watson E Mills and Aubrey Lullard
55 *HSC Ancient History*, Peter Roberts

some occasions, there is intermarriage between brother and sister. (There have even been suggestions that the lineage was passed via the female line, and that this inter-marriage was organised to secure the kingship). In various Egyptian texts, Isis is referred to as the wife and as the sister of Osiris; perhaps this belief in the twin role of Isis gave the incestuous practice legitimacy.

- The intervention of the Hyksos kings did not interrupt the parallel bloodline that maintained the links back to Osiris. Ahmose I, the first pharaoh of the eighteenth dynasty, defeated the Hyksos. This was the last dynasty to rule Egypt before the break created by Ramses I. The eighteenth dynasty commenced what is known as the new kingdom.

There are several occasions where there appear to be a break in the lineage, the principal ones being the following:

- The taking of the pharaonic crown by provincial governors between the sixth and twelfth dynasties
- The beginning of the nineteenth dynasty when the throne was taken by Ramesses I (1293 BCE)
- The beginning of the twenty-fifth dynasty when Nubians invaded Lower Egypt
- The beginning of the Macedonian and Ptolemaic dynasties by Alexander the Great (332 BCE) and the continuation by Ptolemy I

Records for the 200 years following the end of the sixth dynasty are incomplete. Neferkare VII (circa 2140 BCE) was the third pharaoh of the ninth dynasty and his name suggests that he considered himself a legitimate successor of Pepi II Neferkare (2278—2184 BCE) of the sixth dynasty. This link also applies to Neferkare VIII, the second pharaoh of the tenth dynasty, (circa 2130 and 2040 BCE) succeeded by Merykare the last king of this dynasty who presided over the Herakleopolite Kingdom and who attempted to maintain a policy of peaceful co-existence with the adjacent Theban kingdom. If this is a valid analysis, we can reasonably assume that the chronology was valid until the end of the tenth dynasty.

The Theban eleventh dynasty reunified Egypt and held power from 2140 until 1991 BCE when Amenemhat I took the throne. Many of these pharaohs took a Horus name and declared themselves the rulers of the whole of Egypt.

Sehetepibre Amenemhat I was the first ruler of the twelfth dynasty but it is thought not to have been of royal lineage and is believed to have had no direct blood link with the pharaohs of the eleventh dynasty. If there was a link, it must have come through the female line. This pharaoh, whose name meant renaissance worked to re-unite the two lands and to re-establish the old order. Like politicians today, he was a master of propaganda and spin. The importance of his legal right to the throne was enhanced by the writing and publication of a supposed (ancient) prophecy, *The Prophecy of Nefertiti*. This prophecy predicted the advent of a future king called Ameny, who would restore order to the country.

This literary work together with the pharaoh's most notable composition, the *Instructions of Amenemhat* and, in architecture, the reversion to the pyramid-style complexes of the sixth dynasty rulers are all considered to have been manifest attempts to legitimize his rule. The son of his successor, Senusret I, is claimed to have been worshipped as a god for many centuries after his death,[56] indicating that Egyptians at the time believed him to be a legitimate .

There is some debate amongst historians concerning Sekhemre Khutawy Sobekhotep I (1802—1800 BCE), the first pharaoh of the thirteenth dynasty. The records indicate that he reigned close in time to Amenemhat III and this seems to indicate that he was the son of Amenemhat IV of the twelfth dynasty.

We can see, from this brief analysis that it is that it is impossible to accurately cite evidence of a direct and unbroken blood-

---

56 *The Complete Royal Families of Ancient Egypt*, Aiden Dodson and Dyan Hilton

line from the first kings to the end of the thirteenth dynasty. What is evident, is that those kings whose claim to title was suspect, went to great lengths to legitimise their rule through the adoption of full names, the issuing of texts and by the construction of pyramids and other monuments.

Many of the pharaohs' wives have the title King's Daughter indicating that they were the daughter of a pharaoh, but in some instances, such as Neferu I, the first identified queen of the eleventh dynasty, it is not possible to specify precisely which pharaoh is the father. It is of course possible that the pharaohs did legitimise their reign by their choice of queen but we have no evidence of this other than acknowledged tradition.

The first pharaoh of the nineteenth dynasty was Ramses I. His birth name, Ramesses (Ramses Paramessu) means "Re has fashioned him" or "Son of Ra." His throne name was Menpehtyre, which means "Eternal is the Strength of Re." Horemheb's selection of Ramesses as his successor seems to have been carefully thought out. This is illustrated by the fact that Ramesses I chose the Golden Horus name of "He who confirms Ma'at throughout the Two Lands," thus indicating his desire to carry on the work of Horemheb in re-establishing religious order after the heretic rule of Akhenaten. Ramses's name and titles also stress the privileged nature of his relationship with Re or Ra, the sun god.[57] The name Son of Ra is key evidence of his claim to part of the royal line and of his own divinity.

Historians tell us that Ramses I was previously the Vizier, close friend and confidant of the pharaoh Horemheb who, having failed to produce an heir, appears to have bestowed his succession upon his comrade. Ramses must have been of advanced years, probably in his fifties, and was not of royal blood.[58]

One author on the subject makes a tenuous link, which is difficult to substantiate:

Ramses I was about 75 years old when he died in about 1290 BCE, meaning that he must have been con-

---

57 *King Ramses*, Jimmy Dunn
58 *Chronicle of the Pharaohs*, Samy Salah

ceived in about 1365 BCE. This date lies squarely within the reign of Amenhotep III the father of Akhenaton. The only historical information we have about Ramesses I states that his father was called Seti—so which Seti in this era would have been his father? One possibility is evident from the works of Manetho. I have previously identified Armais (Dannus) as being the Armana pharaoh Ay. But, according the Manetho, Armais had a brother called Sethos (Seti) who was also called Argyptus. Since Ay was the brother-in-law of Amenhotep III (and could have been his cousin) it is likely that this Sethos (Seti) was of the right era and age to have been the father of Ramesses I. If this is so, then it would mean that the nineteenth dynasty was simply a continuation of the eighteenth, through a very closely related strand of the Armana family.[59]

After a short reign of two years, Ramses I was succeeded by his son Seti I, who had held the same titles of Vizier and Troop Commander as his father. In order to restore Egyptian fortunes after the instability under the Armana kings, he inaugurated a programme of major construction. He took the additional title of Repeater of Births signifying the beginning of a new and legitimate era. On the basis of inscriptions in the temple of Abydos, the parents of Seti I are assumed to be Ramesses I and Sitre. However, a stele carved under Ramesses II claims Seti I's mother to be named Tia, the same name as the wife of Amenhotep III, a link which was perpetuated when Seti named his daughter Tia and Ramses II (his son) named his daughter Tia-Sitre.

One of Seti's most significant constructions was the grand Temple at Abydos, which incorporated the Abydos King List. The list contains the names of seventy-six kings of ancient Egypt, predecessors whom Seti acknowledged to be legitimate pharaohs. On the other hand, rulers who were considered illegitimate, such as Hatshepsut and Akhenaten were conveniently

59 *Eden in Egypt*, Ralph Ellis

omitted from the List. The list was arranged in three rows, each containing 38 cartouches. The first two rows consisted of the names of his predecessors and the third row is just a repetition of Seti I's throne name and other names.

The Abydos King List, together with the temple reliefs showing Seti being anointed and crowned by the gods, as well as the dedication of the entire Abydos site to Osiris were actions that proclaimed the legitimacy of Seti I's rule and the authenticity of his claim to dynastic succession. The pharaoh's divinity—his relationship and kinship with the gods—was proved by being the son and heir of a divine pharaoh, whose wife had conceived him from the gods or, failing this, by mythology that convinced the world that the king was a heavenly father.

Seti's actions indicate that he was fully aware of the importance of the bloodline that connected the pharaohs back to Osiris and made their God status legitimate. Logic tells is that given this awareness, if there was any question of his own legitimacy, it was very probable that Seti would ensure that his son Ramses II (who was to succeed him) would marry someone who carried the blood of a legitimate queen or king from the eighteenth dynasty. Since there is no evidence of this, we must assume that Seti I believed that he had a direct claim to the throne and that his reign perpetuated the bloodline.

Ramses II came to the throne at the age of twenty-five and reigned sixty-seven years. He would have been conceived in 1304 BCE, which means that like his father and grandfather he was conceived in the Armana period. In his case, this would have happened when Horemheb was on the throne and abundant progeny of Amenhotep III existed. History has named him Ramesses the Great, reflecting the fact that no other pharaoh constructed as many temples or erected as many colossal statues and obelisks as he. He had many wives, but he had two principal wives, Nefertari and Istnofret whom he married at least ten years before Seti's death. Nothing has been able to be proved of their ancestry.

If there was a break in the bloodline, the first three pharaohs of the nineteenth dynasty did nothing to betray it. Their names and the messages carved on their abundant constructions confidently claimed their divinity and their links to the line from Osiris. In all probability there existed connections through marriage, but there are no records to prove this one way or the other. In any event, their actions proclaimed the importance of the bloodline and reinforced its importance for future generations.

Following this interruption to the bloodline (if that is what it was), the Egyptian crown was passed from Nubian, to Assyrian to Libyan, to Persian and Greek Monarchs over an 800 year period that started with the twentieth dynasty in 1190 BCE and culminating in the invasion by Alexander in 332 BCE. The Nubians invaded Lower Egypt and took the throne of Egypt under Usermaatre Piye although they already controlled Thebes and Upper Egypt in the early years of Piye's reign. Piye's conquest of Lower Egypt in 752 BCE established the twenty-fifth dynasty, which ruled until 656 BCE. His first wife Tabiry had the title King's Daughter indicating that she claimed to be the daughter of a pharaoh. Her father was Alara, a Nubian king who has been variously claimed to have been Ary Meryamun and Aryamani (Usermaatre Setepenre) (785—778). If this is the case then the bloodline is protected through her.

Piye's father Kashta had attempted to pre-empt the problem of legitimate succession some years earlier.

Kashta's appearance as King of Upper and Lower Egypt and peaceful takeover of Upper Egypt is suggested by the fact that the descendants of Osorkon III, Takelot III and Rudamun (765—762) continued to enjoy a high social status in Thebes in the second half of the eighth and in the first half of the seventh century BCE as is shown by their burials in this city as well as the joint activity between the Divine Adoratrice Shepenupet I and the god's Wife of Amun Elect Amenirdis I, Kashta's daughter. A stele from Kashta's reign has been found in Elephantine (modern day Aswan)—at the local temple dedicated to the god Khnum—which attests to his control of this region. It bears his royal name or prenomen

Nimaatre. Egyptologists today believe that either he or more likely Piye was the Year 12 Nubian king mentioned in a well-known inscription at Wadi Gasus which associates the Adopted god's Adoratice of Amun, Amenirdis, Kashta's daughter together with Year 19 of the serving God's Wife of Amun, Shepenupet. Kashta's reign length is unknown.

Some sources credit Kashta as the founder of the twenty-fifth dynasty since he was the first Kushite king known to have expanded his kingdom's influence into Upper Egypt. Under Kashta's reign, the native Kushite population of his kingdom, situated between the third and fourth Cataracts of the Nile, became rapidly 'Egyptianized' and adopted Egyptian traditions, religion and culture.[60]

Alexander III of Macedon (356—323 BCE), commonly known as Alexander the Great was a King (Basileus) of the Ancient Greek kingdom of Macedon and a member of the Argead (Greek) dynasty. Doctor Joanne Foster describes Alexander's impact on Egypt and its Royal dynasty:

After conquering Persia's naval bases all along the coastline of Asia Minor and Syria-Palestine, Alexander marched south into Egypt where he remained for some six months. Although generally regarded as little more than an eccentric diversion, Alexander's Egyptian sojourn was essential to his future plans. He needed a strong coastal base for both strategic and commercial purposes, from which he could not only communicate across the Mediterranean but which could also handle the highly lucrative sea-borne trade network he wanted to divert from Phoenicia. With naval reinforcements following his progress down the coast, his Macedonian army covered the hazardous 130-mile distance in only a

---

60 *The Kingdom of Tush*, Laslio Torok

*week to reach the heavily fortified coastal town of Pelu-
sium in late October 332 BCE.*

*With his reputation going before him, Alexander was
met by Egypt's Persian governor Mazaces. With no armed
forces and with no likelihood of any assistance following the defeated Darius's swift departure back east to
Persia, Mazaces simply handed over the treasury's 800
talents and "all the royal furniture." In return he was
kept on as part of the new administration together with
the new governor Cleomenes, who was made responsible
for finance and created the royal mint around 331 BCE.
Cleomenes was a hardheaded, unscrupulous business-
man who quickly amassed a personal fortune of 8,000
talents during his career as governor. Yet he remained
loyal to Alexander with whom he kept up a regular cor-
respondence, sending him such delicacies as smoked
quail by the thousand. After installing a garrison at the
key defensive site of Pelusium, Alexander then ordered
his fleet to sail south up the Nile to the traditional capital
Memphis (Ineb-hedj) at the apex of the Delta where he
himself would arrive by land at the head of his troops.
Passing by the ancient religious site of Heliopolis (Iunu)
with its vast white temples and obelisks, Egypt made an
enormous impression on both the Macedonian troops and
their twenty-four-year-old leader. Brought up with his
formidable mother Olympias's tales of Egyptian gods, the
religiously-minded Alexander must have been completely
dumbstruck in a land so steeped in ritual, where priests
held enormous power wielded inside temples not built
to human scale. Passing by the great pyramids of Giza,
still gleaming in their shining white limestone, he finally
reached Memphis to a genuinely rapturous reception.*[61]

The obvious break in the bloodline caused by the assimilation of a conquering Macedonian king was solved in retrospect,

---

61 *Alexander in Egypt*, Alan M Fildes and Dr Joann Fletcher

at least conceptually, by what has become known as *The Alexander Romance*. This document was composed and written in Alexandria by an unknown author "whom certain manuscripts falsely name as Callisthenes, kin of Aristotle and companion and historian of Alexander the Great"[62] some time before the fourth century AD.

In elaborate prose, the romance tells how Nectanebo II (the last king of the thirtieth dynasty, the final dynasty of native Egyptians) fled to Macedon when Egypt was invaded by the Persians. After his departure, the Egyptian God of the underworld *Sinopos* delivered an oracle, which promised "that King of yours who fled (Nectanebo) will come again into Egypt, not having aged, but rejuvenated. He will subdue your enemies the Persians." In the meantime, Nectanebos uses sorcery to seduce Olympias the Queen of Macedonia who subsequently gives birth to Alexander, the son of Nectanebo and person who was later to drive the Persians out of Egypt. In this scenario, Alexander is a direct descendent of Nectanebo and has legitimate claim via the bloodline to be pharaoh of Egypt

The Alexander Romance was written many years after Alexander's death and represented myths which grew from the short time Alexander spent in Egypt (332—331 BCE). During that time, he instituted remarkable constructions and did everything to present himself as a divine pharaoh. Persia had occupied Egypt for 180 years since the end of the twenty-sixth dynasty in 525 BCE. They have appointed a series of governors to rule the territory. As Dr Joann Fletcher explains:

> *The Persians showed relatively little respect for the ancient traditions and were deeply unpopular, and the Egyptians's had rebelled so often that parts of the country remained virtually independent.*
>
> *Because of this, Alexander was hailed as Saviour and Liberator, and as the people's choice and legitimate*

---

62 *The Romance of Alexander the Great by Pseudo-Callisthenes*, Introduction; Albert Mugrdich Wolohojian

heir, he was offered the double crown of the Two Lands. Anointed as pharaoh in Memphis on 14 November 332 BCE, the culmination of his coronation was the climactic moment when the high priest named him son of the gods according to traditions dating back almost 3,000 years.

Always a devout man who began each day with sacrifices to the gods, Alexander had no difficulty worshipping the Egyptian deities. Equating their gods with his own, he worshipped the Egyptian Amun as a form of Zeus. At the Memphite necropolis of Sakkara the new pharaoh offered sacrifices to the Apis bull, a cult animal of the creator god Ptah, followed by Greek-style games and literary contests in which performers from all over the Greek world took part in a multi-cultural extravaganza. These kinds of events mark the beginnings of Hellenism in their blending of Greek practices and local traditions, and Egypt and Greece would successfully co-exist for the next three centuries.

Alexander is reported to have attended lectures given by the Egyptian philosopher Psammon where he debated the inter-relationship between Greek and Egyptian theology and custom.

For two months, he resided as living god in the royal palace at Memphis, studying Egyptian laws and customs at first hand, he gave orders for the restoration of the Egyptians' religious centres, including the great southern temples of <u>Luxor</u> and Karnak, where he appears in the company of the Egyptian gods wearing traditional Egyptian regalia including the rams horns of Amun as worn by his pharaonic predecessors including Amenhotep III.

Alexander's image was replicated all over Egypt in both monumental statuary and delicate relief, together his with his Greek name translated into hieroglyphs enclosed by the royal cartouche: "Horus, the strong ruler, he who seizes the lands of the foreigners, beloved (son) of Amun and the chosen one of Ra-meryamun sete-penra Aleksandros."

It tells us much that he undertook a perilous desert march to consult the Oracleat Aghurmi. On arrival, he went immediately to the temple of Amun. Plutarch tells us that according to his sources, Alexander was met by the Siwan high priest who greeted him with the words "O, paidion", "Oh, my son," but mispronounced the Greek as "O, pai dios" meaning "Oh, son of god."

The small number of his party waited in the temple forecourt, and after the high priest announced to all present that the god was content, they could proceed with their questions. One of the Macedonians asked the Oracle whether they might give their king divine honours, to which the reply came, "This would please Ammon." Then in his capacity as pharaoh and high priest of all the gods, Alexander was led into to the heavily scented darkness of the inner sanctuary to put his questions personally to the god himself. When he finally emerged into the daylight, he was met by his friends anxious to know exactly what had transpired. Alexander would only say he had been given the answer his heart desired. That the main subject discussed had been the nature of his divine paternity seems the most likely, since he was adamant that the only other person he would tell these secret prophecies to would be his mother, and as he told Olympias in a letter this would only be face to face on his return to Macedonia.

Alexander left Egypt in the spring (mid-April) of 331 BCE having had massive impact on Egypt and having consolidated his own claims to power and influence. Although he would never return alive to see the city he had founded, it would eventually be his final resting place when his embalmed body was returned there for burial ten years later.[63]

---

63 *Alexander in Egypt,* Alan M Fildes and Dr Joann Fletcher

The groundwork done, Ptolemy I (305—285 BCE) was Alexander's appointed successor and together with his descendants, hc adopted Egyptian royal trappings and added Egypt's religion to the Greek tradition, worshipping the gods of eternity and building temples to them. They were even mummified and buried in sarcophagi covered with hieroglyphs.

This adoption of Egyptian culture was the real secret to Ptolemy's rule and that of his descendants. Alexander came and left, as an Emperor and , bringing the rest of the world under his influence, but Ptolemy saw the need to rule according to the customs and traditions of the people he was to rule.

The famed Satrap Stele, on which is carved a decree from Ptolemy (from the same period as his installation as ruler) reads, "I Ptolemy, the satrap, restore to Horus, the avenger of his father, the territory of Patanut [Egypt], from this day forth forever . . . ." In addition to showing respect for the Egyptian religion and beliefs (something previous conquerors had failed to do), this inscription reminded the people exactly who it was who had liberated Egypt from the Persian Empire, thus ensuring much support for the new ruler and the dynasty that would follow him.

The perpetuation of the pharaonic dynasty via Ptolemy I Soter (Saviour), Alexander's successor was attempted in two ways; first via the will and testament of Alexander and secondly by the actions of Ptolemy, after Alexander's death.

The *Alexander Romance* tells us, "And Perdikkas thought that Alexander would leave all his goods to Ptlomeos because he had often spoken to him of Ptlomeos's lucky birth. And Olympias, too, had made it clear that Ptlomeos had been fathered by Philip (Alexander's official father)."

It goes on to speak of Alexander's spoken will allocation: "Egypt goes to Ptlomeos, and let him be given as wife Cleopatra, the sister of Alexander, ruler of the brave."

Being the son of Phillip might have helped secure the Macedonian throne but it did not help with any claim to the throne of Egypt. The main thing that helped Ptolemy's claim to legitimacy was that Alexander, the divine willed Egypt to him.

There is much written about the parents of Ptolemy: Everyone agrees that his mother was Arsinoe but historians disagree about her conception of Ptolemy. On the one hand, it is claimed that she was spouse of Lagus and on the other, that she was a concubine of Phillip II and that Ptolemy I was the result of this association. Whatever the truth of it, the fact that there was claim of a direct link between Phillip and Ptolemy indicates that the concept of legitimate and continuous lineage was thought to be important in a Macedonian context. Ptolemy was shown to be aware of the importance of lineage in relation to Egypt by his sponsorship of Manetho who traced the pharaohs back to Osiris and brought the concept of "dynasty" into the public domain when he published his *Aegyptika*.

The motivation of Ptolemy to establish legitimacy could well explain the myth surrounding Alexander's tomb:

> In 2002, Andrew Chugg, an English aerospace expert and Egyptologist, resurrected the idea that Alexander had indeed been interred in the pharaoh's sarcophagus. The argument was based on old ideas suggesting that in the rush to bury Alexander, Ptolemy had placed the royal mummy in the empty sarcophagus made for, but never occupied by, Nectanebo II. This event it was said, may have inspired the confused legend enshrined in *The Alexander Romance* that Nectanebo II was Alexander's real father, making Alexander the legitimate pharaoh of Egypt. The scattered, ambiguous evidence from the ancient writers Pausanius, Curtius and Diodorus was combed for clues, which were reinforced by the findings of Auguste Mariette at Memphis-Saqqara.[64]

The significance of the divine lineage to Ptolemy I was transmitted and manifested by his son, Ptolemy II Philadelphus. This is explained very clearly by A E Samuel:

---

64 *Alexander's Tomb*, Nicholas J Saunders

It is also clear that the dynastic cult of the Ptolemies never spread throughout the Mediterranean world in the way that we find the worship of Isis and Sarapis did; and this may well indicate a difference in the attitude toward it. In any case, as Dunand points out, the Ptolemies were not directly involved in the propagation of these cults, and their establishment for the most part was a matter of individual initiative. The dynastic cult was largely a phenomenon restricted to Egypt itself, and that has been taken to mean that it existed only where it was supported directly by the crown. On the other hand, cults of individual sovereigns, kings and queens, dedications and temples, combine to show members of the dynasty were treated as divinities, either individually or in assimilation to other deities in Egypt. Similarly, the evidence of sculpture, like the many small stone heads of Philadelphus which were attached to bodies of cheaper materials like wood, are inexplicable unless they were used as cult figures by private persons. Thus, despite all the uncertainties in the material, there is no doubt that the idea of the Ptolemaic monarchy definitely included a notion of the divinity of the king, a notion which extended to the Greeks and Macedonians and was established in the ideology as early as the middle of the reign of Philadelphus.[65]

All in all, these stories about the actions of Ramesses, Seti I, Alexander, Ptolemy and Piye and the significant historical writings that support them indicate clearly that the lineage of the god-King was massively important to them. Even non-Egyptians such as Alexander became enraptured by the glorification provided by the Egyptian tradition and the divine power it bestowed upon its earthly kings.

In those cases where the genealogical succession is unable to be traced, any actual succession would have been achieved through an unknown female line. However, during the years

---

65 *The Ptolemies and the Ideology of Kingship*, A E Samuel

Greg Rigby

since the enthronement of Ramesses I at the beginning of the nineteenth dynasty (1292 BCE) which included invasion by Nubians, Assyrians, Libyans, Persians and Greeks, it is difficult to plot a direct line. The last dynasty that can claim an unbroken connection back to the first pharaohs and thus to Osiris was the eighteenth dynasty.

Whether the line was continuous or not, the pharaohs all made an effort to proclaim their legitimacy and their right to the titles that the kingship bestowed upon them and in doing so they reinforced the importance of legitimate inheritance of the title Son of God and of the line back to Osiris.

CHAPTER 5

The Son of God

As we saw in Chapter 2, the word Moses derives from the Egyptian word mes or mos, which means son. This word was incorporated into the name of many Egyptian pharaohs.

- Dedumose
- Kamose
- Ahmose
- Thutmose
- Rameses

With the exception of Dedu, the prefixes of these names, Ka, Ah, Thut and Ra were all Egyptian spiritual entities: Ka, the spiritual essence of the soul, Ah the God of the Moon, Thut the architect God of the universe and Ra, the God who created all forms of life.

Because of this, Thutmose (for example) was Son of Thut or, in simpler terms, Son of God. These designations were most popular from the commencement of Ahmose I's reign at the beginning of the eighteenth dynasty (circa 1550 BCE), a dynasty that included the rule of Thutmose III. (In Chapter 7, we will discuss how this may have been significant.)

The full name of the pharaoh consists of five names. Examples of some of these names are given in the list of pharaohs detailed in appendix 2. The following were the name titles:

- The Horus name
- The Nebti name
- The golden Horus name

Greg Rigby

- The prenomen
- The nomen

a) The Horus-name

The oldest known part of the royal titulary is the Horus-name, sometimes called the banner-name or the Ka-name. It represents the king as the earthly embodiment of the god Horus, the divine prototype and patron of the Egyptian kings. This name is ordinarily written within a rectangular frame, at the bottom of which is seen a design of recessed panelling, such as we find in the facades of early tombs and in the false doors of many private tombs. The Ancient Egyptian name for this facade was serekh.

On the top of the serekh is perched the falcon of Horus, hence the appellation Horus-name. In the more elaborate New Kingdom examples, Horus is wearing the double crown and is accompanied by the sun and a uraeus (a stylised upright cobra worn as a head ornament).

In the Early-Dynastic Period, the perched falcon of Horus was in fact part of the name of the king. Aha, for instance, was actually called Horus-Aha, "Horus who fights."

The Horus Name was not the birth name of the king, but it was given to him when he ascended the throne. During the first three dynasties, it was the king's official name. His name of birth would not appear in official documents. This has complicated the identification of many early kings mentioned in the king lists, where only the name of birth is mentioned.

Although it would continue to be used throughout the entire Ancient Egyptian history, it lost its importance to the Prenomen en nomen from the end of the Old Kingdom on.

b) The Nebti-name

The Nebti-name shows the king in a special relation to two goddesses: the vulture-goddess Nekhbet of the Upper Egyptian cities of Elkab and Hierakonpolis and the cobra-goddess Uto of the Lower Egyptian city Buto. Both goddesses are the deified personification of Upper and Lower-Egypt respectively, and as such, the Nebti-name denotes the king as "the one of Nekhbet (Upper-Egypt) and Uto (Lower-Egypt)," i.e. as the "one belonging to Upper and Lower Egypt". It is often translated as Nebti or the Two Ladies.

First dynasty King Den is the first to have assumed this Nebti-name. The use of this title by Den may perhaps indicate some governmental reforms that may have occurred during this king's reign.

c) The "Golden Horus" name

The meaning of the third part of the royal titulary, the Golden Horus name is more disputed. It represents the falcon god Horus perched on a symbol that usually represents gold.

Based on the Greek equivalent of this title on the Rosetta Stone, which translates into English as superior to (his) foes, it has been proposed that the hieroglyphs symbolised Horus as victorious over Seth, the Ombite (another possible reading of the hieroglyph on which the falcon is standing). This was, no doubt, the interpretation during Greek times, when the opposition between Horus and Seth was much more pronounced than in earlier times. Significantly, during this period, the Earth's pole position had moved out of Draco and into Ursa Minor, the constellation synonymous with Horus.

If the Golden Horus name symbolised Horus's victory over his enemy Seth, one might expect that the names following this group should be aggressive in nature, but most of the time, those names are far from being bellicose.

In a context dealing with the titulary of Thutmosis III, the king says, "He (Amun) modelled me as a falcon of gold." Thutmosis III's co-regent Hatshepsut calls herself "the female Horus of fine gold." The concept of the golden falcon can be definitely traced back to the eleventh dynasty. An inscription of the twelfth dynasty describes the Golden Horus name as the "name of gold."

The notion of gold is strongly linked to the notion of eternity. The burial chamber in the royal tombs of the New Kingdom was often called the golden room, not (only) because it was stacked up with gold, but because it was there for eternity. The golden Horus name may convey the same notion of eternity, expressing the wish that the king may be an eternal Horus.

d) The Prenomen

The Prenomen is the name that follows the title King of Upper and Lower Egypt. The oldest known example of this title is again dated to the reign of first dynasty king Den, when it was often combined with the Nebti-name, without a distinct name added to it. It would take until the end of the third dynasty before this title really came into use. It would eventually replace the Horus-name as most important official royal name.

The Prenomen itself usually contained the name of the god Re. Typical examples are "pleasing to the heart of Re" (Amenemhat I) and "lord of the heavenly order is Re" (Amenhotep III).

One of the first cases of Re as an element in a king's name is with Khephren of the fourth dynasty (Khaf-Re). The title King of Upper and Lower Egypt can sometimes be followed by the phrase "the Lord of the Two Lands:"

Sometimes this phrase replaces it entirely. A queen can be called the Mistress of the Two Lands.

e) The nomen

The nomen is introduced by the epithet son of Ra. It was added to the royal titulary in the beginning of the fourth dynasty. It was from that time on that the royal titulary became established in the form discussed here.

The name following this title was, as a rule, the king's name of birth. It is almost the equivalent of a surname or a family name. For instance, the eleventh dynasty is reflected in the names Antef and Mentuhotep; the twelfth dynasty in the names Amenemhat and Sesostris; the thirteenth dynasty shows several kings of the name Sebekhotep; and the eighteenth dynasty consists almost entirely of rulers named Amenhotep or Thutmosis.

Sometimes, the phrase "the good god" is placed before the nomen of the king, in addition to or in place of "the "son of Re."

Another title sometimes placed between "son of Re" and the actual nomen was "lord of the apparitions," sometimes also translated as "lord of the crowns."

This title again confirms the narrow link between the king and the sun: the king's apparition on the throne is compared to the rising of the sun on the Eastern horizon.

From the latter half of the Old Kingdom onwards, the principal name is the Prenomen, and this is often found alone or accompanied only by the nomen. The Horus-name would serve only rarely for identification purposes.

Both Prenomen and nomen are almost invariably written within cartouches or royal rings. The cartouche depicts a loop formed by a rope with the ends tied together to give the appearance of a straight line.

Strictly speaking this loop should be round as it conveys the notions of eternity and encompassing the entire creation. It is elongated and oval because of the length of the hieroglyphic names enclosed in it.

Occasionally, one may find the name of a god or goddess in a cartouche. This was especially the case for Osiris-Onnophris and Isis in the temple inscriptions of the Greek-Roman Period.

Cartouches were often followed by either a wish-formula, such as *living eternally*:

$\frac{Q}{4}$ 🐍

Or, *bestowed with eternal life*:

⟨ 𝄞 🐍

Or by a phrase that relates the king to a particular deity, such as *beloved by Amun-Re*:

⟨☉⟩ ⟨⟩

Note the honorific transposition whereby the name of Amun-Re was moved to the start of the phrase.[66]

The title son of God or, in the case of those at the end of the Ptolemaic dynasty, son of God the Father was considered normal when attributed to the Egyptian pharaoh. It was part and parcel of his entitlement to the royal throne as well as his claim to the titles that came with that position. More importantly, the pharaoh was considered divine—the incarnation of God on earth.

As he believed that he had a genuine connection back to Osiris, the incumbent might well have believed the he was a God and may well have referred to Osiris as "the father."

Given this Egyptian tradition, if it could be shown that the person who became known as Jesus Christ was in fact the son of a pharaoh; as such, he had a legitimate claim to the Egyptian throne, and the title Son of Ra and the other attributes would equally have belonged to him. It sounds far-fetched, but for our investigation to be thorough, we are obliged to examine this idea as a genuine possibility.

---

66 *Hieroglyphs Lessons*, Jacques Kinnaer

CHAPTER 6

The Last Known Son of God

If the hypothesis that the Jesus Christ person was to be a legitimate claimant to the Egyptian throne, then his father must have been someone with a rightful claim to the position of pharaoh and he must have been alive at the time of Jesus Christ's conception.

In fact, only two personalities may accurately fit these limiting criteria: Ptolemy XIII, the son of Ptolemy XII Auletes or Ptolemy XIV, the younger brother of Cleopatra VII and Ptolemy XIII. Both of these persons held the Egyptian throne for a short time in the final century BCE and disappeared from office in mysterious circumstances.

Ptolemy XIV

Ptolemy XIV lived from 60 to 44 BCE and reigned from 47 to 44 BCE. He was the brother of Cleopatra and son of Ptolemy XII one of the last members of the Ptolemaic dynasty of Egypt. Following the death/disappearance of his older brother Ptolemy XIII in January 47 BCE, he was proclaimed pharaoh and co-ruler by his older sister and remaining pharaoh, Cleopatra VII. He and Cleopatra were married, but Cleopatra continued to be the lover of Julius Caesar. Ptolemy is considered to have reigned in name only, with Cleopatra keeping actual authority to herself.

Ptolemy XIII Theos Philopator

Ptolemy XIII was twelve years old when he became joint ruler of Egypt (with his sister Cleopatra) in 51 BCE. Because of his youth, Pothinus, alongside the general Achillas and the rhetorician Theodotus of Chios acted as co-rulers of Egypt, with the Roman Republic as their guardians. When Ptolemy and Cleopatra were elevated to the status of senior rulers, Pothinus was maintained as the former's regent. Most Egyptologists believed that Pothinus used his influence to turn Ptolemy against Cleopatra.

In the spring of 48 BCE, Ptolemy XIII and Pothinus attempted to depose Cleopatra VII who had made moves to enhance her status as Queen. Her face appeared on minted coins, for example, while Ptolemy XIII's name was omitted on official documents. It is likely that Ptolemy intended to become sole ruler, with Pothinus acting as the power behind the throne.

Ptolemy and Pothinus managed to force Cleopatra to flee to Syria. However, she soon organized her own army and when she returned to claim her throne, a civil war began in Egypt. At this time, their other sister made her claim the throne as Arsinoe IV. This complicated the situation but without direct Roman support, her influence was short lived.

Defeated Roman general Pompey the Great came to Egypt to seek refuge from his pursuing rival, Julius Caesar. Initially, Ptolemy XIII and Pothinus pretended to accept his request, but on September 29, 48 BC, Pothinus had the General murdered, in hopes of winning favour with Caesar. When Caesar arrived he was presented with the head of his deceased rival and former ally, but reportedly, instead of being pleased, he reacted with disgust and ordered that Pompey's body be located and that he be given a proper Roman funeral.

Cleopatra VII proved more successful in winning Caesar's favour and became his lover. Caesar arranged the execution of Pothinus and the official return to the throne of Cleopatra VII, who never officially annulled her marriage to Ptolemy XIII.

Still determined to depose Cleopatra, Ptolemy XIII allied himself with his sister Arsinoe IV. Jointly, they organized the factions of the army loyal to them against those loyal to Cleopatra VII and the relatively small part of his army that had accompanied Caesar to Egypt. The battle between the warring factions occurred in December of 48 BCE inside Alexandria itself. The city suffered serious damage, including (according to some sources) the burning of some of the buildings that comprised the Library of Alexandria.

The arrival of Roman reinforcements from Pergamum gave the victory to Caesar and Cleopatra VII, forcing Ptolemy XIII and Arsinoe IV to flee the city. Ptolemy XIII reportedly drowned in January 47 BC while attempting to cross the Nile. It is claimed that he was weighed down by a golden suit of armour. Strangely, however, no body was found.

Cleopatra VII remained the unchallenged ruler of Egypt, although she named their younger brother Ptolemy IV (47—44 BC) her new co-ruler.

It was several years later when the first clue was received to the fact that Ptolemy XIII might not in fact be dead.

In Ephesus, Cleopatra's sister, Arsinoe, spared by Caesar after his Alexandrian triumph and transferred to benign imprisonment amongst the priests of Artemis, had suddenly declared herself Queen of Egypt. There were accompanying rumours that their one surviving brother, and her own official husband, Ptolemy XIV, was Arsinoe's accomplice. There was even the rumour of a pretender claiming to be her dead brother, Ptolemy XIII, the one whose golden armour had been dredged from the blooded waters of the Nile. [67]

Upon return to Egypt, Cleopatra found herself and her son in a vulnerable position. By then, Ptolemy XIV would have been about fifteen, old enough to demand equal power and old enough to become a rival. Meanwhile, her sister Arsinoe was up to her usual tricks, working behind the scenes to sow dissent and confusion. In Cleopatra's absence, Arsinoe had tried to pass off an imposter as Ptolemy XIII, alive and well and claiming his place on the throne. [68]

---

67 *Alexandria: The Last Nights of Cleopatra*, Peter Stothard
68 *Cleopatra: Egypt's Last and Greatest Queen*, Susan Blackaby

On March 15 in the year 44 BCE, Caesar was murdered in Rome. Ptolemy XIV disappeared a few months later. Historians have assumed, but it remains uncertain that Cleopatra poisoned her co-ruler to replace him with his nephew Ptolemy XV Caesarion, the infant son of Cleopatra and Caesar, who was proclaimed co-ruler in September 44 BCE.

In 41 BCE, Mark Antony, one of the triumvirate of rulers who filled the power vacuum in Rome following Caesar's death, sent his intimate friend Quintus Dellius to Egypt to summon Cleopatra to Tarsus to meet him. Cleopatra arrived in great state, and so charmed Antony that he chose to spend the winter of 41/40 BCE with her in Alexandria. To safeguard herself and Caesarion, she had Antony order the death of her sister Arsinoe and asked him to remove the threat presented by a young man, who was claiming to be Ptolemy XIII her brother. The execution of Arsinoe was carried out in 41 BCE on the steps of the temple of Artemis in Ephesus. Historians tell us the following.

> *Mark Antony and Cleopatra were forging an alliance of their own. Cleopatra agreed to make her wealth and resources available to Mark Antony in his bid to overtake Pathia. In return he arranged to have Arsinoe assassinated. For good measure he also arranged to have Ptolemy XIII's imposter tracked down and assassinated also.*[69]

> *Cleopatra advised Mark Antony that it was in fact her sister Arsinoe who encouraged Serapion to give the Egyptian fleet to Cassius and Brutus (this may well be true) which made it an easy matter for Cleopatra to persuade Mark Antony to order Arsinoe's execution. Unfortunately, Arsinoe was killed on the steps of the temple of Artemis at Ephesus causing further scandal in Rome. Cleopatra begged clemency for the priests of Artemis who were the guardians of Arsinoe, but extended no such request for Serapion or for the young*

---

69 *Ibid*

pretender who claimed to be Ptolemy XIII, raised from the dead.[70]

And then Antony began doing the things she asked. It was, in the first instance, to have a number of people killed, killed or delivered up to her — her sister Arsinoe, who, since she had been led a captive through the streets of Rome, had taken refuge in the precinct of Artemis at Ephesus, where she was now murdered to gratify Cleopatra's undying hatred; a young man at Aradus, (a small island of the coast of what is now Lebanon) who professed to be her vanished brother Ptolemy XIII; Serapion, the Ptolemaic governor of Cyprus, who had given help to Cassius.[71]

Although Cleopatra asked for clemency for the temple clergy who had hailed Arsinoe queen, Antonius also ordered the execution of Serapion and a young pretender claiming to be the resurrected Ptolemy XIII.[72]

And a man calling himself Ptolemy XIII had appeared, miraculously delivered from the watery grave in the Nile delta marshes.[73]

The above quotations claim that Antony ordered that the young pretender be killed. As this young man had spent time with Arsinoe, the wife and sister of Ptolemy, it is unlikely that she did not recognise him and therefore he was most likely to have in fact been the young king who was still alive. Additionally, if Cleopatra believed him to be dead, she would hardly have imposed upon Mark Antony to have him killed.

The evidence therefore points to the likelihood that Ptolemy XIII was alive. More than that, he was obviously motivated to stay alive. This was a young man who had previously proved

70 *Cleopatra and Mark Antony*, J Hill
71 *The House of Ptolemy*, E R Bevan
72 *Cleopatra the Great*, Joann Fletcher
73 *Cleopatra, Last Pharaoh of Egypt*, M J Trow

himself an expert in self-protection and in the use of disguise and deceit to elude death. Because of that, it cannot be assumed that Mark Antony's orders produced their desired result.

There has never been a claim that Ptolemy eluded capture and escaped. However, until he surfaced in Ephesus and then again, in Aradus there had never been any claims that he escaped when he deceived the Romans into believing that he had drowned in the Nile. In fact, despite the lack of a body, the bulk of today's historians still believe that he was killed when Caesar's forces pursued him in 47 BCE. Another quotation might unintentionally provide a clue to what happened:

> *Yet another enemy was also killed at Cleopatra's request. This was a youth in the Phoenician town of Aradus (Arvad) who claimed to be Cleopatra's half-brother and husband Ptolemy XIII. After the young king's downing in the Nile, in mysterious circumstances Caesar had been afraid that false reports of his survival would get about, and now this person at Aradus had justified his fears by declaring that he himself was the king. So he too was executed at Antony's instructions.*
>
> *In these Syrian territories Antony found that his favour towards Cleopatra had lost him a great deal of support, for the Syrians never forgot that large areas of their country had once been occupied by the Ptolemaic kingdom, and that she was ambitious to re-annex them. Consequently, the seizure of Serapion at her request must have seemed highhanded to his hosts at Tyre; and there were people at Aradus who resented the execution of the Pretender Ptolemy XIII.[74]*

Aradus was a small island two kilometres from the mainland and any visiting Roman soldiers would have been easy to see as their boats approached.

---

74 *Cleopatra*, Michael Grant

When they did arrive, the soldiers would have found it necessary to have their target pointed out to them. If Ptolemy had friends on the island, there would have been enough time to hide him and for locals to point out some foreigner who wasn't as popular as he was. Once this other person had been killed, they would then have protested, in order to persuade Mark Antony and Cleopatra to believe that Ptolemy had been killed.

Ptolemy XIII was only twenty-one years old and would have possessed the athleticism and agile mind of an adroit young man. If he was still in Aradus when Mark Antony's troop of killers arrived and he did evade them, it would have been relatively easy for him to disappear into Syria, and from there he would have had the later opportunity to move south into Palestine.

The group of soldiers that were dispatched to murder Ptolemy were also despatched to eliminate Arsinoe, the sister of Ptolemy XIII and Cleopatra, who had been granted sanctuary by Caesar at the temple of Artemis in Ephesus. Arsinoe lived in the temple for a few years, always keeping a distant but watchful eye on her sister Cleopatra, who perceived Arsinoe as a threat to her power. In 41 BCE, at Cleopatra's instigation, Mark Antony ordered Arsinoe to be executed. She was murdered by Mark Antony's soldiers on the steps of the temple, a gross violation of the temple sanctuary and an act that scandalised Rome. What is significant to our analysis is that the death of Arsinoe was widely reported but there was no report that we are aware of regarding the location of and killing of the pretender Ptolemy XIII.

The emotional games played between Cleopatra and Mark Antony are well documented as was her suicide in 30 BCE. Her son by Caesar, Ptolemy XV Philopator Philometor Caesar known as Caesarion was thirteen years old and was killed at the behest of Octavian in the same year. These deaths ended the official Egyptian monarchy and simultaneously it was thought to have ended the pharaonic bloodline. Cleopatra and Marc Antony did have a daughter—Cleopatra Selene. This daughter married Juba II son off King Juba I of Numidia and the couple had a son known as Ptolemy of Mauretania (9 BCE—40 CE). This person lived in Rome until he was twenty-one when he returned to Mauretania (part of Algeria). He was not of the authentic Royal bloodline and had no claim to the Pharaonic crown.

We have no tangible evidence that Ptolemy XIII survived. If he did survive, he would have lived in hiding, aware that knowledge of him being alive would invite pursuit and assassination. He would most likely have adopted a humble disguise, since anything more would have attracted attention.

What we do know is that there is a strong possibility that he did survive and that the co-incidental emergence of a humble unknown who came to be attributed with the title Son of God points to the fact that he did. At the same time, he would have been aware of the succession difficulties experienced by his father Ptolemy XII and his grandfather Ptolemy XI and the emphasis they had both placed on pharaonic succession.

In 80 BC, Ptolemy XI had been removed from the throne of Egypt after he had killed his coregent and stepmother Berenice III. When he later died without a male heir, the only available male descendants of the Ptolemaic lineage were the illegitimate sons of Ptolemy IX by an unknown Greek concubine. The boys were living in exile in Sinope, at the court of Mithridates VI, King of Pontus. The eldest of the boys, Ptolemy XII was proclaimed king with the title Ptolemy XII Neos Dionysos and he married his sister, Tryphaena. He was coregent with his daughter Cleopatra VI Tryphaena and his wife Cleopatra V Tryphaena. The stumbling block was that Ptolemy XI had left the throne to Rome in his will therefore Ptolemy XII was not the legitimate successor.

To secure his fate and the fate of his dynasty Ptolemy XII adopted a pro-Roman policy. Nevertheless, a patron relationship with Pompey in Rome did not guarantee his permanence on the throne, thus Ptolemy XII soon afterwards travelled to Rome to offer a bribe in exchange for an official recognition of his kingship.

Later, when he was threatened by an uprising Ptolemy XII fled again to Rome, possibly with his daughter Cleopatra VII, in search of safety. His daughter Berenice IV became his successor and ruled as coregent with her sister (or possibly mother) Cleopatra VI. A year after Ptolemy XII's exile, Cleopatra VI

Tryphaena died and Berenice ruled alone over Alexandria from 57 to 56 BCE. Ptolemy XII finally recovered his throne by paying Aulus Gabinius 10,000 talents to invade Egypt in 55 BCE. He had Berenice and her supporters executed. From then on, he reigned until he fell ill in 51 BC.

Around two thousand Roman soldiers and mercenaries, the so-called Gabiniani, were stationed in Alexandria to ensure Ptolemy XII's authority on the throne. In exchange, Rome was able to exert its power over the restored king.

Before his death, Ptolemy XII chose his daughter Cleopatra VII as his coregent. In his will, he declared that she and her brother Ptolemy XIII should rule the kingdom together. To safeguard his interests, he made the people of Rome executors of his will. Since the Senate was busy with its own affairs, Pompey (as Ptolemy XII's ally) approved the will.

> *Throughout his long-lasting reign the principal aim of Ptolemy was to secure his hold on the Egyptian throne so as to eventually pass it to his heirs. To achieve this goal he was prepared to sacrifice much: the loss of rich Ptolemaic lands, most of his wealth and even, according to Cicero, the very dignity on which the mystique of kingship rested when he appeared before the Roman people as a mere supplicant.*[75]

This tells us that Ptolemy XIII would probably have been indoctrinated with the importance of the pharaonic bloodline, an importance that had been emphasised by Ptolemy I through his sponsorship of Manetho's Aegyptika. This, and the drama of his own scenario, would have ensured that Ptolemy XIII was aware that he was the last pharaoh and therefore the last god king. To perpetuate the link to Osiris he would need to have produced a boy child. As with all legitimate pharaohs, such a child, like all its predecessors would then have claim to the pharaonic title and to the title Son of God.

---

75 *Ptolemy and the Romans*, Mary Siani-Davies

CHAPTER 7

The Selection of the Mother of the Son of God

Ptolemy XIII would have been twenty-one years old when Arsinoe was killed. Given that he was a young man, he had plenty of time to arrange habitation and to contrive and organise the continuation of the pharaonic dynasties by siring a son who would inherit the bloodline.

The nativity of Jesus Christ is generally believed to have occurred circa 6 BCE when Ptolemy XIII, if alive, would have been some fifty-six years old.

In a previous chapter, we discussed the fact that the eighteenth dynasty was the last group of kings that could claim to be able to trace their genealogy (sometimes via the female line) back to Osiris without a non-reconcilable break. The spin that had been orchestrated by Ramesses, Alexander and Ptolemy I to hide their illegitimate claim to the kingship was probably known by all subsequent kings and it had most likely been discussed among their close advisors. In particular the priests of Egypt whose raison d'être was to perpetuate the essence of the old religion would have contrived to advise on measures to keep the line intact. Given that Ptolemy I was the sponsor of Manetho, it is most likely that any breaks in the bloodline would have been known to all the pharaohs of the Ptolemaic dynasty. Anyone fixed on the idea of perpetuating the line, might well have wished to correct any anomalies and because of that, the choice of the mother for the next in line would have been very significant.

In all likelihood, Ptolemy XIII had gone into hiding in Syria, a country that, like Palestine, had existed under Egyptian influence for many centuries:

- The Egyptian religion crossed the Jewish boundaries of Palestine and Syria as early as 1479 BCE when Thutmose III invaded the threatening Kadash coalition at Yehem and Meggido.[76]
- Then, in 301 BCE at the battle of Ipsus, Antigonus was killed, and the three allies were finally able to divide the empire between them. Not only did Ptolemy I become supreme ruler of Egypt, but also added Palestine and lower Syria to his empire. Under his rule, all of these territories appear to have prospered.[77]

Because of this enduring influence, Ptolemy XIII would most likely have had access to priests who would be disposed towards him and who would revere him as a god king. He would have been able to use his access to such loyal priests to take refuge where necessary and to get information where he required it. For all these reasons it would seem logical that Ptolemy XIII might use the time he had to search out a woman who had inherited Royal Blood. To do that, he would have needed to use his influence with priests to find a female whose royal ancestry could be traced back to the eighteenth dynasty. In retrospect, we are helped in our understanding of this because Jesus, genealogy is found at two places in the Bible:

Matthew's gospel (Matt. 1:2-16). Starts with Abraham and lists his descendants all the way down to Jesus. There are 41 generations in total.

Luke's gospel (Luke 3:23-38). This genealogy starts with Jesus and follows his line up until God. There are 77 generations mentioned in total.

76 *Future of the God Amen*, Nicholas P Ginex
77 *Ptolemy I Soter, The First King of Ancient Egypt's Ptolemaic Dynasty*, Jimmy Dunn

In each of the two genealogies, every name is different until we reach David, with the exception of Joseph, Zorobabel and Salathiel. Because of this, it is almost impossible to reconcile them by matching the persons and claim that they are listed by different names (as we've seen many times before in the Bible). The fact that there are two different lists suggests that **the two genealogies do not trace the same lineage.** It is easy therefore, to conclude that one of the two genealogies in the gospels must list Jesus's ancestors through his father, while the other must list them through his mother. The preceding verse in Luke tells us that that line from Joseph started with Heli: "Now Jesus himself was about thirty years old when he began his ministry. He was the son, so it was thought, of Joseph, the son of Heli."[78]

Despite the differences, the place where these two lists coincide is with David and it is probably significant that, amongst other titles attributed to him, Jesus was known as Son of David.

David has always been considered significant by those tracing the genealogy of Jesus Christ and for that reason King David's place in history warrants closer analysis.

It is significant that on the basis of what we already know about the authenticity of the eighteenth dynasty, several researchers and Egyptologists have claimed that David was the Egyptian pharaoh Thutmose III, an important pharaoh from this same dynasty:

> *The first segment of Pharaoh Thutmose III's epithet was always written as "Twt," i.e. with three consonants. For some mischievous reasons the middle consonant letter was changed to the vowel "u" by some Egyptologists. When "Twt" was written, in the equivalent Hebrew alphabetical characters, it becomes "Dwd." When "Dwd" is pronounced phonetically, it becomes "Dawood" which the Hebrew name for "DAVID."*[79]

---

78 *Luke 3:23*
79 *Historical Deception: The Untold Story of Ancient Egypt*, Moustaffa Gadalla

The accounts in the Bible of David and his wars and military battles described in the Tanakh (the Jewish Bible) compare with and are similar to the exploits of the eighteenth dynasty Pharaoh Thutmose III, as they were written on the stone walls on the Temple of Karnak in Thebes."[80]

> *It was the Egyptian King David (Thutmose III) who had defeated an earlier coalition of Syrian and Canaanite kings, and as described in the Bible, had established garrisons in these regions in order to permanently secure Egyptian control there. (2 Samuel 8:5, 6)*[81]

There is little evidence of the process of selection that culminated in Mary. The only story that we can reference was The Book of James—Protevangelium.[82] This was an apocryphal Gospel, probably written about 150 CE. It is the oldest source to assert the virginity of Mary not only prior to but during (and after) the birth of Jesus and was quoted by Origen in the early third century. Origen was an early Christian bishop, based in Alexandria whose writings show him to have had an affinity for ancient Egyptian beliefs.[83] The Book of James tells us:

> *Now there was a council of the priests, and they said: Let us make a veil for the temple of the Lord. And the priest said: Call unto me pure virgins of the tribe of David. And the officers departed and sought and found seven virgins. And the priests called to mind the child Mary that she was of the tribe of David and was undefiled before God: and the officers went and fetched her. And they brought them into the temple of the Lord, and the priest said: Cast me lots, which of you shalt weave the gold and the undefiled (the white) and tile fine linen and the silk and the hyacinthine, and the scarlet and the*

80 *Tracing the Hebrew Pharaohs of Egypt*, Craig M Lyons
81 *The Gospel According to Egypt*, Charles N Pope
82 *The Apocryphal New Testament*, M R James
83 *Origen and the Life of the Stars*, A Scott

true purple. And the lot of the true purple and the scarlet fell unto Mary, and she took them and went unto her house. And at that season Zacharias became dumb, and Samuel was in his stead until the time when Zacharias spake again. But Mary took the scarlet and began to spin it.

And she took the pitcher and went forth to fill it with water: and lo a voice saying: Hail, thou that art highly favoured; the Lord is with thee: blessed art thou among women. And she looked about her upon the right hand and upon the left, to see whence this voice should be: and being filled with trembling she went to her house and set down the pitcher, and took the purple and sat down upon her seat and drew out the thread.

And behold an angel/messenger of the Lord stood before her saying: "Fear not, Mary, for thou hast found grace before the Lord of all things, and thou shalt conceive of his word." And she, when she heard it, questioned in herself, saying: "Shall I verily conceive of the living God, and bring forth after the manner of all women?" And the angel/messenger of the Lord said: "Not so, Mary, for a power of the Lord shall overshadow thee: wherefore also that holy thing which shall be born of thee shall be called the Son of the Highest. And thou shalt call his name Jesus: for he shall save his people from their sins." And Mary said: "Behold the handmaid of the Lord is before him: be it unto me according to thy word."

If this document is valid and truthful, it indicates that the priests were looking for a virgin of the tribe of David, and that her introduction to the Lord's emissary was not a random coincidence. In particular, it tells us and that it was not done at the behest of some heavenly inspiration. Interestingly, the King James Bible gives the name of Mary's father as Ioacim, which would point to the genealogy in Matthew as that of Mary. This means that Mary's genealogy was traced by Matthew.

What is obvious therefore is that if David was Thutmose III and Ptolemy XIII selected someone who he knew to have a direct line from King David, he was selecting someone of the royal blood. He was choosing a woman who would assist him to re-establish the authentic Pharaonic line back to Osiris.

The New Testament was written by people with an agenda. They were believers who were disposed towards a supernatural, incarnate God and to his earthly manifestation in the form of his Son, Jesus Christ. For this reason, the gospels must be read with some scepticism, as they may not represent an actual description of what took place. Taking that into account, it would perhaps be worthwhile to look at the Gospels to see if we can find links to Ptolemy XIII, the last Egyptian god king. The Gospels were written in ancient Greek and each Greek word had many possible ways of being translated into English. The first verse relating to the annunciation as described by Luke in Greek reads: Ἐν δὲ τῷ μηνὶ τῷ ἕκτῳ ἀπεστάλη ὁ ἄγγελος Γαβριὴλ ἀπὸ τοῦ θεοῦ εἰς πόλιν τῆςΓαλιλαίας ἡ ὄνομα Ναζαρὲθ.

The traditional English translation of this and the ensuing verses is:

> *The angel Gabriel was sent by God to a town in Galilee called Nazareth, to a virgin betrothed to a man named Joseph, of the House of David; and the virgin's name was Mary. And he went in and said to her; "Rejoice, so highly favoured! The Lord is with you."*
>
> *But she was deeply disturbed by these words and asked herself what this greeting could mean, and the angel said to her, "Mary, do not be afraid; you have won God's favour. And behold! You are to conceive and bear a Son, and you must name him Jesus. He will be great and will be called Son of the Most High. The Lord God will give him the throne of his ancestor David; and he will rule over the House of Jacob forever and his reign will have no end."*

91

And Mary said to the angel; 'How can this come about, since I am a virgin?"

"The Holy Spirit will come upon you," the angel answered, "and the power of the Most High will cover you with its shadow. And so the child will be holy and will be called Son of God. And behold, your kinswoman Elizabeth has, in her old age, herself conceived a son, and she whom people called barren is now in her sixth month, for nothing is impossible to God."

"I am the handmaid of the Lord," said Mary. "Let what you have said be done to me." And the angel left her.[84]

This translation leaves out the first few words of verse one: "In but the sixth month . . . ." These words do not seem to add much to the story until we compute the date claimed for Christ's birth: The earliest source stating December 25 as the date of birth of Jesus was Hippolytus of Rome (170–236), written very early in the third century, based on the assumption that the conception of Jesus took place at the Spring Equinox which he placed on March 25, and then added nine months.[85]

This would have been true if we start at the sixth month of the Hebrew (lunar) calendar of the time, which has the first month of the year as Tishrei (September-October). In fact, Hippolytus devised his own calendar to fit the facts that he wished to present: "Anti-pope Hippolytus replaced the eight-year *Octaeteris* lunar cycle, used by the early bishops and priests of Rome for circa 174 years, with his own ill-conceived sixteen-year cycle."[86]

Another element of Luke's account of the annunciation worthy of comment is the use of the name Gabriel. The Hebrew etymology of this name tells us that the word meant "God's man" or "God's strong man." This definition conjures a picture of a very different individual than some mystical winged being

---

84 Luke 1:26-38
85 *Mercer Dictionary of the Bible*, Mills, McKnight, Bullard
86 *The Calendar of Christ and the Apostles*, Carl D Franklin

from the heavens, when the god in question is an earthly Egyptian king, who is likely to have had a retinue of men to protect and serve him.

This same twist of perspective can be used looking at the end of verse 33. The actual translation from the Greek reads, *"And this royal power itself not will be the last/the end/an end."* This seems to be a logical statement, when interpreted in the context of someone wishing to perpetuate the Egyptian royal bloodline.

Whatever one's disposition or faith, there is no doubt that the person of Mary was chosen to give birth to the Son of God. She was of the house of David, and this could only have been significant in the context of her ancestry. This in turn becomes logical (in the hypothesis we are presenting) and fits the circumstances if David was the eighteenth dynasty Pharaoh Thutmose III—the last known dynasty with authentic links to the primary bloodline. In this reality, Ptolemy XIII believed that by marrying Mary, he would be able to beget a child that would provide an interrupted link in the Royal bloodline back to Osiris. Whilst he personally was the Son of God in name, his son would be Son of God in reality.

CHAPTER 8

The Fulfilment of Prophecy?

Orthodox Christians will claim that the arrival of Jesus was the fulfilment of Old Testament prophecies, in Genesis, Samuel, Isaiah and Micah. The Genesis prophecy relates to the Lord's instruction to Abraham:

> *Get out of your country, from your family and from your father's house, to a land that I will show you. I will make you a great nation; I will bless you and make your name great; and you shall be a blessing. I will bless those who bless you, and I will curse him who curses you; and in you all the families of the earth shall be blessed.*[87]

This quotation, together with the final verses of Genesis Chapter 11, make it clear that the home of Abraham was Haran (in modern Syria) and that Haran was also the name of Abraham's brother. When he and his family leave they journey through Israel, but because of famine, they continued on to Egypt.

This recorded instruction was followed by Abraham's expedition, which took him to Egypt. There he tricked the pharaoh into marrying Sarah his wife, leading to conjecture about who was the father of Sarah's son Isaac and because of that, the inter-relationship between the Abrahamic and Egyptian bloodlines.

It is difficult to know whether Sarah's relationship with the un-named pharaoh was with a king from the thirteenth dynasty

---

87 Genesis 12:1-3

or of a Semitic King from the concurrent fourteenth dynasty. Neither is it clear whether the land Abraham was told to exit was in Egypt or in one of the Canaan territories. Similarly, whilst it is assumed that the great nation was a nation based in Israel, it could equally be referring to one based in Egypt.

In this context, the link to the Egyptian bloodline may well have been established between 1800 BCE (when it is most likely that Abraham was born) and the eighteenth dynasty which commenced in 1550 BCE during which time there was considerable overlapping of the so-called dynasties as is shown in the table below.

The fourteenth dynasty consisted of a local group from the eastern Delta, based at Avaris, that ruled from 1805 BCE until around 1650 BCE. The dynasty comprised many rulers with Western Semitic names, and is thus believed to have been Canaanite or Hebrew in origin.

The fifteenth dynasty was also Semitic, and the people were called Hyksos.

The sixteenth dynasty was a Theban dynasty, which grew out of the collapse of the thirteenth dynasty.

The seventeenth dynasty covers a period when Egypt was split into a set of small Hyksos kingdoms. It consisted mainly of Theban rulers and was contemporary with the fifteenth and sixteenth dynasties.

The end of the seventeenth dynasty ran directly into the eighteenth, which controlled the whole of Egypt and which is generally acknowledged as the legitimate line.

Another Old Testament reference states that God sent Nathan the prophet to David to tell him:

> *When your days are fulfilled and you rest with your fathers, I will set up your seed after you, who will come from your body, and I will establish his kingdom. He shall build a house for My name, and I will establish the throne of his kingdom forever. I will be his Father, and he shall be My son.*[88]

---

88 2 Samuel 7:12-14

This verse in Samuel was written some 800 years after the event. Because of that, we must assume that it is derived from a verbal tradition, with all the inherent defects that such a tradition holds.

According to Jewish belief, the book was written by Samuel, with additions by the prophets Gad and Nathan. Modern scholarly thinking is that the entire history (called the Deuteronomistic history) was composed in the period 630—540 BCE by combining a number of independent texts and traditions of various ages.

Josiah became king of Judah circa 641/640 BCE. To the east, the Assyrian Empire was disintegrating, the Babylonian Empire had not yet replaced it, and Egypt to the west was still recovering from Assyrian rule. In this power vacuum, Judah was able to govern itself for the time being without foreign intervention. However, in the spring of 609 BCE, Pharaoh Necho II personally led a sizable army up to the Euphrates to aid the Assyrians. The Kingdom of Judah ended in 586 BCE when Babylonian forces under Nebuchadnezzar II captured Jerusalem, and removed most of its population and took them back to their own lands. Babylonian rule was toppled however in the 540s, by Cyrus, who founded the Persian Empire in its place.

Given that the prophecy would take into account the existing power bases at his time of writing, it must therefore have been written circa 640 BCE and referred to Israel, or it was written circa 605 BCE and the land referred to was Egypt. Necho the king of Egypt is quoted as saying, "What quarrel is there between you and me, O king of Judah? It is not you I am attacking at this time, but the house with which I am at war. God has told me to hurry; so stop opposing God, who is with me, or he will destroy you."[89]

In this quotation, we can see that Pharaoh Necho II claims that he has direct instruction from God, which, if true, means he will have received instruction via the Oracle. Consulting

---

89 2 Chronicles 35:21

Dates	13th Dynasty	14th Dynasty (a Canaanite group from the eastern Delta, based at Avaris, that ruled from 1805 to 1650 BCE)	15th Dynasty (Hyksos 1674–1535 BCE)	Abydos (an independent dynasty reigning over Abydos from c. 1650 until 1600 BCE)	16th Dynasty (a Theban dynasty emerging from the collapse of the Memphis-based 13th dynasty c. 1650 BC and finally conquered by the Hyksos 15th dynasty c. 1580 BCE)	17th Dynasty (Ruled upper Egypt)
1800						
1775						
1750						
1725						
1700		21 kings				
1675	58 kings					
1650			7 kings	4 kings	15 kings	9 kings
1625						
1600						
1575						
1550						

97

the Oracle was a ritual involving priests and priestesses in the place of the Oracle who interpreted the word of God for the supplicant.

In addition to the question about the source of the instruction, it is difficult to know whether the God referred to is Osiris or Ra, communicated with via the Oracle or whether the God concerned was the divine King of Egypt, and the words spoken were phrased similarly to those of a modern monarch who says "we disapprove" when he means "I disapprove."

These simple analyses put serious question marks to any claims of authenticity of prophecies that in most cases are based on events that have already taken place or are underway. Where they do predict the future they are based on wishful thinking by priests who would always have wished to please their petitioners.

Another prophet whose works are worthy of examination is Isaiah. It is generally thought that his ministry as a prophet began circa 739 BCE. According to Jewish tradition, Isaiah was executed by Manasseh only a few years after he ascended the throne. This would imply that Isaiah prophesied during a period of approximately fifty years circa 739—690 BCE. This is the period when Persians, Assyrians/Babylonians, Egyptians and Greeks were competing for power and during which Judea was overrun and controlled by each of these power bases in turn. In this context, it is easy to see that the bulk of the Isaiah texts were written to bolster the self-belief of the people of Judea and to deprecate the other nations.

Isaiah was called the Messianic prophet based on his prophecies in Isaiah 52 and 53, which indicate that a servant of God would undergo suffering, specifically Isaiah 52:14-15: *"Behold, my servant shall act wisely; he shall be high and lifted up, and shall be exalted. As many were astonished at you—his appearance was so marred, beyond human semblance, and his form beyond that of the children of mankind."*

As the person is not identified other than as "my servant," and much of it is in the past tense, one might be forgiven for assuming that the content of these verses refers to Osiris, the mutilated god king of the Egyptians.

The current Jewish tradition does not believe that the Isaiah predictions were fulfilled in the person of Jesus Christ.

The Isaiah prophecy that is claimed to relate to Mary and the virgin birth of Jesus tells us,

> *"Therefore the Lord himself will give you a sign: The virgin will conceive and give birth to a son, and will call him Immanuel (God is with us)."*[90]

All the great nations of Mesopotamia surrounding Judea on every side had a comprehensive pantheon of religious beliefs combined with long traditions. Many of these included stories of a special individual who was closely associated with God (if not a god himself), and who emanated from a virgin birth:

- Mithras had existed as the savior-god of Persia for 4000 years. He had been born on December 25 of a virgin, was laid in the crib and was visited by three wise men who brought him gold, frankincense and myrrh.
- Zoroaster the Persian God was conceived by a shaft of light circa 1200 BCE, and the reports of his life have many similarities to that of Jesus as recorded in the gospels.
- In the Assyrian/Babylonian tradition, Marduk, who was the head of the Babylonian pantheon since the second half of the second millennium BCE, was created in the heart of Apsu, while "He who begot him was Ea, his father, she who conceived him was Damkina, his mother." In the same Assyrian traditions, the gods created the king Tukulti-Urta (circa 800 BCE) in the womb of his mother.
- The Greek Gods Dionysus, Adonis and Attis were born on December 25 of a virgin or by intervention of Zeus, and Dionysus was placed in a crib among beasts.

---

90 Isaiah 7:14

- **Horus** can be traced to the beginning of Egyptian history, as son of the goddess Isis and the God Osiris. His conception and birth were contrived without intercourse and are to be understood in terms of the Egyptian doctrine of parthenogenesis, which is an asexual form of reproduction found in females where the growth and development of embryos or seeds occur without fertilization by a male.

Living god-kings, sons of God and gods who are the rebirth of the God in Heaven were the order of the day. Conversations with gods and prophecies using the Oracle were the norm. In fact, the book of Isaiah uses the word Oracle in preference to the word prophecy.

In the context of the traditions of the Gods of Persia, Assyria, Greece and Egypt, an attempt to portray a future for Judea, which is a powerful for the Hebrews and as full and symbolism as that of its enemies is understandable. In any event, the fact that events are predicted and then, some 800 years later someone claims that they have been fulfilled does not mean that the 'prophet' actually foresaw the event, neither does it mean that the event actually happened. Accordingly, the fact that there were prophecies and claims that they were fulfilled in the person of Jesus does not offer any tangible confirmation that our hypothesis is invalid. If it sows doubts, then they must be offset by looking deeper into Jesus's known connections with Egypt, in order to locate counterbalancing evidence.

CHAPTER 9

Jesus's Connection with Egypt

The first place in the New Testament Gospels that mentions a connection between Jesus and Egypt is Matthew's second chapter reference to the "slaughter of the innocents" and the "Holy family's flight into Egypt" to protect their newborn son. There, it tells us that Jesus was born when Herod the Great (74—4 BCE) was King of the Jews as well as a client (puppet monarch) of the Roman emperor. Herod rebuilt/upgraded the Temple in Jerusalem, but he is chiefly remembered amongst Christians as the instigator of the Massacre of the Innocents.

The gospels tell us that three wise men from the East informed Herod of the birth of a 'king' in Bethlehem. In response to their failure to reappear and report the child's whereabouts Herod "sent forth and put to death all the male children in that town and in all its districts, from two years old and under" (Matt. 2:16). The story continues and it explains that the Holy Family was able to avoid this massacre by fleeing to Egypt, where they remained until an 'angel' told Joseph that Herod had died.

The massacre of the innocents is not reported outside of the Gospel of Matthew and other later Christian writings based on that gospel. The Roman Jewish historian Josephus does not mention it in his history, Antiquities of the Jews (c. 94 CE). The first twenty verses of Chapter 2 of Matthew's Gospel can be divided into two parts, 1-12 concerning the Magi and birth, and 13-21 concerning the flight into Egypt:

> *In the time of King Herod, after Jesus was born in Bethlehem of Judea, wise men from the East came to*

Jerusalem, asking, "Where is the child who has been born king of the Jews? For we observed his star at its rising, and have come to pay him homage." When King Herod heard this, he was frightened, and all Jerusalem with him; and calling together all the chief priests and scribes of the people, he inquired of them where the Messiah was to be born. They told him, "In Bethlehem of Judea; for so it has been written by the prophet: And you, Bethlehem, in the land of Judah, are by no means least among the rulers of Judah; for from you shall come a ruler who is to shepherd my people Israel." Then Herod secretly called for the wise men and learned from them the exact time when the star had appeared. Then he sent them to Bethlehem, saying, "Go and search diligently for the child; and when you have found him, bring me word so that I may also go and pay him homage." When they had heard the king, they set out; and there, ahead of them, went the star that they had seen at its rising, until it stopped over the place where the child was. When they saw that the star had stopped, they were overwhelmed with joy. On entering the house, they saw the child with Mary his mother; and they knelt down and paid him homage. Then, opening their treasure chests, they offered him gifts of gold, frankincense, and myrrh. And having been warned in a dream not to return to Herod, they left for their own country by another road. Now when they had departed, behold, an angel of the Lord appeared to Joseph in a dream and said, "Rise, take the child and his mother, and flee to Egypt, and remain there till I tell you; for Herod is about to search for the child, to destroy him." And he rose and took the child and his mother by night, and departed to Egypt, and remained there until the death of Herod. This was to fulfil what the Lord had spoken by the prophet, "Out of Egypt have I called my son." Then Herod, when he saw that he had been tricked by the wise men, was in a furious rage, and he sent and killed all the male children in Bethlehem and in all of that region who were two

*years old or under, according to the time which he had
ascertained from the wise men. Then was fulfilled what
was spoken by the prophet Jeremiah: "A voice was heard
in Ramah, wailing and loud lamentation, Rachel weeping
for her children; she refused to be consoled, because they
were no more." But when Herod died, behold, an angel of
the Lord appeared in a dream to Joseph in Egypt, saying,
"Rise, take the child and his mother, and go to the land
of Israel, for those who sought the child's life are dead."
And he rose and took the child and his mother, and went
to the land of Israel.*[91]

There is a debate about whether the Massacre of the Innocents actually took place. The main arguments against the validity of verses 13-21 include:

- Of the four Gospels, only Matthew mentions these
events.
- It is not mentioned in either Roman or Jewish records,
when it is known that historians such as Josephus
carefully recorded Herod's abuses.
- Eminent scholars such as Geza Vermes and E. P. Sanders
regard it as a "creative hagiography."[92]
- It is a story contrived to fulfil prophecy. Various students
of the Bible tell us, "This is a pure invention on
Matthew's part. Herod was guilty of many monstrous
crimes, including the murder of several members of
his own family. However, ancient historians such as
Josephus, who delighted in listing Herod's crimes, do
not mention what would have been Herod's greatest
crime by far. It simply didn't happen. The context of
Jeremiah 31:15 makes it clear that the weeping is for the
Israelites about to be taken into exile in Babylon, and

91 Matthew 2:13-21
92 *The Nativity and Legend*, Geza Vermes

has nothing to do with slaughtered children hundreds of years later."[93]

- "Matthew's purpose is to present Jesus as the Messiah and the Massacre of the Innocents as the fulfilment of passages in Hosea (one of the twelve prophets of the Hebrew Bible) referring to the exodus, and in Jeremiah referring to the Babylonian exile."[94] Such prophecy was used in Matthew to claim that the birth of Jesus fulfilled prophecy (by Micah): *"But as for you, Bethlehem Ephrathah, too little to be among the clans of Judah, from you One will go forth for Me to be ruler in Israel. His goings forth are from long ago, from the days of eternity."*

This is questionable on two counts: (a) The Bethlehem referred to by Micah may well be the name of a person not a place. (b) It talks of someone who is to be the ruler in Israel, which Jesus never was. Bethlehem was a small village with an estimated population of 1000 people. Based on this population size, the maximum number of children under two years old would have been twenty.

We do not know whether the stories of the slaughter of the innocents and the flight into Egypt are true. However, certain elements in these stories bear examination:

- The contradictions created by the differences in the stories of Matthew and Luke
- Why Matthew told the story of the Magi
- Why Herod became so upset about stories of a king being born in a Bethlehem
- Why was the holy family directed to go to Egypt? Or, if the story is untrue, why did Matthew choose Egypt as his reported destination?

Let's examine each of these in turn.

---

93 *New Testament Contradictions*, Paul Carlson
94 *The Birth of the Messiah*, Raymond E Brown

The contradictions between Luke and Matthew

According to Matthew, Jesus was born during the reign of Herod the Great. According to Luke, Jesus was born during the first census in Israel, while Quirinius was governor of Syria.[95] This is impossible because Herod died in March of 4 BC, and the census took place in 6 and 7 AD, about ten years after Herod's death.

In order to have Jesus born in Bethlehem, Luke says that everyone had to go to the city of his or her birth to register for the census. This is again highly unlikely since it would have caused a bureaucratic nightmare. The purpose of the Roman census was taxation and the Romans were interested in where the people lived and worked, not where they were born.

Both Matthew and Luke say that Jesus was born in Bethlehem and Matthew misquotes Micah 5:2 to show that this was in fulfilment of prophecy.

Luke has Mary and Joseph travelling from their home in Nazareth in Galilee to Bethlehem in Judea for the birth of Jesus[96] while Matthew, says that it was only after the birth of Jesus that Mary and Joseph resided in Nazareth, and then only because they were afraid to return to Judea.

This divergence of these reports puts doubt on many that the gospel's claims concerning the events of the Nativity. What they do show however, is that the gospel writers believed it important to claim that the birth took place in Bethlehem and that it was important to reference it to a census.

Why did Matthew tell the story of the Magi?

Without the divine intervention promoted by Christians, how could 'wise men from the East' have known of the Childs birth and what is the reference to a star?

The only way that the wise men would have known of the impending birth is if they had been told about it. It is not difficult to imagine that Ptolemy XIII might have told priests with whom he had sought refuge about the impending birth that would

---

95 Luke 2:2
96 Luke 2:4

secure the pharaonic bloodline. Additionally, at a time when particular days of the year were predicted by the rising and setting of individual stars, and sometimes planets such as Venus that were thought to be stars, it is not difficult to imagine that the date of the child's birth would be predictable, nine months after conception, in relation to the rising of a certain star. This is in line with the Egyptian tradition, maintained by the priests, of tracking the stars and predicting the Egyptian calendar by their rise and fall. It also ties in with the idea that the term Magi was itself related to astrology and the positions of the stars in the heavens.

"The teachings of Zarathushtra were intermingled with the old religion, and the Magi's position was transformed into the priests of the new religion," writes Dariush Jahanian. "Many of the Magian practices were themselves adapted from Mesopotamian religion, such as purity laws and especially astrology. This is how the Magi came to be known in the West as astrologers. The word for magic, as is well known, comes from the word magi. Thus, the magus was known in the Hellenistic world as an astrologer and occultist, even if he were not Persian."[97]

Another strange element of this story is that as the wise men would have been priests or priest/astronomers and would have already known the location of Jesus's birth. As priests, it would have been much easier to make contact with High Priests in Israel than to obtain an audience with the king, and, given the subject matter—the birth of the Messiah—it would have been more likely that a meeting with the High Priests would have been their initial objective.

According to Matthew, after the magi had visited him, the priests of Israel were asked by Herod for the birthplace of the Messiah and he was reminded of the prophecy made in Micah 5:2; *"But you, O Bethlehem Ephrathah, are only a small village among all the people of Judah. Yet a ruler of Israel will come from you, one whose origins are from the distant past."*

This proves conclusively that the Magi would have received similar information if they had spoken with priests. If the Magi

---

97 *The Three Magi: Zoroastrian Pilgrims*, Hannah M.G. Shaper

visit actually happened, the priests of Israel (who had acquired much of their tradition from Egyptian religious teachings) would have been alerted by the Magi or by Herod's interest. In such circumstances, with their interest sparked, they would have involved themselves in the tracing of and (in the event) the protection of their Messiah (the anointed one). The story is puzzling in the extreme. Priests from a foreign religion would have given little credence to the Torah and its predictions; neither would they have been interested in the birth of someone fulfilling those predictions. If there was a visit by such priests, there must have been more to it.

The eastern territories, including Persia and India were conquered by Alexander and administered by the Ptolemies thereafter. The Ptolemies were fanatical about the pharaonic bloodline and by the idea that the pharaoh was a divine king, inheriting lineage back to Osiris. In addition, they controlled the dispensers of religion as a way of controlling their 'subjects'. For these reasons, it is likely that priests and astronomers from the new territories would have been subjected to the essential elements of the Egyptian tradition, particularly those that mirrored their own beliefs. The similarities between Hindu, Zoroastrianism and the Egyptian regions have been noted, but these similarities pre-date any influence by the Ptolemaic dynasties. The important but limited element of the religion that could have interested them was that it descended directly from God and that the pharaonic line had a direct connection with the first God king. This was the only aspect that might have impressed Eastern wise men/magicians sufficiently to travel a long distance to visit a new and unlikely successor to the pharaonic title.

If all of these doubts are not enough, it is interesting to note that the visit of the wise men is almost an exact duplication of the story that was woven around the birth of the ancient Persian God Mithra:

Mithra was born of the usual virgin on December 25th, the Birthday of the Unconquered Sun, which Christians adopted in the 4th century CE and renamed Christmas. Some said Mithra was the child of an incestuous union between the sun god or

Ahura Mazda and his own mother, just as Jesus, who was God, was similarly born of the Mother of God. Mithra's birth was witnessed by shepherds and the 'Three Wise Men', known in Persia as Magi, magicians or seers.[98] Mithra, the mediator between God and man, was visited by Magi at the time of his birth and given gifts of gold, frankincense and myrrh.[99]

Could it be that the story of the Magi was simply a duplication of this aspect of the Mithra nativity legend?

Why was Herod upset?

It was not uncommon in these times that there were Judaic claimants to the title of 'Messiah' (divinely appointed king). Two known ones are Simon of Peraea (who according to Josephus was a pyromaniac), Simon Magnus (the Samaritan), Judas the son of Hezakiah (mentioned in the Acts of the Apostles 5:37) and Anthronges all of whom were rebels and were killed by the Romans.

Simon Magnus was mentioned by Irenaeus, Justin Martyr, Hippolytus and Epiphanius as a magician in Acts 8:9-24. In apocryphal works, including the Acts of peter, Pseudo-Clementines, and the Epistle of the Apostles, Simon also appears as a formidable magician with the ability to levitate and fly at will.

Given the existence of so many claimants, the existence of Jesus would not have been such a dramatic announcement. However, it would have caused anxiety, if the wise men told Herod that the infant was the son of an Egyptian god king, and was therefore divine by birth and the hereditary claimant of all title and territory that such a title involved.

For the previous 300 years, save only for the late interruption of the Romans, Israel had been part of the Ptolemaic empire. It is not difficult to see that the appearance of a new and legitimate King of Egypt, who could claim the kingship of Israel, would certainly have been perceived as a threat to the Herodian dynasty that was being established by Herod the Great.

If the visit of the Magi is a true story and Herod did react, one can imagine that he would have been as keen to locate the father,

98 *Manmade God*, Barbara G Walker
99 *Bible Myths and Their Parallels in Other Religions*, T W Doane

Ptolemy XIII, as he would have been to locate and eliminate the child. It is easy to see therefore why a now aged Ptolemy XIII (if alive) would have stayed in hiding. Conversely, it is hard to imagine why Persian seers who had their own religious traditions and loyalties would have been interested in the birth of someone who would perpetuate either the royal Egyptian bloodline or someone who might fulfil a questionable (in the Persian religious tradition) Hebrew prophecy. On balance therefore, the evidence would seem to indicate the possibility that both the visit of the three wise men and the slaughter of the innocents did not happen.

Why was the holy family directed to go to Egypt?

No historical record shows that the slaughter of the innocents actually took place. Therefore, if it did not happen, Matthew's reason for the flight to Egypt is removed. On that basis, its inclusion must have been to give reason for the family's journey to Egypt or to document a reason for recording the fact that the journey into Egypt took place. Either way, it is difficult to imagine any reason why the journey into Egypt would be mentioned if it did not happen.

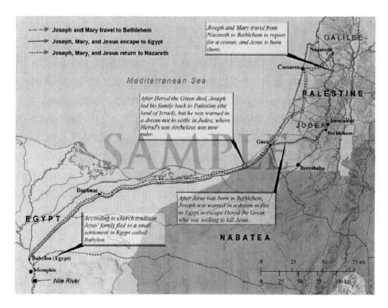

Fig 11 The traditional route taken by the holy family

Greg Rigby

If there is any truth in this story, the journey on foot would have taken some considerable time and would have involved significant risk to the group. There was most likely a trail used by commuters and a non-stop flow of migrants that would have been easy to follow but the needs for shelter, food and water and the needs of an infant would have all been impediments to progress. Additionally, if the group were following a trail and they were in fear for their lives, they would have left themselves exposed to inspection by and confrontation with Roman and Jewish authorities.

The biblical record says nothing about where in Egypt Joseph took his family. If the group consisted of two adults, a donkey and an infant then progress would have been slow. An average of two kilometres per hour was probably the most they could have achieved. On that basis, each 100 kilometres would have taken fifty hours, which would have taken four days non-stop travelling for twelve hours per day. Conventional Christian tradition tells us that Joseph led his family into the delta about midway between the modern cities of Port Said and Suez and wound their way across the delta, making a number of stops. The holy family first stopped at the town of Basta near the large, modern city of Zagazig. Later, according to a local story, the family arrived in the delta town of Belbeis and from there moved on to the Roman fortress Babylon. The final leg took them to Upper Egypt and eventually to the Qousqam Mountains. This is a journey of over 400 kilometres, which (excluding any stopovers) would have taken 16 days non-stop travel. The same tradition says that the Holy Family lived in the Qousqam Mountains in a cave. It is in this cave that the angel is said to have appeared to Joseph, informing him that Herod was dead and instructing him to take the child and Mary back to their home.[100]

---

100 *Biblical Egypt*, S Kent Brown

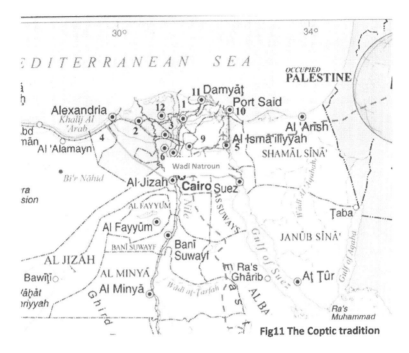

Fig11 The Coptic tradition

Fig12 The Coptic tradition

According to Coptic tradition, the family travelled from Sinai in the east to the Wadi Natroun in the West and then southward to Old Cairo and eventually to Assyut in the heart of Upper Egypt—a journey which have been considerably longer.[101]

Either way, their place of refuge must have been proximate to food and water. In addition, since there was still a strong Semitic presence in Egypt, the likelihood would have been that they would have located themselves with or proximate to people who were sympathetic to them.

Since the work of Emil Schürer in 1896, most scholars have agreed that Herod died at the end of March or early April in 4 BCE. However, Jimmy Akin recently published an analysis of the calculation of the date of Herod's death in the National Catholic Register where he calculates the more likely date to be 1 BCE. If the Emil Shürer tradition is correct, the holy family

---

101 *Jesus: The Complete Guide*, J L Houlden

Greg Rigby

spent almost eighteen months in Egypt. If the Akin analysis is correct, it was over five years.

The more important question is why Egypt?

The travellers would have been able to hide in many other places, which would have resulted in a shorter journey. Crossing the river Jordan would have created much less difficulty than a perilous 400- or 500-kilometre journey, much of it across the northern perimeter of the Sinai desert.

It would seem that there must have been a connection or link of some kind; either a real connection or one in the mind of the author. Egypt seems to be important to the story that was being told.

There are some suggestions that the gospel of Matthew was written by someone who was not Jewish and who was located in Alexandria, a major centre of Judaism at that time:

The most convincing argument against the author being Jewish is that he seems to misunderstand Hebrew poetic technique in Matthew 21:1-11: he has Jesus ride in on both a donkey and a colt, in literal fulfilment of Zechariah 9:9, but any Jew (as well as Mark and Luke) would understand that Zechariah 9:9 refers to only one animal, and the repetition is poetic. Despite this difficulty, however, many scholars still regard the author as a Christian Jew. There is also disagreement about where the Gospel was written. The traditional location, still supported by several scholars, is Antioch, a known centre of Christian Judaism (see Galatians 2:11-14). But Galilee and Alexandria have also been suggested (Galilee as a centre of pharisaic activity that could explain the emphasis on conflict with the Pharisees, Alexandria as another major centre of Judaism). There is more agreement about the date of the Gospel, which almost all scholars regard as being written after the destruction of the Temple in 70 CE. If Matthew used Mark as a source, then this is almost certain. Furthermore, the destruction of the city in the Jewish revolt against the Romans seems to be referred to in Matthew 22:7. The precise date of the Gospel is unknown, but a date in the 80s CE is plausible.[102]

---

102 *Introduction to Matthew's Gospel,* Maxim Cardew

There is no doubt that the author of the Matthew Gospel, who is thought not to have been a contemporary of the person who has become known to us as Jesus Christ, saw a world in which Israel and Egypt were somehow connected.

Another element in the equation that linked Herod, Israel and Egypt was the relationship between Herod and Cleopatra VII and any claims to his territory that Cleopatra, her children or her associations with Rome brought about. There are several versions of this relationship varying from seduction to animosity on the part of Cleopatra.

We are told by historians:

The queen's relationship with Herod was the most frustrating of all her associations. The sole source is Josephus, much of whose material came from someone that both dynasties knew well, Nikolas of Damascus, tutor to Cleopatra's children and then long-time advisor to Herod. The families of Cleopatra and Herod had been in contact with one another since Herod's father Antipatros of Askalon had assisted in the restoration of Ptolemy XII in 55 BC when both future dynasties were in their teens. Eight years later Antipatros aided Caesar in the Alexandrian War and received Roman citizenship for his efforts. Power passed to the younger generation, with Cleopatra and Herod as rulers of their respective territories and eyeing each other suspiciously. Although Herod owed his kingship directly to Antonius and Octavian, the various territorial arrangements from 37 BCE to 34 BCE favoured his rival Cleopatra, who allegedly would have preferred his entire kingdom.

Nikola's account, which made extensive use of Herod's own memoirs, is highly positive; even eulogistic, toward Herod and exceedingly negative about Cleopatra, but it presents a vivid picture of two dynasts, which were highly competitive about their conflicting territories.

Despite such implications by Josephus, it seems unlikely that Cleopatra attempted to further her needs by trying to seduce Herod.[103]

---

103 *Cleopatra: A Biography*, Duane W Roller

When Herod fled from Judea to Alexandria in 40, he was well received by Cleopatra, who offered to appoint him as commander of her army. Anxious to reach Rome, Herod declined. After Herod became king of Judea, enmity developed between them, for his accession had frustrated Cleopatra's plans to annex Judea. Cleopatra incited Antony against Herod. She also lent a ready ear to the complaints of Alexandra, Mariamne's mother, who had quarrelled with Herod for refusing to appoint her son Aristobulus as high priest. Cleopatra openly sided with Alexandra and it was as a result of her intervention that Herod was required to account to Antony for the death of Aristobulus. Though Herod succeeded in saving his throne, he was compelled to cede to Cleopatra Jericho and its environs together with certain areas of Arabia. When Antony prepared for battle against Augustus, Cleopatra ordered Herod to take up arms against the Arabians who had failed to discharge their debts. Herod, though fully aware of Cleopatra's enmity toward him, realized the extent of her influence on Antony, to whom he owed his kingdom and accordingly took pains to prevent their personal differences from jeopardizing his position. Therefore, it is highly unlikely that Herod had counselled Antony to do away with Cleopatra, as was rumoured to Augustus. It is possible that Cleopatra's feelings toward Herod may have caused her evident dislike of the Jews of Alexandria. Cleopatra ruled for over 20 years, taking her life at the age of 39 after Augustus' victory over Antony. There is a reference in the Talmud (Tosef., Nid. 4:17; Nid. 30b) to Queen Cleopatra of Egypt, but it is unclear which Cleopatra is meant.[104]

Whatever the truth of it, it is most certainly the case that rumours of a child of Ptolemy XIII who had a directly inherited claim to the Egyptian pharaonic crown (and the territories that this post would claim to be rightfully theirs) would have been seen as a threat to the Herodian dynasty that Herod had struggled to establish. It would certainly have been a much greater

104 *The Jewish Virtual Library*

threat to Herod than news of a hypothetical Messiah brought to him by a group of Persian magicians.

There is one additional aspect of this analysis, which warrants examination. This is the inclusion in Matthew 2:14-15 of the following verses: *"And he rose and took the child and his mother by night, and departed to Egypt, and remained there until the death of Herod. This was to fulfil/perfect what the Lord had spoken by the prophet, 'Out of Egypt have I called my son'."*

The prophet mentioned is believed to refer to Hosea 11:1-2: *"When Israel was a child, then I loved him, and called my son out of Egypt. As they called them, so they went from them: they sacrificed unto Baalim, and burned incense to graven images."*

Matthew is saying that in confirmation of Hosea 11:1, God first called His son Israel out of Egypt. In his second verse, the prophet Hosea says, *"As they called them, so they went from them: they sacrificed unto Baalim, and burned incense to graven images."* In other words, the Israelites were called out of Egypt, but they served the Baalim and the graven images instead of the true God.

What Matthew tells us is that in Jesus, this history was perfected. The Israelites were called out of Egypt, but were imperfect in serving Baalim. But Jesus was called out of Egypt, and unlike his predecessors he was perfect.

We can deduce therefore that the Israelites brought traditions out of Egypt, which were tied to and were a continuation of the rites of the Egyptian religion. This is confirmation of the passages in the book of Genesis, which tell us that Moses threatened with death those who held onto the Egyptian religious traditions. What Matthew also tells us by implication is that during his stay, Jesus had encountered the same Egyptian tradition.

The Gospel of Matthew attempts to portray the principal subject of his stories as someone whose existence and actions fulfilled Old Testament prophecies. In addition, it endeavours to portray Jesus as someone more than human by many references to God, the Son of God and the Son of (a) Man. In the process, it displays an ongoing and underlying link between Jesus and Egypt and portrays elements of the Egyptian pharaonic religion.

Greg Rigby

In doing this, it helps to provide further circumstantial evidence in support of our general hypothesis, and it gives no information or claim to preclude the hypothesis from being valid.

Over and above the underlying connections between Hebrews and Egypt brought about by many centuries of residence in Egypt, ongoing longstanding transmigration and by being ruled and influenced by Egyptian pharaohs and their priests there seems to have been a special relationship between Jesus and Egypt established very early in his life. This relationship appears to have been directed by those persons guiding/instructing Jesus's parents.

CHAPTER 10

Clues in the New Testament

The most obvious places in the New Testament where we should search for passages that would negate our hypothesis, would be references to God, references to Jesus as Son or any mentions by Jesus of his father.

Where appropriate we will attempt to determine whether the statements could be a reference to an earthly father, or to a divine status that might have been brought about by his or his father's pharaonic status.

Matthew makes many references to God, the father and the son, some of which are listed below. Interestingly, each of these can be explained in the context of ancient Egyptian beliefs:

5:34—Do not swear at all: either by heaven, for it is <u>God's throne</u>; *35* or by the earth, for it is his footstool;

5:16—In the same way, let your light shine before men, that they may see your good deeds and praise your <u>Father in heaven</u>.

5:48—Be perfect, therefore, as <u>your heavenly Father is perfect</u>.

6:9—This, then, is how you should pray: <u>Our Father in heaven</u>, hallowed be your name.

7:21—"Not everyone who says to me, 'Lord, Lord,' will enter the kingdom of heaven, but only he who does <u>the will of my Father who is in heaven</u>

10:32—"Whoever acknowledges me before men; I will also acknowledge him before <u>my Father in heaven</u>.

11:25-27—At that time Jesus said, "I praise you, <u>Father, Lord of heaven</u> and earth, because you have hidden these things from the wise and learned, and revealed them to little children. Yes, Father, for this was your good pleasure. All things have been committed to me by my Father. <u>No one knows the Son except the Father, and no one knows the Father except the Son and those to whom the Son chooses to reveal him.</u>

16:16—Simon Peter answered, "You are the (anointed one), <u>the Son of the living God.</u>"

16:27—For <u>the Son of Man</u> is going to come in his Father's glory with his angels, and then he will reward each person according to what he has done.

18:10—For I tell you that their angels in heaven always see <u>the face of my Father in heaven.</u>

26:64—Jesus replied. "But I say to all of you: In the future you will see the <u>Son of (a) Man sitting at the right hand of the Mighty One</u> and coming on the clouds of heaven."

28:18—Then Jesus came to them and said; "<u>All authority in heaven and on earth has been given to me.</u>"

To explain how these quotations have a link to ancient Egyptian beliefs, it is necessary to outline key elements of these beliefs that could be pertinent to our analysis: Many of the Egyptian beliefs are laid out in the Book of the Dead. This book, which is collection of authentic Egyptian texts, tells us that Heaven and the Court of the Gods was in and around the constellation of Ursa Major, described as the Thigh or the Great Bear: "The Osiris Ani saith: I am he who sendeth forth light over the Thigh of heaven. I come forth in heaven."[105]

"As for those gods, the Lords of Justice. They are Seth and Isdes, Lord of the West. As for the tribunal which is behind

---

105 The Book of the Dead, the chapter of Lifting Up the Feet, and of Coming Forth on the Earth, E A Wallis Budge

Osiris, Imsety, Hapy, Duamutef and Qebehsenuef, it is these who are behind the Great Bear in the northern sky."[106]

In ancient times, the North Pole position was in the Ursa Major constellation, and the group of seven stars we know as the plough revolved around the pole position.

> *"Behold my shape is turned upside down. I am Wen-nefer, season by season, whose attributes come unto him one by one when he travels around."[107]*

From Egypt, the constellation was low in the northern sky. It rotated around the pole position and as it did so, it crossed the Sky, backwards and forwards, across the bottom arc and top arc of its circular movement, but it did not fall below the horizon. Inside the cup of the constellation is the shape of a regular pentagon and the everlasting and infinite shape of a pentagram star.[108]

> *Happy are you O Osiris! You have appeared in glory, you have power, you are a spirit; you have made your shape everlasting; and your face is that of Anubis. Ra rejoices over you and he is well disposed towards your beauty. You have seated yourself on the pure throne which Geb, who loves you, made for you; you receive him in your arms in the West, you cross the sky daily.[109]*

> *The imperishable stars are under thy supervision, and the stars which never set are thy throne.[110]*

> *The stars which never rest sing hymns of praise unto thee, and the stars which are imperishable glorify thee as thou sinkest to rest in the horizon of Manu.[111]*

---

106 *The Book of the Dead, Spell 17*, R O Faulkner
107 *The Book of the Dead; Spell 42*, R O Faulkner
108 *The God Secret*, Greg Rigby
109 *The Book of the Dead; Spell 181*, R O Faulkner
110 *The Book of the Dead; Hymn to Osiris*, E A Wallis Budge
111 *The Book of the Dead;* A HYMN OF PRAISE TO RA WHEN HE RISETH

One other single important element of Egyptian belief that is pertinent to this analysis is the Egyptian conviction that upon the death of a pharaoh, he ascended to the heavens (the area around Ursa Major) and joined Osiris and the other god kings and that they were visible as a major star in or near the constellation. Ordinary people who lived good lives ascended to become stars and they too could be seen in the northern sky. Thus, we can see that the quotations from Matthew above are all consistent with these essential elements of Egyptian religious belief.

> As astronomer-priest's observations became more sophisticated, the Egyptians came to believe that when the sun came up and hid the northern stars, it travelled through the underworld, allowing the circumpolar stars to rotate to their (morning) starting position the next day. "The Pyramid texts also reflect a belief in an astral afterlife among the circumpolar stars . . . ."[112]

[In] the Egyptian religion, old beliefs were rarely discarded; new ideas and concepts were merely tacked on, even when in direct contradiction to existing views. That is why the Egyptians could believe in an afterlife in which the deceased would spend eternity in the company of the circumpolar stars as an *akh*, at the same time as being restricted to the burial chamber and offering chapel of the tomb as a *ka*, but also visiting the world of the living, inhabiting the Elysian Fields and travelling across the sky and through the underworld with the sun god as a *ba*.[113]

If Jesus Christ's father was Ptolemy XIII, and if we assume that the popular date of the Nativity of 6 BCE to be correct, the child would have been conceived when his father was some 55/56 years old. This means that if Ptolemy were still alive at the time Jesus started his ministry, he would have been 85 years old. This means that (if alive) Ptolemy XIII would have been an old

---

112 *The Book of the Dead; Introduction*, R. O. Faulkner
113 *Ibid*

man at the time of Jesus reported baptism by John. In relation to Jesus's baptism, Matthew 3:13-17 tells us:

> *Then Jesus came from Galilee to the Jordan to be baptized by John. But John tried to deter him, saying, "I need to be baptized by you, and do you come to me?" Jesus replied, "Let it be so now; it is proper for us to do this to fulfil all righteousness." Then John consented. As soon as Jesus was baptized, he went up out of the water. At that moment heaven was opened, and he saw the Spirit of God descending like a dove and alighting on him. And a voice from heaven said, "This is my Son, whom I love; with him I am well pleased."*

This claim that the father's voice was heard is duplicated in the other three gospels (Mark 1:1-8, Luke 3:1-20, John 1:19-28). These assertions by the gospel writers that a heavenly voice was heard (who claimed to be Jesus's father) at the Baptism of Jesus (and also at the transfiguration) would seem to indicate that the writers believed Jesus's father to be dead and living in heaven. This view is suspect; a voice from Heaven would have frightened and scattered the throng at the crowded baptism ceremony and since such a fright is not mentioned, the interpretation is most implausible. The claim was probably made therefore to embellish the text and enhance the emerging view that Jesus was divine, (in the sense of mystical) and that he was directly linked to a God that was almighty, eternal, incarnate and at the same time interested in the inhabitants of the tiny planet named earth, occupied by humanity.

If the words were said, they were more likely to have been spoken by a human voice and heard (and reported) by the group of followers who had accompanied Jesus to the event.

Returning to the extracts from Matthew, at the beginning of this chapter, each of them (other than the first) can be explained in the context of Egyptian religious belief and Jesus's earthly Father (Ptolemy) either still alive or departed to live in Heaven. In this latter context, "my father in Heaven," "our father in Heaven," "your heavenly father," or "Father, Lord of Heaven"

Greg Rigby

would refer to the eternal Egyptian God of Heaven, with all his various names and configurations (Ra, Amen, Tuth, Seth, Osiris) or to Ptolemy himself if he had died and was believed to have joined the pantheon of gods in the heavens.

Jesus is quoted as calling himself the Son of (a) man and claims that "all authority in heaven and on earth has been given to me"—a claim that could only be made by a legitimate pharaoh who has the designation Son of God, and who is claiming his title and the authority of his position.

The reference to God's throne in Matthew 5:34 (the first in the list above) is a direct reference to one of the cornerstones of the Egyptian religious tradition where heaven is the part of the sky that houses the Ursa Major constellation and the throne embedded within it:

> *It is I who causes Osiris to be a spirit, and I have made content those who are in his suite. I desire that they grant fear of me and create respect of me among those who are in their midst, for I am lifted aloft on my standard, on my throne and on my allotted seat.*[114]

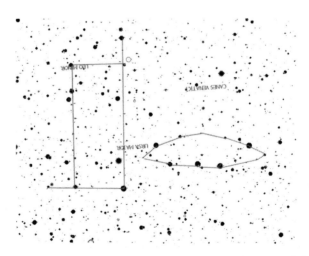

Fig 13 The throne and the eye that spell Wsir—the name of Osiris in the heart of the Ursa Major constellation

114 *Book of the Dead, Spell 85*, R O Faulkner

This is confirmed in the Book of Revelation, which tells us,

> *"Peace from the (one) who is and the (one) who was and the (one) who coming and from the seven spirits which are before the throne of him." (Rev. 1:4) And behold a throne is set in Heaven and on the throne a sitting one. (Rev. 4:2).*

References to God, the father and the son in the other three Gospels are shown below and the explanation of each in the context of ancient Egyptian religious belief is shown alongside the quotation:

Mark 1:1—The beginning of the gospel about Jesus Christ, the Son of God

This claim that Jesus was the Son of God can be explained by him, as the legitimate pharaoh () having this title as his *nomen*.

Mark 1:24—"What do you want with us, Jesus of Nazareth? Have you come to destroy us?

I know who you are—the Holy One of God!"

In the Book of the Dead, Osiris is usually described as holy:

"And the gods who live in the horizon ascribe unto me praises, as the divine Spirit-body, the Lord of mortals. I am exalted like that <u>holy god</u> who dwelleth in the Great House."[115]

Mark 3:10-12—For he had healed many, so that those with diseases/plagues were pushing forward to touch him. Whenever the unclean (evil) spirits beheld him, they prostrated themselves before him and cried out, "You are the Son of God." But he gave them strict orders not to tell who he was.

Jesus asking anyone not to tell who he was does not ring true. Why would he want this to be hidden? The only logical reason would be that these three verses of Mark's gospel relate to Jesus having been recognised as the Son of Ptolemy XIII and he was instructing those that recognised him to keep it quiet. This in turn implies that they had seen Jesus in the company of

---

115 The Book of the Dead, the chapter on being transformed into the Prince of the Tchatchau Chiefs, E A Wallis Budge

his father, and it is entirely possible that this could have happened during the thirty years prior to the commencement of his ministry.

Mark 8:38—If anyone is ashamed of me and my words in this adulterous and sinful generation, the Son of Man will be ashamed of him when he comes known/is established in/by his Father's /judgement/splendour with/behind the holy angels

Again we have similarities to quotations from the Book of the Dead that give us clues to the Egyptian creed:

> *If any god, or any goddess, attack the Osiris Ani, whose word is truth, when he setteth out, the Ancestor of the year who liveth upon hearts [Osiris] shall eat him when he cometh forth from Abydos, and the Ancestors of Ra shall reckon with him, and the Ancestors of Light shall reckon with him. [He is] a god of splendour [arrayed in] the apparel of heaven, and he is among the Great Gods.*[116]

Mark 15 34 And at the ninth hour Jesus cried out in a loud voice; "Eloi, Eloi, lama sabachthani?"—which means, "My God, my God, why have you forsaken me?"

Eminent historians have claimed that this outcry from the cross was spoken in Egyptian: The words assigned to the sufferer, are Egyptian: Lama or *Rama*, denotes weeping; *Remi* was the weeper in Rem-Rem. *Sabak* means to be prostrate and utterly subdued, *Tani*, is to bow the forehead. Instead of these words John says; *"When Jesus received the vinegar he said, It is finished; and he bowed his head and gave up his spirit."* Now it is noteworthy that the one version should be a rendering of the other, (the gospels of Mark and John) according to Egyptian. Heli (Heri) means it is finished ended, to fly away, give up the ghost, and ascend as a sprit. Any Egyptologist will know that *Heli-heli-lama-Sakak-tanti* contains and conveys the sense of *heli*, to *be ended* (in giving up the ghost); *lama*, to weep; *sabak* be prostrate; and *tani*, to bow down the forehead. He will also

---

116 Ibid THE Chapter OF ADVANCIN.G TO THE TCHATCHAU CHIEFS OF OSIRIS

know that as such it is a description by another speaker and not a dramatic utterance by the sufferer; and John's version is a descriptive narrative except in the words "*it is finished,*" which as *Heli-heli*" might express the giving up the spirit by whomsoever they were said. If the words were Egyptian, *heli* would naturally become *eli*, as a Semitic form.[117]

As an observer of logic, it is the author's view that the phrase could equally have been an incantation of God's names; **Eli, Eli, Ra Ma'at, Sebek Hathor Neith.** Eli was one of the two most frequently used deity names amongst Proto-Jewish Western Semites.[118] 'L' and 'R' are interchangeable when used in Egyptian pronunciation of the unilateral hieroglyphic and only the 'Ma' of '**Ma'**at' would have been heard.[119] Most of these names are those of Egyptian Gods and would substantiate the view that in an extreme situation the person called out in his natural tongue, which if this is valid, would appear to have been Egyptian.

Luke too refers to Jesus as the Son:

> *Luke 1:32—He will be great and will be called the Son of the Most High. The Lord God will give him the throne of his father David.*

This could be interpreted to mean the Jesus was a descended from Thutmose III and had legitimate claim to the pharaonic throne

> *Luke 2:48-50—When his parents saw him, they were astonished. His mother said to him, "Son, why have you treated us like this? Your father and I have been anxiously searching for you." "Why were you searching for me?" he asked. "Didn't you know I had to be in my Father's house?" But they did not understand what he was saying to them.*

117 *The Natural Genesis, Vol 2*, Gerald Massey
118 *Collected Works of Sri Bhati Anada Goswami*
119 *Egyptian Language; Phonetic System and Pronunciation*, Luigi Tripani

The translation of the Greek word τοῖς as 'the house' is creative translation. The word appears to be plural not singular. In addition, there is an abundance of possible translations for πατρός (chosen as 'father') and the word itself is genitive—therefore the translation could be more accurate if it read, *"I was obliged to be with these of my ancestry."* This in turn provokes the question: what ancestry?

> *Luke **10:22**—"All things have been committed to me by my Father. No one knows who the Son is except the Father, and no one knows who the Father is except the Son and those to whom the Son chooses to reveal him."*

It is interesting that this reads "knows who the father is" rather than "knows the father"—obviously the author wished to portray that the identity of the father and son was of significance. This would make sense if the father were an earthly father, who was keeping his identity secret. If it became known the Ptolemy XIII was the father of Jesus and that he was still alive, the safety of both father and son would have been unsure.

> *Luke **22:29**—And I confer on you a kingdom, just as my Father conferred one on me, **30** so that you may eat and drink at my table in my kingdom and sit on thrones, judging the twelve tribes of Israel.*

Here Jesus acknowledges that a kingdom was conferred upon him. This would make sense if Jesus thought that he had claim to the kingdom of Egypt and its territories.

> *Luke **22:66-71**—At daybreak the council of the elders of the people, both the chief priests and teachers of the law, met together, and Jesus was led before them. "If you are the Christ (anointed one)," they said, "tell us!" Jesus answered, "If I tell you, you will not believe me, and if I asked you, you would not answer. (Some time) from now, but the Son of Man also will be sitting at*

the right hand of the power of God." They all asked, "Are you then the Son of God?" He replied, "You say I am." Then they said, "Why do we need any more testimony? We have heard it from His own lips."

If Jesus believed himself to be of the royal bloodline, this statement may well relate to his belief concerning his physical place in the heavens after his death.

***John 1:51**—He then added, "I tell you the truth, you shall see heaven opened, and the angels/emissaries of God ascending and descending on/over the Son of Man."*

This verses gives an interesting description of heavenly events and may well relate to the fact that the sky appears to rotate and therefore, all stars external to those at the centre of the rotation appear to rise and/or fall over/above the stars nearer the centre. The emissaries/messengers of God may also be the planets that move independent of the heavenly rotation of the stars around the northern pole position.

***John 5:43**—I have come in my Father's name.*

In addition to the nomen given to all pharaohs (son of Ra), the name of Ptolemy XIII was 'Theos Philopator' (Θεός Φιλοπάτωρ), meaning "God loving His Father." This statement in John attributes to Jesus the inherited qualities of his father. If John 5:43 does not relate to Theos Philopator as its definition of his father's name, what father's name does it refer to? Nowhere in John is there a statement of Jesus's father's name other than Joseph, and we must assume that, as it is not given, the reader is expected to know what it is. Even the more esoteric documents from the period avoid specifying the father's name.

The Gospel of Truth, one of the Nag Hammadi scrolls (that will be discussed in more detail in a later chapter) contains extensive commentary on the question of the name of the father. Despite that, it does not actually specify what the name is:

Who, then, has been able to pronounce a name for him, this great name, except him alone to whom the name belongs and the sons of the name in whom the name of the Father is at rest, and who themselves in turn are at rest in his name, since the Father has no beginning? It is he alone who engendered it for himself as a name in the beginning before he had created the Aeons, that the name of the Father should be over their heads as a lord—that is, the real name, which is secure by his authority and by his perfect power. For the name is not drawn from lexicons nor is his name derived from common name giving, But it is invisible. He gave a name to himself alone, because he alone saw it and because he alone was capable of giving himself a name. For he who does not exist has no name. For what name would one give him who did not exist? Nevertheless, he who exists also with his name and he alone knows it, and to him alone the Father gave a name. The Son is his name. He did not, therefore, keep it secretly hidden, but the son came into existence. He himself gave a name to him. The name, then, is that of the Father, just as the name of the Father is the Son. For otherwise, where would compassion find a name—outside of the Father? But someone will probably say to his companion, "Who would give a name to someone who existed before himself, as if, indeed, children did not receive their name from one of those who gave them birth?"

Above all, then, it is fitting for us to think this point over: What is the name? It is the real name. It is, indeed, the name which came from the Father, for it is he who owns the name. He did not, you see, get the name on loan, as in the case of others because of the form in which each one of them is going to be created. This, then, is the authoritative name. There is no one else to whom he has given it. But it remained unnamed, unuttered, till the moment when he, who is perfect, pronounced it him-

self; and it was he alone who was able to pronounce his name and to see it.[120]

This passage compounds the problem; why is no actual name given? If the name of the father is so important, why cannot it be known? Or is it that those writing these texts were endeavouring to be careful *not* to stipulate it? Were they hiding the name for a practical reason—that to announce it would be dangerous for them or that it would serve to destroy the foundations of the theology they were endeavouring to establish. Either way, it implies that the authors knew the origins of the secret that their words were trying to perpetuate.

An interesting alternative explanation lies in the definition of the ancient Hebrew word for 'Son'; This Hebrew word is derived out of the parent root בּן (*ben*, Strong's #1121). In the original Hebrew alphabet, this word was written as:

The first picture is a picture of a tent, our house. The second picture is of a germinating seed, but it can also mean to "continue" as a seed continues the next generation. When combined these letters mean "continue the house," the Hebrew word for a "son," the one who continues the line of the house.[121]

If this is what the authors were trying to say, then they must have been aware of the importance of the bloodline and were talking about the only lineage of that time that could have been of any significance; the line of the god-kings of Egypt.

Other interesting mentions of father and son in John's Gospel are somewhat more philosophical and include references to Jesus relationship with his father: *Then they asked him, "Where is your father?" "You do not know me or my Father," Jesus replied. "If you knew me, you would know my Father also." (John 8:19)*

---

120 *The Gospel of Truth (Nag Hammadi Library)*, translated by Robert M Grant
121 *Biblical Word of the Month—Stone*, Jeff A. Benner

There are two possible meanings to this statement: either Jesus is talking to Hebrews who are ignorant of the Egyptian tradition and who would not therefore know of the location of the father in the heavens or he was talking about his earthly father Ptolemy XIII. On balance it is likely that he meant the latter, since this would fit with "you do not know me," meaning, you do not know that I am the son of Ptolemy XIII and the rightful God king in the Pharaonic tradition.

> ***John 8:28***—*So Jesus said, "When/as long as you have lifted up/exalted/honoured the Son/posterity of Man/mankind/God, then you will know that I am/exist and that I do/form/make/constitute/ produce nothing on my own but speak just what/these (words) the Father has taught me."*

The Greek words that constitute this verse have many possible meanings when they are translated into English. Whatever the translation, it seems most likely this statement relates to the lifting up or exaltation of Jesus's father Ptolemy XIII (the son of God). In other words Jesus is saying, "I wait to take my place as the Son of God until my father is in Heaven—then you will know me in my new role, and then I speak the words my father has taught (that are pertinent to the role)." For this to be an accurate meaning Ptolemy XIII would have needed to still be alive at the time the words were spoken and for this to be the case, Ptolemy XIII would have needed to be circa 85/86 years old. The verse could be read as an announcement of Jesus's father's approaching death, which (if so) would probably have been mentioned in tThe story of death that fits well with such a scenario is the later visit by Jesus to Bethany (where he had enemies and had previously been abused) to visit the dead/dying Lazarus, where reportedly Jesus wept, and it was said, "See how he loved him!" In the context of Egyptian religion, the raising of a pharaoh can mean the raising of him to be a star in heaven. This could account for the wording in John, where he never actually states that Lazarus comes back to life only that "the dead man came out, his hands and feet wrapped in strip of linen"—in other words, he did not walk and was probably carried out. It is possible therefore that Lazarus was a pseudonym for Ptolemy, and the story relates to the death of Jesus's true father. Significantly, the coverage of this story in John 11 tells us that one member of Lazarus's family is Mary, who many eminent students of the New Testament believed to have been Mary Magdalene, a subject that we will return to in a later chapter.

> ***John 8:54-55****—Jesus replied, "If I glorify/praise myself, my glory/opinion means nothing. My Father, whom you claim as your God, is the one who glorifies/honours/praises me. Though you do not know him, I know him. If I said I did not, I would be a liar like you, but I do know him and I keep his word.*

This verse (as was the previous verse we examined) was part of the Sermon on the Mount and was addressed to the "Jews who believed him." In a later chapter, we will show that this probably referred to the Essenes, the forerunners of Gnostic Christians who were the Jews that protected many of the ancient the sacred Egyptian traditions that linked them back directly to Isis and Osiris and who would have revered the holder of the bloodline as a god-king. In this context, Jesus's words indicate that he follows the instructions that he was given by his father and that he is an obedient son who will protect the instructions that his father has given him.

> ***John 10:34-36****—Jesus answered them; "Is it not written in your Law, 'I have said you are gods/judges'? If he called them 'gods,' to whom the word of God came—and the Scripture cannot be broken—what about the one whom the Father sanctified/blessed (set apart as his very own) and sent into the world? Why then do you accuse me of blasphemy because I said, 'I am God's Son'?"*

This verse refers to Psalm 82 which talks of people making judgements of those less fortunate than themselves and reinforces the fact that those addressed are gods in that they make judgements of others but that "ye shall die like men and fall like one of the princes." It was spoken at the Festival of Dedication (Hanukkah) in Jerusalem when opponents picked up stones to stone him for blasphemy. The words as quoted indicate that Jesus had a fervent belief in his status, and he was attempting to explain it. It is interpreted by Christians to mean that Jesus was claiming to be the Son of God incarnate. The words could equally have been those of Jesus claiming his heritage as the first son of the last surviving god-king, Ptolemy XIII.

> *John 12:49-50—For I did not speak of my own accord, but the Father who sent me commanded me what to say and how to say it 50 I know that his command leads to eternal life. So whatever I say is just what the Father has told me to say."*

These verses could well refer to Jesus's earthly father Ptolemy XIII who has given Jesus strict instructions of about what he should say and how he should say it.

The Egyptian context can be illustrated by "A Hymn of Praise to Ra" and by the first of the chapter of "Coming Forth by Day" contained in the Book of the Dead:

> *Let me not be kept captive [by the tomb], and let me not be turned back [on my way]. Let the members of my body be made new again when I contemplate thy beauties, even as are the members of all thy favoured ones, because I am one of those who worshipped thee upon earth. Let me arrive in the Land of Eternity, let me enter into the Land of Everlastingness. This, O my Lord, behold thou shalt ordain for me."* [122] *"Ra commanded Thoth to prove true the words of Osiris before*

---

122 *The Papyrus of Ani; The Book of the Dead*, E A Wallis Budge

his enemies; what was commanded [for Osiris], let that be done for me by Thoth. [123]

John 16:25-27—*"Though I have been speaking figuratively, a time is coming when I will no longer use this kind of language but will tell you plainly about my Father. In that day you will ask in/with (the memory of) my name. I am not saying that I will ask/question the Father on your behalf/concerning you. No, the Father himself loves you because you have loved me and have believed that I came from God.*

The verses are conclusive in their statement that Jesus has been talking figuratively. In them, we are being told quite clearly and unambiguously that it has been necessary to read between the lines to get to the truth.

The passage goes on to say that "a time is coming"—in other words, it hasn't arrived yet—"when I will tell you plainly about my Father." In fact, there is nothing in the following chapters of John that might constitute such an explanation of the father. This can only mean that if there ever was an explanation, it was removed or that it was included in a way that it is not immediately obvious. A removal is the most plausible explanation and it would be understandable if the text removed flew in the face of the Christian proclamation of Jesus as the divine Son of God incarnate, the central proposition of Pauline Christianity.

All of these verses can relate to Jesus's knowledge of, his relationship with and the instructions he might have received from his earthly father. Ptolemy XIII would have believed that he was the Son of God who would, through Jesus, perpetuate what he believed to be a divine bloodline back to Osiris.

One of the most profound instructions relating to the Father that was attributed to Jesus was in The Lord's Prayer, which defined Jesus's suggested way of praying to God the Father. This prayer is mentioned in Matthew 6:9-13 and in Luke 11:1-4:

123 *Ibid*

Matt. 6:9-13—Thus therefore pray you; Father of us, which (is) in the heavens, hallowed be the name of you, let come the kingdom of you, let be done the will of you, as in heaven (so) also on/over earth, the bread of us daily give us today and forgive us the debts of us as also we forgive the debtors of us. And not lead us into temptation but deliver us from evil. For yours is the kingdom and the power and the glory for the ages AMEN.

Luke 11:2-4—Father of us who (is) in heaven hallowed be the name of you, let come the kingdom of you, let be done the will of you as in heaven also upon earth. The bread of us daily give us each day and forgive us the sins of us also indeed ourselves we forgive everyone indebted to us and not lead us into temptation but deliver us from evil.

Both versions include the invocation "hallowed be the name of you," which seems strange since it does not state the name to which it refers.

The name of God in Egyptian, Greek and Hebrew is traceable in the stars in and around the constellation of Ursa Major, and this illustration is alluded to in various chapters of the Book of Revelation:

Rev. 2:13—I know where thou dwellest where (is) the throne of the Satan and <u>thou holdest the name of me</u> and not thou didst deny the faith of me even in the days of Antipas.
Rev. 2:17—And on/over the stone <u>a name new written</u> which no man knows except the (one) receiving (it)
Rev. 9:11—They have over them a king the angel of the abyss name to him <u>in Hebrew Abaddon </u>and in <u>the Greek name he has Apollyon.</u>
Rev. 19:12—The (ones) but eyes of him a flame of fire and on/over the head/top of him <u>diadems many having a name written</u> which no one knows except he.

Rev. 19:16—And on/over the thigh of him <u>a name</u> <u>written</u> king of kings and lord of lords.

Possible representations of these names of gods can be obtained by joining up stars in the Ursa Major constellation. The following illustrations depict these names from the Book of Revelation:

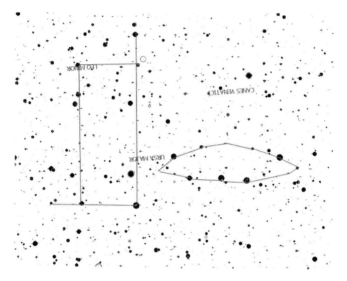

Fig 14 *Wsir*, **the name of Osiris (in Ursa Major) in heaven**

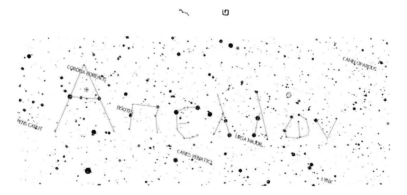

Fig 15 The name of Apollo (over Ursa Major) in the heavens

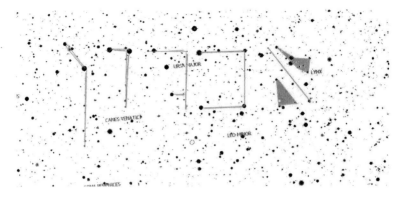

**Fig 16 The name Abaddon (in Hebrew) written
in the stars of Ursa Major**

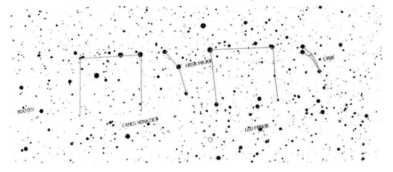

**Fig 17 The name Yahweh—the God of the Hebrews written
in the stars of Ursa Major**

Such representations may be appropriate in light of the first verse of John's Gospel: "In the beginning was the Word, and the Word was with God, and the Word was God," since we know that in the Egyptian pantheon, God was an aspect of these same stars. In this context, it is perhaps strange that Jesus did not suggest any of these possibilities as the name to be hallowed.

The word hallowed means holy or respected. The exhortation "hallowed be thy name" could fit with the Hebrew name Yahweh, since by early post-biblical times, the name Yahweh had ceased to be pronounced aloud, except once a year by the High Priest in the Holy of Holies. However, if this or any of the other names written in Heaven are the name alluded to in the Lord's Prayer, and the followers of Jesus were aware of the name being referred to, it would not fit that they were not perpetuated in the Christian tradition.

Going back to the words of the Lord's Prayer, Matthew's gospel may provide a simpler answer to the exhortation to hallow the lord's name. This version of the prayer clearly and explicitly states, "For yours is the kingdom and the power and the glory for the ages. AMEN."

Amen is the name of the Egyptian God of Gods, and in his role as Amon-Ra, he could certainly have been thought of as Father/King of the Gods. Together with Osiris Amun-Ra, he is the most widely recorded of the Egyptian gods and was the chief deity of the Egyptian religion. Amun-Ra also came to be worshipped outside of Egypt and came to be identified with Zeus in Ancient Greece and Jupiter in the Roman pantheon.

Amun/Amon/Amen was sometimes known as Amaunet and is mentioned at length in the Old Egyptian pyramid texts. His name Amun (written *imn*, pronounced Amana in ancient Egyptian), means hidden.

Certainly, the ongoing, repetitive use of Amen (the name of one of Egypt's greatest gods) throughout the Christian world would seem to indicate the wish expressed in the second line of the Lord's prayer. "Hallowed be they name" has not been knowingly achieved. No one considers the word/name Amen to be holy, yet it is only ever used in the context of prayer and religious ceremony, which gives it a hallowed connotation.

Perhaps it is important that we ask why no one has ever queried the routine use of the Egyptian God of Gods' name at the end of their prayers and to the other references to the name of an Egyptian god in the gospels:

> *Matt. 28:19—Therefore go, and make disciples of all nations, baptizing them in the name of the Father and of the Son and of the Holy Spirit, teaching them to observe all things that I commanded you. Behold, I am with you always, even to the end of the age. Amen.*
> *Mark 16:19-20—So then after the Lord had spoken unto them, he was received up into heaven, and sat on*

the right hand of God. And they went forth, and preached everywhere, the Lord working with them, and confirming the word with signs following. Amen.

*   **Luke 24:53**—*And were continually in the temple, praising and blessing God. Amen.*

These links to the constellation of Ursa Major and to the name Amen, the name of the Father of the Gods, are confirmed in the Book of Revelation:

*   **Rev. 3:1**—*These things says the one having the seven spirits of the one God and the seven stars, I know your deeds that the characterisation you have that you are alive and yet dead you are.*
*   **Rev. 3:14**—*These things says the Amen, the witness, the one faithful and true, the beginning of the creation of the one God.*

Christian zealots have attempted to confuse the faithful by claiming that Amen means *so be it.*[124] Others have claimed that it means truly,[125] or that the use of Amen in early Judeo/Christian times was similar to the phrase "God bless you" as it used today[126].

The word is used 129 times in the New Testament, and we acknowledge that it would be impossible for Christian theologians to admit that it refers to the Egyptian God of Gods, Amen-Ra. If they did so, it would (by definition) mean that the God of Christians was the same person as the ancient God of the Egyptians, and that would mean that Jesus had as much claim to eternity as did Osiris, the first mythical Son of God. That being said, it is strong evidence of the link between Jesus and the Egyptian pantheon.

We have not analysed the New Testament line by line, a task we will vacate to far more eminent un-biased scholars than ourselves.

---

124 *Baker's Evangelical Dictionary of Biblical Theology - Amen*
125 *Ibid*
126 *Use of the Word Amen*, R Dean Anderson, Jr

All in all, however, it can be seen clearly from this brief analysis that the New Testament could well be referring to Jesus in his role as the rightful pharaoh, the son of Ptolemy XIII and Mary, the direct descendant of Thutmose III. Seen in that light, his claims to the title Son of God could relate to his divine birthright as defined by the Egyptian tradition and to his position in the sacred pharaonic bloodline that goes back to Osiris, the first God king.

Christians will condemn this hypothesis as it undermines their faith. They will perhaps call on the miracles Jesus that is reported to have performed and more significantly the death and resurrection of Jesus that is claimed in the gospels as evidence that he was/is God incarnate.

It is certainly true that if Jesus Christ actually lived and died, and was resurrected three days after his death, there would exist a significant argument to back the Christian claim.

We were not there, however; therefore, we cannot know what actually happened. The best we can do is look at the reports and play devils' advocate to identify interpretations of the texts that might permit us to question Christian orthodoxy and promote our hypothesis. To that end we must look at Jesus reported death and resurrection.

Our examination first looks at the descriptions of Jesus's death in the four gospels, and attempts to find any discrepancies:

> *Luke 23:46, 49—And Jesus, crying out with a loud voice, said, "Father, INTO YOUR HANDS I COMMIT MY SPIRIT." Having said this, He breathed His last. And all his acquaintances and the women that followed him from Galilee, stood afar off, beholding these things.*
> *Matthew 27:50, 55—And Jesus cried out again with a loud voice, and yielded up His spirit. Many women were there looking on from a distance, who had followed Jesus from Galilee while ministering to him. Among them was Mary Magdalene and Mary the Mother of James and Joseph, and the mother of the sons of Zebedee.*
> *Mark 15:37, 40—And Jesus uttered a loud cry and breathed his last/gave up the ghost. There were also*

some women looking on from a distance, among whom was Mary Magdalene and Mary the mother of James the Less and (of) Joses, and Salome.
    John 19:26-27, 30-35*—When Jesus then saw His mother, and the pupil/disciple whom He loved standing nearby, He said to His mother, "Woman, behold, your son/pupil!" Then He said to the disciple/pupil, "Behold, your mother!" From that hour the disciple/ pupil took her into his own household. Therefore when Jesus had received the sour wine, He said, "It is finished!" And He bowed His head and gave up His spirit/ the ghost. But coming to Jesus when they saw that he was already dead, they did not break his legs. But one of the soldiers pierced His side with a spear and immediately blood and water came out. And he who has seen has testified and his testimony is true; and he knows that is telling the truth (and he testifies) so that you also may believe.*

The first and most obvious inconsistency is that between the gospels of Matthew, Mark and Luke, which state that the women in attendance were standing afar off or at a distance, and that of John, which claims that Jesus saw the disciple he loved and his mother nearby. The justification given in John is that the person testifying was there, implying that the authors of the other three gospels were not and that their versions are inaccurate. If this is true, the versions in Matthew, Mark and Luke would be based on hearsay and the veracity of Christ's death as reported hinges entirely on the version given in the gospel of John.
    The next most significant statement that invites scepticism is again in the testimony attributed to John, which states that Jesus was dead and that when pierced with the spear blood immediately came from the wound. This contradicts what is known about the body's functions after death. At the moment of death, the heart stops, and blood is no longer being pumped throughout the body. The process of gravity will mean that it will fall to the body's lowest extremities, which means if the

body is pierced in the lateral area, there may be seepage, but no spurt or significant flow of blood will occur.

These two inconsistencies are exacerbated by the intense assertion in John that the testimony is true, leading us to speculate why the author believed that his testimony might be doubted. He admits that the testimony is written as it is "so that you also might believe," but this assertion itself creates doubt in the veracity of the statements made.

Given the importance of Jesus being dead (if it would be claimed that he had risen), we can only speculate that Jesus was not in fact dead, and that the elaborate scene to put the author (or the person relating this story to the author) within earshot of the last gasping words of Jesus was contrived in order to add reinforcement to a required belief in the authenticity of Jesus's death.

Jesus's resurrection, which required his death, proved that Jesus was God incarnate. Without his death, he could not have risen from the dead.

With regard to the resurrection, there are three possibilities:

1. Jesus did not die, and there was no resurrection. The story was a fabrication.
2. Jesus did die, but there was no resurrection, and the stories of such an event were false.
3. Jesus did die, and he was resurrected.

None of the four gospels tells of the actual awakening of Jesus from the dead. In John, Mary Magdalene found the tomb open and went to Peter and 'the other disciple Jesus loved' to tell him that the body had been moved. They went to the tomb and found the linen Jesus had been wrapped in but no body. Peter leaves then Mary has an encounter with Jesus.

In all the other three gospels, Mary Magdalene and other women were met by a man "in bright clothes" who tells them, "He has risen!" In Luke, the women are reminded that Jesus had prophesied that he would be crucified and after three days rise again. In Mark, they were instructed to "go tell His disciple and

Peter," and in Matthew, they were told to "go quickly and tell his disciples!"

Again, we have discrepancies concerning the attendees between the gospel accounts. In particular, "the disciple Jesus loved" was in attendance in the gospel of John and in none of the other three. At the very least, this means that the stories are written by people who were not there and that they rely on accounts that have been transmitted by word of mouth. At worst, it implies some dishonesty in the reports of the most important event in the life of Jesus Christ.

One strange element of text concerning the resurrection occurs in a Gnostic gospel of Marcion (refuted as a heresy by Hippolytus) and in the canonical Gospel of Luke and confirmed in Jesus encounter with Thomas:

> But they were terrified and affrighted, and supposed that they had beheld a phantom. And he said unto them, "Why are ye troubled? and wherefore do reasonings arise in your hearts? Behold my hands and my feet, that I am myself: for a spirit hath not flesh and bones, as ye see me have."[127]

> "See My hands and My feet, that it is I Myself; touch Me and see, for a spirit does not have flesh and bones as you see that I have."[128]

> Then He said to Thomas, "Reach here with your finger, and see My hands; and reach here your hand and put it into My side; and do not be unbelieving, but believing."[129]

These texts claim that Jesus showed himself to be flesh and bones. In other words he was corporeal and in any human sense of the word, alive. Does this point to the possibility that Jesus did not die?

---

127 *Fragments of the Faith Forgotten: The Gospel of Marcion* translated by G R S Mead
128 Luke 24:39
129 John 20:27

The Jesus prophecy (mentioned in the Luke version of the resurrection) is mentioned in three gospels, and in two of these, it is mentioned twice. If these were instructions rather than predictions, then Jesus was trying hard to ensure that the events would unfold in a particular way.

Luke 9:22—*"The Son of Man must suffer many things and be rejected by the elders and chief priests and scribes, and be killed and be raised up on the third day."*

Matthew 16:21—*From that time Jesus began to show his disciples that he must go to Jerusalem and suffer many things from the elders and chief priests and scribes, and be killed and be raised up on the third day.*

Matthew 20:17-19—*As Jesus was about to go up to Jerusalem, He took the twelve disciples aside by themselves and on the way he said to them. Behold we are going to Jerusalem and the Son of Man will be delivered to the chief priests and scribes and they will condemn him to death, and will hand him over to the Gentiles to mock and scourge and crucify Him and on the third day he will be raise up.*

Mark 8:31—*And he began to teach them that the Son of Man must suffer many things and be rejected by the elders and the chief priests and scribes and be killed and after three days rise again.*

Mark 10:33-34—*"Behold we are going to Jerusalem and the Son of Man will be delivered to the chief priests and the scribes; and they will condemn Him to death and will hand him over to the Gentiles. They will mock Him and spit on Him, and scourge Him and kill Him and three days later, he will rise again.*

Whilst the gospels report that these predictions were made to the disciples, something must have happened to make them have common knowledge.

Matthew 27:62-63—*Now on the next day, the day after the preparation, the chief priests and the Pharisees*

143

gather together before Pilate, and they said, "Sire we remember that when he was alive that deceiver said, 'After three days I am to rise again.'"

This implies that the information about Jesus's prediction must have been passed to those who claimed that they remembered it. When added to Jesus' clear attempt prior to the crucifixion to ensure the course of events that would take place this has all the hallmarks of a setup—a series of contrived events with (presumably) a known outcome.

Jesus is reported to have mentioned the resurrection when he visited Bethany at the time that he attended Lazarus:

__John 11:23-25__—Jesus said to her, "Your brother will rise again." Martha said to Him, "I know that he will rise again in the resurrection on the last day." Jesus said to her, "I am the resurrection and the life. Whoever believes in me, though he die, yet shall he live."

A link to an ancient Egyptian view of the last day, judgement and resurrection is well illustrated in the many coffin texts:

As for the tribunal which judges the needy, you know that they will not be lenient on that day of judging the poor; in the hour of exercising (their) function, wretched is he who is accused as a wise man. Do not put your trust in length of years, for they regard a lifetime as an hour; a man survives after death, and his deeds are laid before him in a heap. Existence yonder is eternal, and he who complains of it is a fool, but as for him who attains it, he will be like a god yonder, striding forward like the lords of eternity.[130]

Jesus's words are allegorical, and we cannot be sure of their meaning. However, they can be understood in the context of the Egyptian view of the afterlife and the judgement by the court of

---

130 *Ancient Egyptian Texts: The Instructions of Merikare*, R O Faulkner

Gods that were placed behind the Ursa Major constellation (the imperishable stars that never set) in the northern sky.

Whether Jesus did or did not rise from the dead, he had obviously worked hard to set down a prediction that he could fulfil. Why was there such a prediction? There was nothing in the Old Testament that predicted these events and created an agenda that must be fulfilled. There are many predictions of a Messiah, but none that predict the resurrection. Therefore, whether contrived or real, it did not occur in order to fulfil some ancient Hebrew prophecy.

From the clues given in the gospels, Jesus is calculated by theologians to have died on April 3 CE 33,[131] fourteen days after the vernal equinox. Traditionally, throughout all the ancient civilisations, the vernal equinox was the time of rebirth.

The story of Easter as a time of rebirth, renewal and resurrection of life in general was found in the myths of many non-Christian deities such as the Greco-Phrygian god Attis and the Greco-Syrian god Adonis, among others.[132] Some Christian apologists demonstrate the dying-and-rising theme overall to be sound.[133]

There are many Gods with similar profile aspects to Jesus Christ:

- Krishna—who was crucified and resurrected
- Romulus—who was "snatched away to heaven" and who makes post mortem appearances
- Dionysus—born on December 25 and hung on a tree or crucified
- Zoroaster—killed, and his followers expected a second coming
- Attis—born December 25, crucified on a tree and resurrected after three days
- Horus—crucified and resurrected after three days
- Osiris—slaughtered and subsequently resurrected

131 *7 clues*, Jimmy Akin
132 *The Resurrection of Spring*, D M Murdock and S Acharya
133 *The Riddle of Resurrection*, Dr. Tryggve N. D. Mettinger

- Odin—hanged himself for nine days and was subsequently resurrected
- Tammuz/Adonis—was resurrected from the kingdom of the dead
- Bel/Marduk—crucified on a hill and resurrected
- Baal—Baal is announced dead and is subsequently resurrected
- Heracles—was killed and was resurrected

This list and the tradition it implies does not mean that the claim that Jesus had died and been resurrected was either true or false. However, the blatant contrivances admitted in the gospels concerning this critical aspect of the life of the person being reported give cause to doubt the normal Christian interpretation. These, together with the traditions of resurrection do mean that the claims regarding the death and resurrection of Jesus Christ are not proven. In particular, the link to Osiris (if such a link was an imperative in Jesus's life) could be significant. Some quotations from the Egyptian Book of the Dead may well indicate that Jesus and the incarnate God have Egyptian origins:

> *And I, Osiris Ani, have come into thy presence, so that I may be with thee, and may behold thy Disk every day. Let me not be kept captive [by the tomb], and let me not be turned back [on my way]. Let the members of my body be made new again when I contemplate thy beauties, even as are the members of all thy favoured ones, because I am one of those who worshipped thee upon earth. Let me arrive in the Land of Eternity, let me enter into the Land of Everlastingness. This, O my Lord, behold thou shalt ordain for me.*[134]
>
> *The Osiris Ani saith: Hail, thou One, who shinest from the moon. Hail, thou One, who shinest from the moon. Grant that this Osiris Ani may come forth among thy multitudes, who are at the portal. Let him be with the*

---

134 *A Hymn of Praise to Ra; The Book of the Dead,* E A Wallis Budge

Light-God. Let the Tuat be opened to him. Behold, the Osiris Ani shall come forth by day to perform everything which he wisheth upon the earth among those who are living [thereon].[135]

As mentioned several times, we do not actually know what happened and the analysis in this chapter does not prove things one way or the other. What we do know is that our hypothesis has been strengthened not weakened and has certainly not been disproved.

There is one thing we can surmise with some confidence; if the hypothesis that Jesus was the son of Ptolemy XIII is accurate, Jesus would only have submitted to his captors and died (or make it look as though he had died) if the bloodline and the secret that his father had given him to protect were both secure. In other words, for our hypothesis to have foundation there would have needed to be children of Jesus living at the time of his death, or he would have needed to be alive after his reported death in order to father children. We will investigate these possibilities in a later chapter.

First, we will look more closely at the so-called Gnostic gospels, to see if we can discover any elements of them that might consolidate the connection to Egypt and to the Egyptian royal bloodline in particular. From there, we will look at what we know of Mary Magdalene, the likely bearer of Jesus's issue.

---

135 THE Chapter OF COMING FORTH BY DAY AND OF LIVING AFTER DEATH; Ibid

CHAPTER 11

The Gnostic Gospels: The Nag Hammadi Scrolls

Gnosis is defined as the knowledge of transcendence arrived at by way of interior, intuitive means. It implies the possibility of a direct relationship with the higher universal power that we normally describe as God.

In the accepted Gnostic philosophy, there is a true, ultimate and glorious God, who created and is above and beyond all created universes. The basic Gnostic allegory has many variations, but all of these refer to Aeons, who are intermediate deific beings that exist between the ultimate, true god and us. They, together with this true god, comprise the infinite realm (Pleroma) wherein the power of God operates.

One of the aeonian beings who bears the name Sophia (Ma'at in Egypt) is of great importance to the Gnostic worldview. In the course of her journeying, Sophia emanated a flawed consciousness; an entity that became the creator of the physical and spiritual whole, all of which she created in the image of her own imperfection. This being, unaware of its origins, imagined itself to be the ultimate and absolute God. Since it took the already existing divine essence and fashioned it into various forms, it is also called the Demiurgos or half-maker. There is a genuine half, a true deific component within creation, but it is not recognized by the half-maker or by his/her cosmic minions, the Archons or rulers. Herein lays the essence of the cosmic conflict of which we are a part.

Through time, almost all early writings that did not conform to the Christian orthodoxy came to be described as Gnostic. The

148

so-called Gnostic Gospels are a collection of about 52 ancient texts based upon the teachings of several spiritual leaders, written from the second to the fourth century CE. The documents that comprise this collection were not discovered at a single time, but rather as a series of finds. The Nag Hammadi Library was discovered accidentally by two farmers in December 1945 and was named after the area in Egypt where it had been hidden for centuries. An overview of these documents, many of which refer to Jesus Christ directly, is provided online by the Nag Hammadi Library, where they are described as detailed in the paragraphs below:

Writings of creative and redemptive mythology, including Gnostic alternative versions of creation and salvation: The Apocryphon of John; The Hypostasis of the Archons; On the Origin of the World; The Apocalypse of Adam, The paraphrase of Shem.

Observations and commentaries on diverse Gnostic themes, such as the nature of reality, the nature of the soul, the relationship of the soul to the world: The Gospel of Truth; The Treatise on the Resurrection; The Tripartite Tractate; Eugnosis the blessed; The Second treatise of the Great Seth; The Teachings of Silvanus; The Testimony of Truth.

Liturgical and initiatory texts: The Discourse on the Eighth and Ninth; The Prayer of Thanksgiving; A Valentinian Exposition; The Three Steles of Seth; The Prayer of the Apostle Paul; (The Gospel of Philip, listed under the sixth category below, has great relevance here also, for it is in effect a treatise on Gnostic sacramental theology).

Other writings: dealing primarily with the feminine deific and spiritual principle, particularly with the Divine Sophia: The Thunder, Perfect Mind; The Thoughts of Norea; The Sophia of Jesus Christ; The Exegesis of the Soul.

Writings pertaining to the lives and experiences of some of the apostles: The Apocalypse of Peter; The Letter of Peter to Philip; The Acts of Peter and the Twelve Apostles; The (First) Apocalypse of James; The (Second) Apocalypse of James; The Apocalypse of Paul.

Scriptures which contain sayings of Jesus as well as descriptions of incidents in His life: The Dialogue of the Saviour; The Book of Thomas the Contender; The Apocryphon of James; The Gospel of Philip; The Gospel of Thomas.

In this chapter, we will look at those scripts that seem in any way relevant to our hypothesis that Jesus was the son of the Egyptian pharaoh, Ptolemy XIII. In each case we will extract passages from the gospels we examine and comment on them;

The Gospel of Truth: The most significant extract from this gospel that concerns the name of the father has already been included and discussed in the previous chapter.

The Treatise on the Resurrection: This was an unorthodox interpretation of Christian teaching concerning existence after death, written (originally in Greek) between 170 and 200 CE:

> *How did the Lord proclaim things while he existed in flesh and after he had revealed himself as Son of God? He lived in this place where you remain, speaking about the Law of Nature—but I call it Death.*
>
> *Now the Son of God, Rheginos (risen), was Son of Man. He embraced them both, possessing the humanity and the divinity, so that on the one hand he might vanquish death through his being Son of God, and that on the other through the Son of Man the restoration to the Pleroma (totality of divine powers) might occur; because he was originally from above, a seed of Truth, before this structure had come into being. In this many dominions and divinities came into existence.*[136]

Jesus as the son of a divine Pharaoh is most likely to have revealed his identity and title to trusted initiates. The second part of the passage seems to refer to the Egyptian God Osiris who had many names and aspects (divinities). The document enhances our hypothesis and does nothing to invalidate it.

---

136 *The Nag Hammadi Library; The Treatise on the Resurrection translated by Malcolm L Peel*

The Testimony of Truth: This document or codex was written between 150 and 200 CE. It was probably written by Julius Cassianus of Alexandria,[137] who was intent on presenting his version of the the truth—a version of Gnostic Christianity which contrasted with the opinions and practices of what he saw as heretical opponents.

I will speak to those who know to hear not with the ears of the body but with the ears of the mind. For many have sought after the truth and have not been able to find it because there has taken hold of them the old leaven of the Pharisees and the scribes of the Law. And the leaven is the errant desire of the angels and the demons and the stars. As for the Pharisees and the scribes, it is they who belong to the archons who have authority over them.

For no one who is under the Law will be able to look up to the truth, for they will not be able to serve two masters. For the defilement of the Law is manifest; but undefilement belongs to the light. The Law commands (one) to take a husband (or) to take a wife, and to beget, to multiply like the sand of the sea. But passion, which is a delight to them, constrains the souls of those who are begotten in this place, those who defile and those who are defiled, in order that the Law might be fulfilled through them. And they show that they are assisting the world; and they turn away from the light, who are unable to pass by the archon of darkness until they pay the last penny.

But the Son of Man came forth from imperishability, being alien to defilement. He came to the world by the Jordan River, and immediately the Jordan turned back. And John bore witness to the descent of Jesus. For it is he who saw the power which came down upon the Jordan River; for he knew that the dominion of carnal procreation had come to an end. The Jordan River is the

---

137 *Ancient Gnosticism: Traditions and Literature*, Birger A Pearson

Greg Rigby

*power of the body, that is, the senses of pleasures. The
water of the Jordan is the desire for sexual intercourse.
John is the archon of the womb.*

This provocative testimony tells us that we have to read
between the lines. It could well be an allegory relating to Ptolemy
XIII escaping death from drowning. In more recent times, he begot
Jesus and in doing so perpetuated the bloodline of the god kings.

This interpretation would have given legitimacy to the Ptolemaic claim to a power base in Egypt that had most recently been
occupied by kings whose position and offspring were based on
carnal procreation.

The Thunder, Perfect Mind: This document is written as if
by the God of many nations, who is male and female and who is
presented in the text in the first person singular; in many ways
it expands on the Egyptian funeral texts. It could equally be a
proclamation of someone who believes him/herself to be a rep-
resentation of God, as did the pharaohs:

I was sent forth from the power,
and I have come to those who reflect upon me,
and I have been found among those who seek after me.
Look upon me, you who reflect upon me,
and you hearers, hear me.
You who are waiting for me, take me to yourselves.
And do not banish me from your sight.
And do not make your voice hate me, nor your hearing.
Do not be ignorant of me anywhere or any time. Be on
  your guard!
Do not be ignorant of me.
For I am the first and the last.
I am the honoured one and the scorned one.
I am the whore and the holy one.
I am the wife and the virgin.
I am the mother and the daughter.
I am the members of my mother.
I am the barren one

and many are her sons.
I am she whose wedding is great,
and I have not taken a husband.
I am the midwife and she who does not bear.
I am the solace of my labour pains.
I am the bride and the bridegroom,
and it is my husband who begot me.
I am the mother of my father
and the sister of my husband
and he is my offspring.
I am the slave of him who prepared me.
I am the ruler of my offspring.
But he is the one who begot me before the time on a birthday.
And he is my offspring in (due) time,
and my power is from him.
I am the staff of his power in his youth,
and he is the rod of my old age.
And whatever he wills happens to me.
I am the silence that is incomprehensible
and the idea whose remembrance is frequent.
I am the voice whose sound is manifold
and the word whose appearance is multiple.
I am the utterance of my name.
Why, you who hate me, do you love me,
and hate those who love me?
You who deny me, confess me,
and you who confess me, deny me.
You who tell the truth about me, lie about me,
and you who have lied about me, tell the truth about me.
You who know me, be ignorant of me,
and those who have not known me, let them know me.
For I am knowledge and ignorance.
I am shame and boldness.
I am shameless; I am ashamed.
I am strength and I am fear.
I am war and peace.
Give heed to me.

Greg Rigby

I am the one who is disgraced and the great one.
Give heed to my poverty and my wealth.
Do not be arrogant to me when I am cast out upon the earth,
and you will find me in those that are to come.
And do not look upon me on the dung-heap
nor go and leave me cast out,
and you will find me in the kingdoms.
And do not look upon me when I am cast out among those
    who
are disgraced and in the least places,
nor laugh at me.
And do not cast me out among those who are slain in violence.
But I, I am compassionate and I am cruel.
Be on your guard!
Do not hate my obedience
and do not love my self-control.
In my weakness, do not forsake me,
and do not be afraid of my power.
For why do you despise my fear
and curse my pride?
But I am she who exists in all fears
and strength in trembling.
I am she who is weak,
and I am well in a pleasant place.
I am senseless and I am wise.
Why have you hated me in your counsels?
For I shall be silent among those who are silent,
and I shall appear and speak,
Why then have you hated me, you Greeks?
Because I am a barbarian among the barbarians?
For I am the wisdom of the Greeks
and the knowledge of the barbarians.
I am the judgement of the Greeks and of the barbarians.
I am the one whose image is great in Egypt
and the one who has no image among the barbarians.
I am the one who has been hated everywhere
and who has been loved everywhere.

154

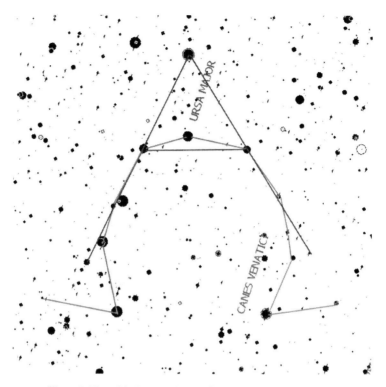

Fig 18 The Alpha and the Omega in Ursa Major

I am the one whom they call Life,
and you have called Death.
I am the one whom they call Law,
and you have called Lawlessness.
I am the one whom you have pursued,
and I am the one whom you have seized.
I am the one whom you have scattered,
and you have gathered me together.
I am the one before whom you have been ashamed,
and you have been shameless to me.
I am she who does not keep festival,
and I am she whose festivals are many.[138]

---

138 *The Nag hammadi Library, The Thunder, Perfect Mind,* translated by George W Macrae

We are unsure of the context in which this document was written, who wrote it or who it was aimed at. It makes claims that are presented, as if from a single God with many aspects. We have duplicated the first half of the full text and underlined the words that link to the Book of Revelation (I am the first and the last) and others that tell us of the claimant's Egyptian connection.

The "one whose image is great in Egypt" seems to refer to the pattern or patterns that represent all the aspects of God that can be traced around the seven key stars of Ursa Major. Interestingly, a picture of the Alpha and the Omega can be traced in the same place (Fig 18). It could, of course, refer to the Great Pyramid at Giza, which as we have shown earlier (Fig 5) could also be an image of a shape to be found in the same constellation. It does little to support or detract from the hypothesis we propose, other than to re-enforce the Egyptian connection.

The Sophia of Jesus Christ: This document (translated by Douglas M Parrott) is written by someone pondering and providing answers to fundamental questions about the nature of the Universe and of humanity. The author claims that the questions were set by the twelve disciples of Jesus and seven women to a resurrected Jesus, which group met at "the mountain of divination and joy." Such a meeting is in part confirmed in Matthew 28:16, which says that "the eleven disciples proceed to Galilee, to the mountain which Jesus had designated." The meeting and its content, which was summarised in Matthew, was not specifically mentioned by the other gospel writers in the New Testament. Below are several paragraphs from the Sophia:

After he rose from the dead, his twelve disciples and seven women continued to be his followers, and went to Galilee onto the mountain called "Divination and Joy." When they gathered together and were perplexed about the underlying reality of the universe and the plan, and the holy providence, and the power of the authorities, and about everything the Saviour is doing with them in the secret of the holy plan, the Saviour appeared—not

*in his previous form, but in the invisible spirit. And
his likeness resembles a great angel of light. But his
resemblance I must not describe. No mortal flesh could
endure it, but only pure, perfect flesh, like that which he
taught us about on the mountain called "Of the Olives"
in Galilee. And he said: "Peace be to you, My peace I
give you!" And they all marvelled and were afraid. The
Saviour laughed and said to them: "What are you thinking about? Are you perplexed? What are you searching
for?"*

*The Perfect Saviour said to them, "I want you to
know that Sophia, the Mother of the Universe and the
consort, desired by herself to bring these to existence
without her male (consort). But by the will of the Father
of the Universe, that his unimaginable goodness might
be revealed, he created that curtain between the immor-
tals and those that came afterward, that the consequence
might follow ...[BG 118:]... every aeon and chaos—that
the defect of the female might <appear>, and it might
come about that Error would contend with her. And these
became the curtain of spirit. From <the> aeons above
the emanations of Light, as I have said already, a drop
from Light and Spirit came down to the lower regions
of Almighty in chaos, that their moulded forms might
appear from that drop, for it is a judgment on him, Arch-
Begetter, who is called Yaldabaoth. That drop revealed
their moulded forms through the breath, as a living soul.
It was withered and it slumbered in the ignorance of the
soul. When it became hot from the breath of the Great
Light of the Male, and it took thought, (then) names were
received by all who are in the world of chaos, and all
things that are in it through that Immortal One, when
the breath blew into him. But when this came about by
the will of Mother Sophia—so that Immortal Man might
piece together the garments there for a judgment on the
robbers <he> then welcomed the blowing of that breath;
but since he was soul-like, he was not able to take that*

157

Greg Rigby

power for himself until the number of chaos should be complete, (that is) when the time determined by the great angel is complete."[139]

In his supplementary commentary to the translation, Parrott writes:

The notion of three divine men in the heavenly hierarchy appears to be based on Genesis 1-3 (Immortal Man = God; Son of Man = Adam [81, 12]; Son of Son of Man, Saviour = Seth). Because of the presence of Seth (although unnamed in the tractate), *Eugnostos* must be thought of as Sethian, in some sense. However, since it is not classically Gnostic and lacks other elements of developed Sethian thought, it can only be characterized as proto-Sethian. Egyptian religious thought also appears to have influenced its picture of the super-celestial realm.

The probable place of origin for *Eugnostos*, then, is Egypt. A very early date is suggested by the fact that Stoics, Epicureans and astrologers are called "all the philosophers." That characterization would have been appropriate in the first century BCE, but not later. *Eugnostos* and *The Sophis of Jesus Christ* may have influenced the Sethian-Ophites, as described by Irenaeus. Some have proposed an influence by *Eugnostos* on Valentinianism. Because of the dating of *Eugnostos*, it would not be surprising if the text had been composed soon after the advent of Christianity in Egypt; the latter half of the first century CE. That possibility is supported by the tractate's relatively non-polemical tone.[140]

Had the events been exactly as described, one must assume that Matthew's gospel would have been less broad brush and

---

139 *The Nag Hammadi Library, The Sophia (Wisdom) of Jesus Christ*, translated by Douglas M Parrott
140 *Novem Testamentum, Gnosticism and Egyptian religion*, Douglas M Parrott

would have contained considerably more detail, since it the content would truly have represented enlightenment.

> *28:17-20—When they saw Him, they worshiped Him; but some were doubtful. And Jesus came up and spoke to them, saying, "All authority has been given to Me in heaven and on earth. "Go therefore and make disciples of all the nations, baptizing them in the name of the Father and the Son and the Holy Spirit, teaching them to observe all that I commanded you; and lo, I am with you always, even to the end of the age."[141]*

The author of The Sophia (circa 50-150 CE) is believed to have written two other Nag Hammadi documents (below) entitled *Eugnostos the Blessed* and *The Holy Book of the Great Invisible Spirit* or to have been influenced by them.

All in all, The Sophia does nothing to disprove our hypothesis unless we believe its description of the meeting and the presentation of Jesus, literally and in detail, meaning that Jesus appeared to the gathering as a resurrected spirit. Had that been the case, we believe that more would have been made of it by orthodox Christians. It seems more likely that the author was using the drawing power of Jesus to promote his own views and that the appearance of Jesus as described is unlikely to have happened.

Eugnostos the Blessed: The person Eugnostos is not known in any other context than that related to the texts found at Nag Hammadi and as we have seen above, he may have had a personal agenda. In Greek, eugnostos is an adjective composed of eu, meaning good or well, and gnostos, which means known; therefore, Eugnostos means well known, familiar (cf. Plato Lysias, frag. 17.3) or even easy to understand. Here in the title of the text, this adjective is treated as a proper name, indicating the name of the author of the tractate. The name Eugnostos also appears in another Nag Hammadi document, the Holy Book

---

of the Great Invisible Spirit (NHC III, 2; IV, 2). In the final portion of this text (the colophon or copyist's note), the author introduces himself with his two names: Eugnostos, his spiritual name, and Gognessos, his ordinary, everyday name.[142] Quotations from the Eugnostos text are included blow:

> *He-Who-Is is ineffable. No principle knew him, no authority, no subjection, nor any creature from the foundation of the world, except he alone. For he is immortal and eternal, having no birth, for everyone who has birth will perish. He is unbegotten, having no beginning, for everyone who has a beginning has an end. No one rules over him. He has no name, for whoever has a name is the creation of another. He is unnamable. He has no human form, for whoever has human form is the creation of another. He has his own semblance—not like the semblance we have received and seen, but a strange semblance that surpasses all things and is better than the totalities. It looks to every side and sees itself from itself. He is infinite; he is incomprehensible. He is ever imperishable (and) has no likeness (to anything). He is unchanging good. He is faultless. He is everlasting. He is blessed. He is unknowable, while he (nonetheless) knows himself. He is immeasurable. He is untraceable. He is perfect, having no defect. He is imperishably blessed. He is called Father of the Universe.*
>
> *Through Immortal Man appeared the first designation, namely, divinity and kingdom, for the Father, who is called Self-Father Man' revealed this. He created a great aeon for his own majesty. He gave him great authority, and he ruled over all creations. He created gods and archangels and angels, myriads without number for retinue.*
>
> *Now through that Man originated divinity and kingdom. Therefore, he was called God of gods, King of kings.*

---

142 *The Nag Hammadi Scriptures*, Marvin W Meyer, M Scopello

Again we can see the link with the Greek/Egyptian notion of an ineffable God and the links between this God and Man. Scopello continues her analysis and makes comment on the location of the writer; "The original Greek text of Eugnostos the Blessed was probably composed in Egypt as early as the end of the first century."

The text does nothing to invalidate our hypothesis or to cast light on the real identity of Jesus.

The Apocryphon (Secret Book) of James: This book was written by several writers and assembled sometime between 100 and 150 CE. As with The Sophia of Jesus Christ, it purports to be a pre-ascension dialogue between Jesus and his disciples. As Francis Williams tells us, "The reporting of a special post resurrection appearance of Jesus, and the appeal to James as a source of secret and superior tradition, are means that Gnostics often used to legitimate their message."[143] Several paragraphs are included below:

They all answered and said, "If you bid us, we come." He said, "Verily I say unto you, no one will ever enter the kingdom of heaven at my bidding, but (only) because you yourselves are full. Leave James and Peter to me, that I may fill them." And having called these two, he drew them aside and bade the rest occupy themselves with that which they were about.

"Therefore, trust in me, my brethren; understand what the great light is. The Father has no need of me, for a father does not need a son, but it is the son who needs the father - though I go to him. For the Father of the Son has no need of you."

"These are the things that I shall tell you so far; now, however, I shall ascend to the place from whence I came. But you, when I was eager to go, have cast me out, and instead of accompanying me, you have pursued me. But pay heed to the glory that awaits me, and, having opened

143 *The Nag Hammadi Library in English*, Francis Williams

your heart, listen to the hymns that await me up in the heavens; for today I must take (my place at) the right hand of the Father. But I have said (my) last word to you, and I shall depart from you, for a chariot of spirit has borne me aloft, and from this moment on, I shall strip myself, that I may clothe myself. But give heed; blessed are they who have proclaimed the Son before his descent, that when I have come, I might ascend (again). Thrice blessed are they who were proclaimed by the Son before they came to be, that you might have a portion among them."

Having said these words, he departed. But we bent (our) knee(s), I and Peter, and gave thanks, and sent our heart(s) upwards to heaven. We heard with our ears and saw with our eyes the noise of wars and a trumpet blare, and a great turmoil.[144]

Secret James can be dated to the first half of the second century, while its sources for the sayings of Jesus may go back to the first century. Ron Cameron tells us that the internal evidence shows Egypt to be its provenance.[145]

The things that are described when he departed are in the imagination of the author. Had they been a general and physical manifestation, the other disciples who were nearby and occupied with what they were about would have been able to see and hear the drama that is described and such an incident would have been more widely documented. This being the case, the words are no more evidence to Jesus's true nature than those of a sincere and charismatic Christian teacher today.

The Gospel of Philip: One translator of this Gospel tells us, "Because of the contents, the eccentric arrangement, and the literary types exhibited, it is likely that The Gospel of Philip is a collection of excerpts mainly from a Christian Gnostic sacramental

---

144 *The Nag Hammadi Library, The Apocryphon of James* translated by Francis E Williams
145 *Early Christian Writings on the Other Gospels, Sayings, Traditions in the Apocryphon of James* by Ron Cameron

catechesis. It explains the significance of sacramental rites of initiation, the meaning of sacred names, especially names of Jesus, and provides paraenesis for the life of the initiated. It interprets Biblical passages, particularly from the book of Genesis, makes use of typology, both historical and sacramental, and, as catechists do, argues on the basis of analogy and parable. In these and other ways The Gospel of Philip resembles the orthodox catechisms from the second through fourth centuries."[146]

The document is thought to have been composed in Greek between 180 and 250 CE and because of that, it does not have any firsthand knowledge of Jesus. The following are some extracts that might be relevant to the hypothesis we are investigating:

One single name is not uttered in the world, the name which the Father gave to the Son; it is the name above all things: the name of the Father. For the Son would not become Father unless he wore the name of the Father. Those who have this name know it, but they do not speak it. But those who do not have it do not know it.

The words and their presentation are intriguing and on the basis of this logical construction, the paragraph describes a name that can never be known to anyone except father and son. Could this refer to the fact that Ptolemy XIII was keeping his identity hidden?

"Jesus" is a hidden name. "Christ" is a revealed name. For this reason, "Jesus" is not particular to any language; rather he is always called by the name "Jesus." While as for "Christ," in Syriac it is "Messiah," in Greek it is "Christ." Certainly all the others have it according to their own language. "The Nazarene" is he who reveals what is hidden. Christ has everything in himself, whether man, or angel, or mystery, and the Father.

---

146 *The Nag Hammadi Library in English*, Wesley W Isenberg

How can Jesus be a hidden name? Jesus is the English form of Ιησους (Iesous), which was the Greek form of the Aramaic name יֵשׁוּעַ (Yeshu'a). Yeshu'a is itself a contracted form of Yehoshu'a, the name known in English as Joshua. Perhaps the author meant that Jesus was a name that hid the identity of the bearer.

> The apostles who were before us had these names for him: "Jesus, the Nazorean, Messiah," that is, "Jesus, the Nazorean, the Christ." The last name is "Christ," the first is "Jesus," that in the middle is "the Nazarene." "Messiah" has two meanings, both "the Christ" and "the measured." "Jesus" in Hebrew is "the redemption." "Nazara" is "the Truth." "The Nazarene" then, is "the Truth." "Christ" [...] has been measured. "The Nazarene" and "Jesus" are they who have been measured.

The author appears to be trying to justify the name of Jesus. The words "the redemption" (in our hypothesis) could refer to redemption from persecution and the attempted elimination of the bloodline. The word "measured" would be the attribute of something or someone that/who fits the dimensions allocated.

> Compare the bridegroom and the bride. They have come from the [...]. No Jew [...] has existed. And [...] from the Jews. [...] Christians [...] these [...] are referred to as "The chosen people of [...]," and "The true man" and "Son of Man" and "the seed of the Son of Man." This true race is renowned in the world [...] that the sons of the bridal chamber dwell.

Here we have a direct and unambiguous reference to the bloodline of Jesus as the true race that is renowned to the world. The author of this Gospel would appear to have been cognisant of the importance of both the name of Jesus and his inheritance.

Light and Darkness, life and death, right and left, are brothers of one another. They are inseparable. Because of this, neither are the good, good, nor evil, evil, nor is life, life, nor death, death. For this reason each one will dissolve into its earliest origin. But those who are exalted above the world are indissoluble, eternal.

These claims seem to relate to the ancient Egyptian belief that the exalted will rise and become stars in the heavens around the polar constellation in the northern sky:

There is the Son of Man and there is the son of the Son of Man. The Lord is the Son of Man, and the son of the Son of Man is he who creates through the Son of Man. The Son of Man received from God the capacity to create. He also has the ability to beget. He who has received the ability to create is a creature. He who has received the ability to beget is an offspring. He who creates cannot beget. He who begets also has power to create. Now they say, "He who creates begets." But his so-called "offspring" is merely a creature. Because of [...] of birth, they are not his offspring but [...]. He who creates works openly, and he himself is visible. He who begets, begets in private, and he himself is hidden, since [...] image. Also, he who creates, creates openly. But one who begets, begets children in private.[147]

Here we are told that the name is known but that it is kept secret and that the Son of (a) Man is a human creature, who was begotten by the normal rules of procreation and has the ability to beget. Presumably, this human ability to beget in private was important and could refer to Jesus's role in the perpetuation of the bloodline. The Son of (a) Man in this paragraph would be Ptolemy XIII and Jesus would fulfil the role of the son of the Son of (a) Man.

---

147 *The Nag Hammadi Library, The Gospel of Philip*, translated by Wesley W. Isenberg

Greg Rigby

The Gospel of Philip is a long document, and because of that, we have extracted paragraphs that may be pertinent to our research. All in all, the gospel says nothing that would invalidate our hypothesis and says much that would validate it. Some additional paragraphs refer to Mary Magdalene; these will be covered in a later chapter.

The Gospel of Thomas: This Gospel is a collection of sayings, anecdotes and parables that are written as the words of Jesus. It is believed to have been compiled from a collection of Greek and Coptic fragments (which vary in content). The Coptic compilation was written circa 350 CE but the individual fragments were probably written nearer 200 CE based on an earlier oral tradition. The only verses that add to our analysis of Jesus's identity and purpose are the following:

> *(113) His disciples said to him, "When is the kingdom going to come?" Jesus said, "It is not by being waited for that it is going to come. They are not going to say, 'Here it is' or 'There it is.' Rather, the kingdom of the father is spread out over the earth, and people do not see it."[148]*
> *(114) Simon Peter said to them, "Let Mariham go out from among us, for women are not worthy of the life." Jesus said, "Look, I will lead her that I may make her male, in order that she too may become a living spirit resembling you males. For every woman who makes herself male will enter into the kingdom of heaven."[149]*

The first verse (113) refers to a kingdom of the father spread out over the earth. The earth at this time would have implied the known world and this could well have referred to the Egyptian kingdom, which would have still had tenure in the mind of the last remaining pharaoh, Ptolemy XIII.

---

148 *The Gnostic Scriptures, Translation of the Gospel of Thomas*, Bentley Layton
149 *The Gospel of Thomas* translated by Beate Blatz

An analysis of the second verse is included in the chapter on Mary Magdalene (Chapter 15). It is perhaps worth noting here that the Egyptian Kingdom of Heaven was in the stars that surrounded the constellation of Ursa Major. Those stars were believed to be the pharaohs or the sons of God. Could it be that the comment attributed to Jesus was based on his belief that she would join the great and the good in the stars of the northern sky?

The Nag Hammadi Scrolls indicate that intellectuals and religious philosophers, who were mainly based in Alexandria, were keen to advocate their view of each individual's way of connecting with/to an incarnate and unassailable God, who was creator of all things visible and invisible. The authors of these scrolls either piggybacked on the life and sayings of a person who they believed would become a popular legend in their time or they reflected knowledge of Jesus's true identity.

We are investigating whether this person could have been someone whose purpose was to perpetuate the Pharaonic blood-line and (perhaps) re-establish the Kingdom of God over the known world. If he was the son of Ptolemy XIII he would have believed that he had a vital role in that connection.

His claims were carefully phrased but it is possible that they were interpreted in different ways by those hearing (of) them. Some came to interpret them as the claims of an incarnate divine individual who was an aspect (son) of God eternal. This may even have been the result of Jesus himself believing that his inheritance gave him a claim to divinity as a direct descendent of Osiris and that he would be raised to join him at his ascension. Others may well have seen them as the rightful assertions of the claimant to the pharaonic throne and to all that that entailed.

Whatever the truth of it, there is nothing in the Nag Hammadi Scrolls, which invalidates our hypothesis.

CHAPTER 12

Other Texts and Codices

The Dead Sea Scrolls

This is a collection of some 981 different texts discovered between 1946 and 1956 in eleven caves from the immediate vicinity of the ancient settlement at *Khirbet Qumran* in the West Bank. The caves are located about two kilometres inland from the northwest shore of the Dead Sea, from which they derive their name. The parchments and the ink on them has been dated to between 385 BCE and 33 CE, the early part of which they would have been under the influences of the philosophical thinking of Israel, Rome, Greece and Egypt.

The view among scholars, almost universally held until the 1990s, is the "Qumran–Essene" hypothesis originally proposed by Roland Guérin de Vaux and Józef Tadeusz Milik, though independently both Eliezer Sukenik and Butrus Sowmy of St Mark's Monastery connected scrolls with the Essenes well before any excavations at Qumran.

The Qumran–Essene theory holds that the scrolls were written by the Essenes, or by another Jewish sectarian group, residing at Khirbet Qumran. They composed the scrolls and ultimately hid them in the nearby caves during the Jewish Revolt sometime between 66 and 68 CE. The site of Qumran was destroyed and the scrolls never recovered. A number of arguments are used to support this theory.

- There are striking similarities between the description of an initiation ceremony of new members in the Community Rule and descriptions of the Essene initiation ceremony

mentioned in the works of Flavius Josephus, a Jewish–
Roman historian of the Second Temple Period:

- Josephus mentions the Essenes as sharing property
  among the members of the community, as does the
  Community Rule.
- During the excavation of Khirbet Qumran, two inkwells and
  plastered elements thought to be tables were found, offering
  evidence that some form of writing was done there. More
  inkwells were discovered nearby. De Vaux called this area
  the "scriptorium" based upon this discovery.
- Several Jewish ritual baths (Hebrew: miqvah = הוקמ)
  were discovered at Qumran, offering evidence of an
  observant Jewish presence at the site.
- Pliny the Elder (a geographer writing after the fall of
  Jerusalem in 70 CE) describes a group of Essenes living
  in a desert community on the northwest shore of the
  Dead Sea near the ruined town of Ein Gedi.

The Essenes and some early Christians espoused a pious,
ascetic life, deserting the city and the secular world for a life
of solitary or communal prayer and self-denial, but the Essenes
were not a Christian group. Their writings make no mention
of John the Baptist, Jesus, or Jesus's followers (by name). The
Dead Sea Scrolls reveal, if anything, that Christianity was not
a unique spiritual and religious phenomenon, but had much in
common with the Essenes who mention in some detail a religious leader named The Teacher of Righteousness. Some elements of these texts are duplicated below that we believe might
help with our analysis. In addition, we include appropriate sections of the Essene codices mentioned above.

The Gospel of Mary

This text was found in the *Berlin Gnostic Codex* (*Papyrus
Berolinensis 8502*). This very important and well-preserved
codex was apparently discovered in the late-nineteenth century
somewhere near Akhmim in Upper Egypt. It was purchased in

1896 by a German scholar, Dr. Carl Reinhardt, in Cairo and then taken to Berlin. This text will be discussed in chapter 15 dedicated to Mary Magdalene.

The Divine Throne Chariot

This text draws its inspiration from Ezekiel (1:10) and is related to the Book of Revelation. It depicts the appearance and movement of the Merkabah, the divine Chariot supported and drawn by the cherubim, which is at the same time a throne and a vehicle. The "small voice" of blessing is drawn from 1 Kings 19:12: it was in a "still small voice" that God manifested himself to Elijah.[150] In Ancient Egypt, this primal pattern was called the Mer-Ka-Ba. It was actually three words, not one. *Mer* meant a kind of light that rotated within itself. *Ka* meant spirit, in this case referring to the human spirit. And *Ba* meant the human body, though it also could mean the concept of Reality that spirit holds. And so the entire word in ancient Egypt referred to a rotating light that would take the spirit and the body from one world into another.[151]

> *The ministers of the Glorious Face in the abode of the gods of knowledge fall down before him, and the cherubim utter blessings. And as they rise up, there is a divine small voice and loud praise; there is a divine small voice as they fold their wings.*
>
> *The cherubim bless the image of the Throne-Chariot above the firmament, and they praise the majesty of the fiery firmament beneath the seat of his glory. And between the turning wheels, angels of holiness come and go, as it were a fiery vision of most holy spirits; and about them flow seeming rivulets of fire, like gleaming bronze, a radiance of many gorgeous colours, of marvellous pigments magnificently mingled.*
>
> *The Spirits of the Living God move perpetually with the glory of the wonderful Chariot. The small voice of*

---

150 *The Gnostic Society Library, Dead Sea Scrolls Texts, Introduction to the Divine Chariot* by Geza Vermes
151 *A Vehicle of Ascension*, Drunvalo

blessing accompanies the tumult as they depart, and on the path of their return they worship the Holy One, Ascending they rise marvellously; settling, they stay still. The sound of joyful praise is silenced and there is a small voice of blessing in all the camp of God.
And a voice of praise resounds from the midst of all their divisions in worship. And each one in his place, all their numbered ones sing hymns of praise.

These passages create a direct link to the constellation of Ursa Major, known as the chariot in some philosophies, the throne that houses the God of Egypt in all his/her aspects. "Not only useful in the physical realm, its connection to the sun might indicate that, in the afterlife, the chariot aided the transformation of the king from the mortal plane to the divine. While he lived, the king became the dazzling sun-disc in his chariot, showing his association with Ra. Even more telling is that the chariot was considered to be the earthly counterpart of the solar bark"[152]

The manuscript adds little to our research into the true identity of Jesus Christ but shows that the Essenes, with whom Jesus was thought to have been associated retained many of the central concepts of the Egyptian religion.

The Great Isaiah Scroll

This Scroll (1QIsaa) is one of the original seven Dead Sea Scrolls discovered in Qumran in 1947. It is the largest (734 cm) and best preserved of all the biblical scrolls, and the only one that is almost complete. It is dated circa 125 BCE. The fifty-four columns contain all sixty-six chapters of the Hebrew version of the biblical Book of Isaiah. We have selected extracts that illustrate the links between the thinking of the author and the Egyptian religious tradition.

Chapter 7:14—Therefore [the Lord] himself will give to you {a sign} {Behold} the virgin shall conceive

---

152 *Chasing Chariots,* edited by Andre J Veldmaijer and Salima Ikram

*and bring forth a son and he shall call his name Imman-
uel (God is with us).*

This text was discussed earlier in Chapter 8. It has been used
extensively by Christian theologians to support their assertions
regarding the virgin birth of Jesus.

> *Chapter 9:5-9—Because a child shall be born to us
> and a son is given to us and the government shall be
> upon his shoulders and he shall be called wonderful,
> counsellor, mighty God, everlasting father the prince of
> peace. Of the increase of his government and his peace
> there shall be no end upon the throne of David and over
> his kingdom to order it and to establish it in judgement
> and in righteousness from and until eternity; The zeal of
> YHWH of Hosts will perform this.*

This text illustrates that a royal bloodline of which David is a
link between its beginning and its continuance was an important
and established concept.

> *Chapter 22:20-24—And it will be in that day that I
> will call to my servant to Eliakim, son of Hilkiah. And
> I will cause him to be dressed in your tunic and will
> strengthen him with your girdle and I will give your gov-
> ernment into his hand and he shall be as a father to the
> inhabitants of Jerusalem and to the house of Judah. And
> I will give him the key of the house of David upon his
> shoulder and he will open and no one shall shut and shut
> and no one will open. And I will drive him as a nail in
> an established place and he shall be for a throne of glory
> for his father's house. And they shall hang upon him all
> the glory of the house of his father, and all the offspring.*

Again, we see confirmation of the importance of the offspring of the house of David, who, as we have previously discussed, could well have been the pharaoh Thutmose III.

Chapter 57:14-15—And he shall say, Cast up, cast up, [the thing cast up] prepare the way, raise up the stumbling block from the way of my people. Because thus says the Father of exaltation and the lifted up One who inhabits eternity, whose name is Holy; He inhabits the high and holy place, with the contrite and lowly spirit, to make alive the spirit of the lowly, and to make alive the heart of the contrite.

The words "he inhabits the high and holy place" seem to be a direct reference to the area around Ursa Major, classified as heaven by the Egyptians. The text itself is similar to many found in the Egyptian Book of the Dead:

I open the door in heaven. I rule my throne. I open the way for the births which take place on this day. I am the child who traverseth the road of Yesterday. I am To-day for untold nations and peoples. I am he who protecteth you for millions of years. Whether ye be denizens of heaven, or of the earth, or of the South, or of the North, or of the East, or of the West, the fear of me is in your bodies. I am he whose being hath been wrought in his eye. I shall not die again. My moment is in your bodies, but my forms are in my place of habitation. I am "He who cannot be known."[153]

Despite the efforts of Moses and those that came after him to present God as someone different from the gods that had gone before, we see in the quote above the enduring close link between the Hebrew and Egyptian views of God and heaven.

Chapter 59:20-21—And the Redeemer shall come to Zion, and to those who repent of transgression in Jacob, says YHWH. And I, [m..As for me] this is my covenant

---

153 The Book of the Dead, The Papyrus of Ani, The Chapter of Driving Back the Slaughters which are Performed in Hensu, translated by E A Wallis Budge

with them, says YHWH; My spirit that is upon you, and my words which I have put in your mouth, shall not depart out of your mouth, nor out of the mouth of your seed, nor out of the mouth of your seed's seed, from now and forever.

The word redeemer in the Hebrew rabbinical tradition generally denotes a person who as the nearest relative of another and is charged with the duty of restoring the rights of another and avenging his wrongs. It can also mean saviour or restorer. This is not a prophecy about Jesus. We know that it refers to God and redemption from Jerusalem's then current state of iniquity as shown in chapter 52 of this scroll, which tells us, "Break out, sing together, waste places of Jerusalem: because YHWH has comforted his people, he has redeemed Jerusalem."

Chapter 63:17-19—Why, YHWH, have you made us to wander from your ways, and hardened our heart from your fear? Restore for your servants' sake, the tribes of your inheritance. The people of your holiness have possessed it but a little while: our adversaries have trodden down your sanctuary. We are yours: from antiquity you never bore rule over them; they were not called by your name.

Here we have an inference that the emergence of the Hebrew religious tradition was new, and that in antiquity, their allegiance was to different beliefs and practices. Such a claim reinforces the view that there was a close and inherited link between the Egyptian and the Hebrew religious traditions.

Our examination of the Isaiah Scroll has confirmed the fact that the Hebrew religion grew out of the Egyptian religious tradition. It does nothing to confirm the identity of Jesus Christ and only provides evidence of the background into which he was born.

The Pesher to Habakkuk

This commentary consist of many fragments and talks about The Teacher of Righteousness who some believe might have been Jesus. We include a single extract, which might be an oblique reference to Jesus's identity. The translation by Fred P Miller uses bold print for the actual text and the other parts are commentary. He does not believe this text refers to Jesus Christ or to Christians in any way and believes that over the years, Christians have made this claim to "discredit Caparnaum and his followers":

> *You have set them for judgement, O Rock, you have established them for correction. (You have) purer eyes (parts of 1:12 and 13).*
> *. . . than to view evil and you are not able to consider wickedness (part of 1:13)*
> *Pesher about the saying that God is not able (to save) his people from the hand of the Gentiles*
> *. . . and God gives judgement in the hand of his "Chosen one" (to) all the Gentiles and in their reproaches*
> *. . . and their guilt to all those doing evil to my people which keep my commandments.*

If this text did refer to Jesus, the term "chosen one" could add weight to our hypothesis, particularly in the context of finding and selecting the right person to be his mother. The words 'my people' might well indicate a race or group who showed allegiance to their ruler. This would enhance the view that the chosen one (if it was Jesus) was someone who believed himself to be such a ruler.

Pistis Sophia

The full text, which contains 148 chapters, was probably written between the third and fourth centuries CE. The author is unknown, but researchers believe that it was probably constructed in Egypt. It is a comprehensive Gnostic document covering aspects of the life of Jesus, almost every facet of existence and man's relationship with God. Specifically, it claims that Jesus remained with his disciples for eleven years after his reported death. We have included extracts that might throw some light on the Jesus identity.

Chapters 2-5 describe the transfiguration in terms that are similar to a hallucinogenic experience. This narrative was compiled many years after the reported event and is most likely a tailored aggrandisement of the transfiguration as reported in Matthew 17, Mark 9 and Luke 9.

In Chapter 6, Jesus admits that he was sent for a ministry, which the author then shrouds in Gnostic embellishment (chapters 7 and 8) in order to portray Jesus as a divine, supernatural being.

Chapters 10-16 develop the Gnostic theme by describing the third vesture in terms of the glory of the name of the mystery of all orders of the emanations and Jesus's interaction with them.

In Chapter 18, Mary speaks openly:

> *Concerning this word then, my Lord, the power which was in the prophet Isaiah, hath spoken thus and proclaimed afore time in a spiritual similitude, discoursing on the Vision about Egypt: 'Where then, O Egypt, where are thy consulters and horoscope-casters and those who cry out of the earth and those who cry out of their belly? Let them then declare unto thee from now on the deeds which the lord Saba th will do!*
>
> *None of the rulers will know what thou wilt do from now on, for they are Egypt, because they are matter.*

This provides us with a direct and unequivocal link to Egypt.

Chapters 19—86 unfold the mystery of light, the seven voices, the seven amen, the five trees, the seven virgins, their fifteen helpers and all their aspects and access to each aspect.

In Chapter 96, Jesus says, *"But Mary Magdalene and John, the Virgin, will tower over all my disciples and over all men who shall receive the mysteries in the Ineffable. And they will be on my right and on my left. And I am they, and they are I."*

If Jesus is basing his announcement on the mysteries that he has learned from his father and he believes that he himself will join the Ineffable in the form of Osiris, then this verse would seem to indicate that John the Virgin is the eldest son of Jesus who will later inherit his claim to the divine title. This title will be that attributed the next legitimate pharaoh (after Jesus) and that Mary will bc acknowledged as his wife and as "wife of the king." This perspective appears to be confirmed in chapter 97: *"He, therefore, who shall receive the [first] mystery of that First Mystery, and it shall be at the time that he cometh out of the body of the matter of the rulers, then the retributive receivers come and lead the soul of that man out of the body."*

Chapter 99 describes how long a year of light is. In the description, it calculates a year as being 365 days. This would seem to indicate that Jesus was talking in terms of an Egyptian year since a Hebrew year could be 353, 354, 355, 383, 384 or 385 days long.

Another oblique reference to Egyptian belief occurs in chapter 110, where the disciples say, *"Now, therefore, because of these great deeds of which thou tellest us, our souls have become frenzied and they have pressed very exceedingly, yearning to go forth out of us on high to the region of thy kingdom."*

Chapter 121 makes direct reference to kings of the earth:

If today a king who is a man of the world, giveth a gift to men of his like, and also forgiveth murderers and those who have intercourse with males, and the rest of the very grievous sins which are deserving of death, if it becometh him who is a man of the world, to have done this, much more then have the Ineffable and the First Mystery, who are the lords of the universe, the authority to act in all things as it pleaseth them, that they forgive everyone who shall receive mysteries.

While there is a question mark over these being the actual words of Jesus, they may explain how, as someone who believed himself to be a king with a divine inheritance, he had the power to forgive sins. (Luke 7:48, Mark 2:5, Matthew 9:2)

Chapter 131 gives a clear indication that the dragon is a pattern in the stars and not some spirit being. In giving this explanation, the author gives another clue to the Egyptian connection:

177

Greg Rigby

> *The Saviour answered and said unto Mary, "When the light of the sun is outside [? above the world], he covereth the darkness of the dragon; but if the sun is below the world, then the darkness of the dragon abideth as veiling of the sun and the breath of the darkness cometh into the world in form of a smoke in the night—that is, if the sun withdraweth into himself his rays, then indeed the world is not able to endure the darkness of the dragon in its true form; otherwise would it be dissolved and go to ruin withal."*

In other words, when the sun is up, you cannot see it, and when the sun has set, you can.

Chapters 136 to 148 refer to a time after Jesus's claimed resurrection. They consist of Jesus talking about the afterlife and the powers to be found there, and the chastisement of sinners. These chapters include reference to the twelve houses of astrology and to the names of Greek Gods such as Zeus, Kronos, Ares, Aphrodite and Hermes. In several chapters, he names the father of his father (his grandfather) as Yew.

The Yew *Taxus baccata* is an ancient tree species that has survived since before the Ice Age and as such as been revered and used by humankind throughout the ages. Some Yew trees are believed to be 4000 years old. The Yew is sacred to Hecate, and the Crone aspect of the Triple Goddess; both are guardians of the underworld, death and the afterlife. The Yew is considered the most potent tree for protection against evil, a means of connecting to your ancestors, a bringer of dreams and otherworld journeys and a symbol of the old magic.[154]

Ptolemy XIII's father was Ptolemy XII Auletes, otherwise known as Ptolemy Neos Dionysus Theos. When we examine these names, it is possible to find an interesting connection. Dionysus (sometimes known as Bacchus) was the Olympian God of wine, vegetation and pleasure and festivity, and Virgil tells us "he loves open hills and the yew tree." In Greek mythol-

---

154 *The Yew, Sacred Tree of Transformation and Rebirth*, Glennie Kindred

ogy, he is a god of foreign origin, and while Mount Nysa is a mythological location, it is invariably set far away to the east or to the south. The Homeric Hymn to Dionysus places it "far from Phoenicia, near to the Egyptian stream."

It is likely (in the hypothesis we propose) that real names were not used by Ptolemy XIII and/or Jesus, for reasons of secrecy. Because of that, they could well have resorted to the use of nicknames. Could the name Yew be a record of the actual nickname used by Jesus for his grandfather, thus providing us with a link between Jesus and his grandfather Ptolemy XII?

Pistis Sophia presents Jesus as someone who is claiming to have knowledge of God and the many aspects of God. The words, if they are represented as they were spoken could well have been those of someone who sincerely believed his divine (Egyptian) inheritance and who had been taught the intricacies of a theology he was to champion in his role as legitimate King and Son of God. Looked at from this perspective, there is nothing in this text that would invalidate our hypothesis and there is much to promote it.

The Bruce Codex

It comprises Coptic, Arabic and Ethiopic manuscripts and originally contained seventy-eight papyrus leaves making up two separate manuscripts, the Book of Jeu and the Untitled Text.

The First Book of Ieou

The Books of IEOU probably represent notes attached initiation rituals and meditation directed towards producing altered states of spiritual consciousness. They are very much in the Gnostic tradition of the time and like Pistis Sophia, they give Jesus commentary of the Plemora, the light, the emanations and the treasuries. The following text is extracted from *The Books of JEU and the Untitled text in the Bruce Codex* translated by Carl Schmidt:

> *The living Jesus said again, "When you become heavenly, you will become the Midst because it is noth-*

ing, for the . . . rulers and the wicked powers (exou-siai) will you and they will envy you because you have known me, because I am not from the world, and I do not resemble the rulers and the powers (exousiai) and all the wicked ones. They do not come from me. And furthermore he who (is born) in the flesh of unrighteous-ness has no part in the Kingdom of my Father, and also he who me . . . according to the flesh has no hope . . . Kingdom of God the Father."

Like other Gnostic texts, it was written a long time after Jesus ministry. It appears to be telling us that Jesus believed himself to be different because his genealogy was true and that it was the envy of earthly rulers.

The Untitled Text in the Bruce codex
The text discusses the All-Father, the All-Mother and the Only Begotten Son. It is likely that this treatise; "was dependent upon a document attributed to Nicotheos, which in turn seems to have depended at least in part upon the first part of *Marsanes* that summarises the doctrine of the paternal perfect invisible triple-powered one noted by Nicotheos".[155] Extracts included here provide no proof of Jesus identity but may provide good background material:

This is the mother-city of the only-begotten one. This is the only begotten of whom Phosilampes spoke: "He exists before the All." It is he who came forth from the endless, characterless, patternless and self-begotten aeon who has begotten himself, who came forth from the ineffable and immeasurable one, who exists verily and truly. It is he, in whom exists the truly existent one; that is to say, the incomprehensible Father exists in his only-begotten Son. The All rests in the ineffable and unutter-able, unruled and untroubled one, of whose godhood

155 *Sethian Gnosticism and the Platonic Tradition*, John Douglas Turner

which is itself no godhood, no one is able to speak. And when Phosilampes understood, he said: "Those things which verily and truly exist and those which do not exist are for his sake. This is he, for whose sake, are those that truly exist which are secret, and those that do not truly exist which are manifest."

The extract could well have been referring to the God and Son as they would have been thought of by priests and initiates of the Ancient Egyptian religion in the persons of Ra and Osiris.

Verse 15 could equally refer to Jesus's earthly father, whose true identity was kept hidden and who fled and hid from persecution: *And I will give to them the mystery of my hidden Father because they have loved what is theirs, and they have fled from him who persecutes them with violence.*

The Gnostic texts we have quoted all perpetuated the same theme: Reading them without bias or commitment to any point of view, it is easy to see that Jesus may well have been trying to explain what he believed to be the essential nature of the ancient Egyptian religion.

The Greek Ptolemaic regime that took the crown of Egypt had a yen to re-establish the essence of this Egyptian Religion, which they and others had caused to be diluted. Their efforts started with Ptolemy I who compiled the Egyptian history (via Manetho) entitled Aegyptika and completed in 271 BCE. This work did much to consolidate the Ptolemaic desire for a return to the ancient traditions and for a continuous and pure bloodline. It traced the king back to the Gods and god kings (including Osiris) who they believed ruled Egypt prior to the dynastic kings.

This history was written at a time when the Egyptians themselves seemed to have lost direction. We are told by historians, "The Egyptians themselves, according to Greek writers, looked back to a time when their initiated priesthood was in possession of greater wisdom than was theirs in later times; they confess that they had fallen away from this high standard and had lost the key to much of their knowledge."[156]

The Egyptian religious beliefs evolved over a span of three thousand years. In the later periods, this evolution was affected by the impact of Persian and Hellenistic cultures and beliefs, which conflicted with the oral traditions that clung to the old religion. Evidence of this is seen in the diversity of hieroglyphic signs for the same person; there were seventy-three signs for the name of Osiris.

During the Ptolemaic dynasty, Egyptian mysteries (of Osiris and Isis) were brought into the public arena. The Ptolemies were so filled with wonder in the ancient beliefs that they wished to open them up to the Egyptian people and thereby bring them back to their sacred roots. Festival re-enactments of sacred stories took place, involving the death, rebirth and an initiatic vision of the "midnight sun" as shown in many the Egyptian texts that spoke of the Netherworld. The Greek/Hellenistic influence accounts for Thoth being renamed or conjoined with Hermes.

Thoth played a part in many of the myths of pharaonic Egypt: he played a role in the creation myth, he was recorder of the gods, and he was the principal pleader for the soul at the judgment of the dead. In fact, Thoth invented writing. He wrote all the ancient texts, including the most esoteric ones, including The *Book of Breathings*, which taught humans how to become gods. He was connected with the moon and thus was considered the ruler of the night. Thoth was also the teacher and helper of the ancient Egyptian trinity of Isis, Osiris, and Horus; it was under his instructions that Isis worked her sacred love magic whereby she brought the slain Osiris back to life.

"It is thought by some researchers that the Hermetic philosophy of a single god hidden in the multiplicity of things, whose name was secret, was given prominence in the Ramesside period (1290-1070 BCE), and may well have gained momentum earlier during the heretical rule of Akhenaton, thus commencing

156 *Fragments of Faith Forgotten*, G R S Mead

the influence of an Egyptian "hermetic" philosophy into later European and Jewish thinking."[157]

Ptolemy XIII's father was Ptolemy XII, who would have been available to influence the thinking of his son during his second reign between 55 and 51 BCE. At this time, Ptolemy XIII was between seven and twelve years old. With the blessing of Rome, Ptolemy XII chose Cleopatra as his co-regent during his final years. His final legacy was the beginning of family in-fighting when he declared that he wanted his daughter Cleopatra VII and his son Ptolemy XIII to rule together. We are told by researchers, "Throughout his long-lasting reign the principal aim of Ptolemy was to secure his hold on the Egyptian throne so as to eventually pass it to his heirs. To achieve this goal he was prepared to sacrifice much: the loss of rich Ptolemaic lands, most of his wealth and even, according to Cicero, the very dignity on which the mystique of kingship rested when he appeared before the Roman people as a mere supplicant."[158]

If it is true that Ptolemy XIII managed to evade execution by Mark Antony's death squad, he had some thirty-five years to contemplate his circumstance before he eventually sired Jesus. He would then have had a further thirty years to ensure that his now valuable son was indoctrinated with the essential elements of the religion he believed in. Interestingly, the gospels give us a clue to Jesus intent in this regard when he spoke to his disciples in Caesarea:

And I tell you, you are Peter, and on this rock I will build my church, and the gates of hell shall not prevail against it.[159]

The Greek word ἐκκλησίαν from the original texts has conventionally been translated as church. It can also mean; assembly, gathering of people in a public place for deliberation, a throng of men assembled by chance or those in a community who are united into one body. It does not mean religion. Its use

---

157 *The Secret Lore of Egypt: Its Impact on the West* by Erik Hornung; review by Lee Irwin
158 *Ptolemy and the Romans*; Mary Siani-Davies
159 Matthew 16:18

therefore implies that the religion had been already established, and that Peter's job was to be the hub of its propagation.

All in all the various Gnostic texts do nothing to disprove our central hypothesis. If anything, they enhance the idea that the words of Jesus, which, if accurately reported were to propose his view of what God, the All and the Heavenly Host entailed.

It is possible that Jesus's views were an up-to-date revelation of the Egyptian Religion and the Egyptian Mysteries as taught to him by his father and the priests with whom his father would have been associated. In such a scenario, it is likely that they would have been expressed to prepare the ground for an eventual re-establishment of the kingdom of Osiris (God) on earth.

CHAPTER 13

The Epistles

Epistles in the New Testament

An epistle is usually a stylish and formal instructive letter. The epistle genre of letter writing was common in Ancient Egypt as part of the scribal-school writing curriculum. The letters in the New Testament from The Apostles to Christians are usually referred to as The Epistles. Those letters traditionally attributed to Paul are known as Pauline Epistles and the others as Catholic Epistles.

The canon of the New Testament includes the Four Canonical Gospels, the Acts of The Apostles, the Epistles or letters of the Apostles and the Book of Revelation. The books of the canon of the New Testament were supposedly written mostly in the first century and finished by the year 150 CE. For the Orthodox, the recognition of these writings as authoritative was formalized in the Second Council of Trullan of 692, although it was almost universally accepted in the mid-300s.

If the hypothesis we propose is correct then Jesus or his children were alive at the stage these letters were written. For that reason, we examined them for any evidence of this and for any clues to our general hypothesis concerning Jesus's identity. Any such evidence is difficult to find since generally, the letters re-enforce the messages in the Gospels concerning Jesus and the message each author believes Jesus to have given. Any change of emphasis relates to the implementation of the message and the dangers to those who transgress. This is unsurprising, as thirteen of the twenty-one epistles of the New Testament are attributed to Paul, who was not a disciple and who had acquired

Greg Rigby

all his information second hand. Like most converts, he was a fanatic.

Below are extracts from the Acts of the Apostles along with several from the canonical epistles that may be useful to our examination. We start with a quotation from Acts 2:

> *Acts 2:16-17—But this is what was spoken of through the prophet Joel: "And it shall be in the last days," God says, "that I will pour forth of my spirit on all mankind; and your sons and your daughters shall prophecy, and your young men shall see visions, and your old men dream dreams."*

The prophet Joel lived circa 950 BCE when there was a strong and growing Hebrew community in Northern Egypt. This prophecy of God's view of the last days is mirrored by the view of the supplicant portrayed in The Papyrus of Ani known as the Egyptian Book of the Dead. The following quote is taken from the appendix of the Papyrus of Nebseni:

> *And let them see the Great God in the shrine on the day of the counting of souls, and let them hold converse with Osiris, whose habitations are hidden, and those who guard the members of Osiris, and who keep ward over the Spirit-souls, and who hold captive the shadows of the dead, and who would work evil against me, so that they shall [not] work evil against me. A way shall be for KA with thee, and thy soul shall be prepared by those who keep ward over the members of Osiris, and who hold captive the shadows of the dead.*

Once more, we see that elements of the Egyptian belief system have carried through into the thoughts of the founders of Christianity.

Some other extracts from the Acts and the Epistles which seem to be worthy of note are those that mention John who was called Mark. The wording seems to indicate that there a

186

person in the group who was named John, who for seem reason unstated was known as Mark. It also states that he was the son of Mary. It does not say which Mary, but if it is Mary the Mother of Jesus, then this person would be Jesus brother and if it is Mary Magdalene it could be Jesus's son;

> ***Acts 12:12, 25***—*And when he (Peter) realised this, he went to the house of Mary, the mother of John who was also called Mark, where many were gathered together and were praying. And Barnabas and Saul returned from Jerusalem when they had fulfilled their mission, taking along with them John, who was also called Mark.*

This same person is mentioned again in Acts 15:

> ***Acts 15:36-39***—*After some days Paul said to Barnabas, "Let us return and visit the brethren in every city in which we proclaimed the word of the Lord, and see how they are." Barnabas wanted to take John, called Mark, along with them also. But Paul kept insisting that they should not take him along who had deserted them in Pamphylia and had not gone with them to the work. And there occurred such a sharp disagreement that they separated from one another, and Barnabas took Mark with him and sailed away to Cyprus.*

The verses imply that John-named-Mark was young and needed guardianship. There has been much speculation concerning the identity of this person and some believe that he is same Mark the Cousin of Barnabas mentioned by Paul (Col. 4:10) and (2 Tim. 4:11):

> ***Col. 4:10***—*Aristarchus, my fellow prisoner, sends you his greetings; and also Barnabas's cousin Mark (about whom you received instructions; if he comes to you, welcome him).*

Greg Rigby

> *2 Tim. 4:11—Only Luke is with me. Pick up Mark and bring him with you, for he is useful to me for service.*

It is proposed by some that this John/Mark is John the beloved, who is mentioned six times in John's Gospel and who is proposed by Christian theologians to be John the Evangelist, writer of John's gospel. This uncertainty inclined us to consider the mentions of John in John's gospel and in particular at the references to "the one who Jesus loved": In the original Greek, verse 19: 26 of John's gospels is written thus:

ησοῦς οὖν ἰδὼν τὴν μητέρα καὶ τὸν μαθητὴν παρεστῶτα ὃν ἠγάπα, λέγει τῆμητρί, Γύναι, ἴδε ὁ υἱός σου.

> This translates to *Jesus then saw the mother and the pupil/disciple standing beside/present/at hand who/that he loved dearly, he said to the mother/woman/wife, "Lo/ behold/look the son of you."*

Most translations of this text say that Jesus saw HIS mother. It does not! If it was meant to refer to his mother it would have probably been written conventionally as τὴν μητέρα αὐτοῦ *the mother of him.* Thus, if we use the correct translation, we can see that it is possible that the reported words of Jesus were directed at Mary Magdalene and to the disciple whom Jesus loved. In other words, 'the disciple who Jesus loved' could have been his own son. If that were the case, the son's identity most likely would have been protected. Assuming that John/Mark is the same person as John the beloved, this in turn might account for the use of the pseudonym of *Mark,* as mentioned in the extracts from the Acts of the Apostles above.

The Epistles of John are attributed to John the Evangelist, traditionally thought to be the author of the Gospel of John and the other two Epistles of John. The first Epistle was probably written in Ephesus between the years 95–110 CE and contains some verses of interest, when compared with Egyptian texts:

188

1 John 1 5—His is the message we have heard from Him and announce to you, that God is Light, and in Him there is no darkness at all.

Once more, we can see a link between this text and the Egyptian Book of the Dead:

Book of the Dead: MAKING THE TRANSFORMATION INTO THE GOD WHO LIGHTENETH THE DARKNESS

The Osiris the scribe Ani, whose word is truth, saith: I am the girdle of the garment of the god Nu, which giveth light, and shineth, and belongeth to his breast, the illuminer of the darkness, the uniter of the two Rehti deities, the dweller in my body, through the great spell of the words of my mouth. I am Hem-Nu, the lightener of the darkness. I have come to lighten the darkness; it is light. I have lightened the darkness. I have overthrown the ashmiu- fiends. I have sung hymns to those who dwell in the darkness. I have made to stand up the weeping ones, whose faces were covered over; they were in a helpless state of misery. Look ye then upon me. I am Hem-Nu. I will not let you hear concerning it. [I have fought. I am Hem-Nu. I have lightened the darkness. I have come. I have made an end to the darkness which hath become light indeed.

The ancient Egyptian beliefs were probably literal, in that they believed that the light from God referred to the light from the sun eliminating and overcoming the darkness of the night on a daily basis. There is a possibility that light in John's Epistle was meant in a more ethereal or spiritual sense but there is no doubt that the concept of God being light was one that was inherited by the Christians from an earlier Egyptian belief.

Another significant text occurs in John's second epistle which he directs at 'the chosen lady'. Interestingly, the word *lady* (κυρία) seems to be a form of address, both here and in 2 John 1:5. At that time, it was not usual to apply the title of *lady*

189

Greg Rigby

to any but the Roman empress. Some theologians have suggested that it is proper name, which is unlikely, and others that it is directed towards Mary the mother of Jesus. If Jesus had a family, there is also the possibility that it was directed at the mother of Jesus's children, who (in our hypothesis) might have been thought of as a queen.

> *2 John 1:—1The elder to the chosen lady and her children, whom I love in truth; and not only I, but also all who know the truth. 5Now I ask you, lady, not as though I were writing to you a new commandment, but the one which we have had from the beginning, that we love one another. 9Anyone who goes too far and does not abide in the teaching of Christ, does not have God; the one who abides in the teaching, he has both the Father and the Son. 12Though I have many things to write to you, I do not want to do so with paper and ink; but I hope to come to you and speak face to face, so that your joy may be made full. 13The children of your chosen sister greet you.*

Looked at from the perspective of the hypothesis that we are proposing, phrases such as "the chosen lady and her children" and "all who know truth" conjures a picture of a special family and some secret, known only to a select few. Verse 12 intimates that there is something special and joyous that John wants to communicate to the lady in question. The words would imply some news of this the lady's son, and might explain why John was reticent to expose the son or himself by expressing this news in writing.

The only other extract from the New Testament Epistles that is of interest to us is in the Epistle to the Hebrews. The author of this Epistle is unknown and it has been suggested that he is Paul and/or Priscilla who was Jewess and a prominent Christian evangelist who had been expelled from Rome.

> *Hebrews 1:4-5—[God's Son] . . . having become so much better than the angels, as He has inherited a more*

190

excellent name than they. For to which of the angels did He ever say, "You are my son, today I have begotten you"? And again, "I will be father to him and he will be son to me"?

In this text, we see that the Son being spoken to inherited his name, which was more excellent than the names of the angels. The word inherited implies that it was the possession of the father before being inherited by the son. This is significant because in early Christian tradition, there was never a suggestion that the Father had ever been the Son. In the Egyptian tradition the only way that a Son of God could inherit this, the father's name would have been for him to be a legitimate , in the line from Osiris. On balance this is excerpt indicates that Jesus inherited the title Son of God and gives us a clue to the route that would have provided such an outcome. By implication, it tells us that Jesus was inheritor of the title and (by extrapolation) that he must have been a link in the royal bloodline.

Other Epistles

One epistle from a person who was living at the time of Jesus was not included in the New Testament—an anonymous epistle attributed to Barnabas; known as The Epistle of Barnabas. We know from the contents that it was written after the destruction of the Jewish temple but before the Jewish Rebellion in 132, and because of that, it is a book written between 70 and 130 CE. Nothing certain is known as to the author other than his name was Barnabas, but scarcely any scholars now ascribe it to the illustrious friend and companion of St. Paul.

External and internal evidence here come into direct collision. The ancient writers who refer to this Epistle unanimously attribute it to Barnabas the Levite, of Cyprus, who held an honourable place in the infant church, Clement of Alexandria does so again and again (Strom., ii. 6, ii. 7, etc.). Origen describes it as "a Catholic Epistle" (Cont. Cels., i. 63), and seems to rank it among the Sacred Scriptures (*Comm. in Rom.*, i. 24). Despite its questionable authorship, it contains one assertion that is of interest.

XII (180) Jesus who was manifested, both by type and in the flesh, (181) is not the Son of man, but the Son of God.

This statement is in direct contradiction to Jesus's many claims that he was the Son of (a) Man. One explanation for the contradiction is that Barnabas was aware of Jesus's divine inheritance, he knew that Ptolemy XIII was dead and that Jesus was now the legitimate holder of the Pharaonic crown. The other possibility was that Jesus was now dead and He had assumed his enthroned position in the Heavens.

If the author is the same Barnabas who took protective care of John-Mark who in turn could well have been the son of Jesus, then Barnabas would have been close to the study and contemplation of such questions. Because of that, he could have had inside information and his claim would have been educated and understandable. The one thing we can be sure of is that Barnabas was not trying to argue with Jesus's claim that he was the Son of (a) Man, as represented in the four Gospels.

There were a great number of letters and texts exchanged between early Christian fathers, philosophers and theologians including Mathetes, Polycarp, Ignatius, Justin, Ireneus, Tatian, Athenagorus, Clement, Tertullian, Felix, Origen, Hippolytus, Cyprian, Dionysius, Malchion, Alexander and Methodius. Most of these men were converts, some by way of the apostles, and they had no firsthand knowledge of the new religion. They had acquired their beliefs by listening to missionaries and zealots and by reading texts and letters that were circulated between the early centres of belief.

It is evident from their letters and communications that many of the early bishops and advocates of Christianity actually believed that Jesus was the incarnate, ineffable Divine Son of an omnipotent and eternal God and that he had been made flesh in order to intercede with God the Father for the sins of mankind. If Christian theology emerged out of the religion of ancient Egypt, this fact had been hidden from many of these early converts and what on the one hand had been literal statements of Truth for the Egyptians had evolved into spiritual, mystical and metaphysical concepts for the Christian philosophers who were teaching the new faithful. Strains of the words used in the Nicene Creed can be found in some of the letters, which were written several hundred years before the Council of Nicea was convened. They show that the spin of modern day politicians was not new and that a dogmatic and self-righteous approach was taken to encourage converts to the new faith.

One early church father worthy of mention is Origen, who was one of the prominent Christian philosophers in the second and third centuries CE. He was based in Alexandria and along with Clement, competed for influence of the faithful with Rome. He suggests in his letters that Satan is a fallen star and that "the redeemed" will take his place "among the stars of heaven." Commenting on Revelation 12: 7-9, which says that Michael and his angels cast down the dragon and his angels from heaven, Origen writes, "Do you not see that the dragon fought with the angels, and when he was hard pressed he was thrown down from Heaven. As he fell he drew with him a third of the stars. It is likely that these stars were divine powers which had revolted with him, and they were borne down with the dragon, as Isaiah said, 'How the morning star fell from Heaven.'" [160]

In chapter 7 of de Pricipiis on incorporeal and corporeal beings, Origen says, "We think, then, that they may be designated as living beings, for this reason, that they are said to receive commandments from God, which is ordinarily the case only with rational beings. 'I have given a commandment to all the stars,' says the Lord."

Origen does not look overtly towards Egyptian theosophy to validate his claims. Rather he calls on the Hebrew Scriptures and the prophets and quotes many of the claims of Paul and the other Apostles to substantiate his reasoning. In our next chapter, we will see evidence that there was an intertwining of many of the Hebrew and Egyptian traditions since Ptolemy II. Because of that, there might not have been need for a Jewish philosopher

---

160 *Origen and the Life of the Stars*, Alan Scott

who had converted to Christianity to acknowledge the Egyptian roots of his beliefs.

There is nothing in any of these works to invalidate our hypothesis. The writers appear to have been sincere believers that Jesus was the only begotten son of an eternal, all-powerful God who was the creator of all things. If our hypothesis is valid, the real identity of Jesus was either known to the authors of these works or they did not know and they truly believed in His divinity as the Son of an eternal and everlasting God almighty.

The identity and ancestry of Jesus was probably only known to a small and a select few but those that did know could have been convinced that someone from the true and unbroken bloodline from Osiris was in fact divine. Certainly, as far as we can tell from Egyptian inscriptions the Egyptian people believed in the divinity of their pharaoh.

Whatever their beliefs, it is likely that they would have been equally true regarding the existence and locations of any children of Jesus. Such children would be Sons of God, whether their father was God in the sense of being a pharaoh of the royal and sacred bloodline from Osiris or whether he was God incarnate, who took living form and died for humanity to atone for our sins against God the Father.

In order to discover more precise clues, it is perhaps necessary to look at the beliefs and activities of others living at the time who were not believers and who held a less bigoted perspective.

CHAPTER 14

Clues Found in the Refutation of Heretical Beliefs

In addition to works published at the time that condemned Christianity, there were several works published by the early Christian fathers that condemned heresies against the faith and the church that proclaimed it. An analysis of these works may be helpful in our attempt to determine the true identity of Jesus, in that they identify those beliefs that the Christian zealots knew to be common at the time and which they thought might be a threat to their own inflexible theosophy.

One famous criticism was Origen's criticism of Celsus's *The True Word*. This work was lost but portions of Celsus's *View of Christians and Christianity* is available.

The two most prominent exposures of heresies were *Against Heresies* by Irenaeus and *The Refutation of All Heresies* by Hippolytus.

Origen against Celsus

Celsus was a second-century Greek philosopher and opponent of Early Christianity. He is known for his literary work, *The True Word* (also *Account, Doctrine* or *Discourse*; Greek: Λόγος Ἀληθής), which survives exclusively in Origen's quotations from it in Contra Celsum. This work circa 177 CE is the earliest known comprehensive attack on Christianity. Here we include extracts from Origen's refutation, which are relevant to our discussion:

195

*Celsus accuses Him of having "invented his birth from
a virgin," and upbraids Him with being "born in a certain
Jewish village, of a poor woman of the country, who gained
her subsistence by spinning, and who was turned out of
doors by her husband, a carpenter by trade, because she
was convicted of adultery; that after being driven away
by her husband, and wandering about for a time, she dis-
gracefully gave birth to Jesus, an illegitimate child, who
having hired himself out as a servant in Egypt on account
of his poverty, and having there acquired some miraculous
powers, on which the Egyptians greatly pride themselves,
returned to his own country, highly elated on account of
them, and by means of these proclaimed himself a God.*

This account by Origen indicates that there existed a proposal that Jesus was a result of human birth and that he spent
his formative years acquiring skills in Egypt, which he subsequently used to market himself as a god figure.

Our next quotation is even more significant to the discussion
in that it deals directly with Jesus's parentage:

*When she was pregnant she was turned out of doors
by the carpenter to whom she had been betrothed, as
having been guilty of adultery, and that she bore a child
to a certain soldier named Panthera.*

Origen quotes Celsus as someone who gives us a name for
Jesus's father and the claim that he (Jesus's father) was a soldier. In
relation to this name, we are told, "A common appellation for Jesus in
the Talmud was Yeshu'a ben Panthera, an allusion to the widespread
Jewish belief during the earliest centuries of the Christian era that
Jesus was the result of an illegitimate union between his mother and
a Roman soldier named Tiberius Julius Abdes Panthera."[161]

This parentage is mentioned by other authors: "We encountered the name Pandera in Bavli Shabbat/Sanhedrin; the Tosefta

---

161 *The Bible Fraud*, Tony Bushby

(with Pandera in the Qohelet Rabba Parallel) and (it) is the earliest attestation of this name in rabbinical sources"[162]

"We now know that Pantera/Panthera was a Greek name that shows up in a number of Latin inscriptions from the period, especially as the surname of Roman soldiers."[163]

The extent of Celsus's credibility is unknown. What is known is that Origen's refutation was a significant document and that its existence means Celsus and his opinions were believed to be a serious threat. It certainly adds weight to the argument that Jesus existed, and that he was fathered by human intervention. In relation to Jesus's genealogy and Celsus's assertions, Origen states:

> *"The framers of the genealogies, from a feeling of pride, made Jesus to be descended from the first man, and from the kings of the Jews." And he (Celsus) thinks that he makes a notable charge when he adds that 'the carpenter's wife could not have been ignorant of the fact, had she been of such illustrious descent'.*

Origen does not refute this quotation in a way that reveals where the Gospel writers obtained their information, which, if it did not come directly to them from Mary or from Jesus himself would have required compendious research. This would add weight to the argument that Jesus's father must have been more than a random Roman soldier impregnating a Jewish peasant girl. The alternative is that the entire story was the construct of some Christian zealots. There have been claims of links to the Essenes but there is no evidence of this as the causation of the Christian religious establishment.

All in all, this refutation by Origen does more to compound our belief that Mary was descended from David and that David was Thutmose III, himself a link in the Pharaonic bloodline back to Osiris. It also adds weight to our hypothesis that the father of her child was Ptolemy XIII who is most likely to have been living under an assumed name at the time.

---

162 *Jesus in the Talmud*, Peter Schäfer
163 *The Jesus Dynasty*, James A Tabor

Greg Rigby

Origen writes that Celsus made several statements regarding the resurrection of Jesus. These statements are important since, if it is true that Jesus died and was resurrected in corporeal form then he would have needed to have access to the supernatural and it would be proof of his divinity:

> *His power to say that He voluntarily withdrew from the sight of men, and seemed only to die, without really doing so; but, appearing again, made a juggler's trick of the resurrection from the dead.*

Celsus added,

> *If Jesus had really wished to manifest his divine power, he ought to have shown himself to those who ill-treated him, and to the judge who condemned him, and to all men universally, without reservation. For he had no longer occasion to fear any man after his death, being, as you say, a God; nor was he sent into the world at all for the purpose of being hid.*

Celsus claimed that the resurrection was a contrived fiction. He goes on to add substance to his claim, by claiming that if Jesus wanted to use his resurrection as proof of his divinity, he would have appeared to the world in general, not just to the select few disciples who would then have the job of convincing the world without any evidence to back them up.

Origen refuted these suggestions with emotive statements:

> *But a clear and unmistakable proof of the fact I hold to be the undertaking of His disciples who devoted themselves to the teaching of a doctrine which was a danger to human life,—a doctrine they would not have taught with such courage had they invented the resurrection of Jesus from the dead.* [164]

---

164 *Origen against Celsus, Book 2, I.VI*

Celsus was clear in his assertion that the Hebrews were actually Egyptians by descent, and that Egyptian theology had much to offer: "The Hebrews, being (originally) Egyptians, dated the commencement (of their political existence) from the time of their rebellion."

Furthermore, he states, "We ridicule the Egyptians, although they present many by no means contemptible mysteries for our consideration, when they teach us that; such rites are acts of worship offered to eternal ideas."

These extracts from Celsus's work show clearly that some philosophers and theologians at the time claimed Hebrew descent from Egypt and that they showed respect for the Egyptian traditions.

It is quite remarkable how Origen was open-minded enough to believe the now strange idea of stars being "intermediate beings between angels and men."[165] At the same time, he was dogmatic and self-righteous in his condemnation of Celsus's assertions regarding the Jesus story, no matter how logical. He quoted Paul in response to the above, who said, *"We speak wisdom among them that are perfect; not the wisdom of this world, nor of the princes of this world, who come to naught, but we speak the wisdom of God in a mystery, even the hidden wisdom, which God ordained before the world unto our glory; which none of the princes of the world know."*[166] The Faith was established quickly and became entrenched in the dogma of the Church. The early Fathers were closed-minded when any suggestions were raised that the story contained even the slightest flaw and they resorted to the Gospels, the Epistles and to the Hebrew Scripture to substantiate their arguments.

In his refutation, Origen does more to give substance to the claims of Celsus than to eradicate them. Because of that, his refutation enhances the hypothesis that Jesus was of the royal Egyptian bloodline.

---

165 *The Demiurge in Ancient Thought*, Carl Séan O'Brian
166 1 Corinthians 2:6

Greg Rigby

Irenæus's Against Heresies

The work of Irenæus's *Against Heresies* (circa 180 CE), known as *The Detection and Refutation of False Knowledge* is one of the most precious remains of early Christian antiquity. It is devoted, on the one hand, to an account and refutation of those multiform Gnostic heresies which prevailed in the latter half of the second century; and, on the other hand, to an exposition and defence of the Catholic faith. The inclusion of a reference to any belief or practice indicates that that belief or practice was known to Irenæus and that it was of some significance at the time.

There are 142 chapters to Irenæus's work, most of which are focussed on the doctrine of the Most High God, the Father of all, and the part of Jesus as the Son of God in Christian theology. We have extracted here, two sections that might contribute some small light on the true identity of Jesus:

> *But again, those who assert that He (Jesus) was simply a mere man, begotten by Joseph, remaining in the bondage of the old disobedience, are in a state of death having been not as yet joined to the Word of God the Father.*[167]

Specifically, in relation to the divinity of Jesus, he also quotes Caprocrates (circa 130 CE) and the Ebionites, who believed that Jesus was a man:

> *The Ebionites, following these, assert that He was begotten by Joseph; thus destroying, as far as in them lies, such a marvellous dispensation of God, and setting aside the testimony of the prophets which proceeded from God.*[168]
>
> *They (Caprocrates followers) also hold that Jesus was the son of Joseph, and was just like other men, with the exception that he differed from them in this respect, that inasmuch as his soul was steadfast and pure.*[169]

---

167 Irenaeus: Against Heresies, Book III, Chapter XIX, I
168 Ibid; Book 3, Chapter XXI, 1
169 Ibid; Book 1, Chapter XXV, 1

From these quotations we can see, that there must have been a strong body of opinion claiming that Jesus was just a man. The heretics who made this claim were in many cases men of learning who themselves refuted the idea that Jesus was divine and the Son of God. Their arguments are based on logic as they saw it but they take us back to the basic question we are attempting to address: If Jesus was human, how did the Christian movement get established? What was it that provoked the idea that Jesus was linked to the divine? How did so many people conclude that Jesus was the Son of God? On what basis did Jesus himself propose his claim?

Irenæus suggested that the reason for their scepticism was the fact that they were not yet believers, which by any standards is tautological reasoning and adds nothing constructive to the argument.

The second extract from Irenaeus's refutation indicates clearly that the author believed in the intertwined nature of Egyptian and Hebrew scriptures:

> *Since, therefore, the Scriptures have been interpreted with such fidelity, and by the grace of God, and since from these God has prepared and formed again our faith towards His Son, and has preserved to us the unadulterated Scriptures in Egypt, where the house of Jacob flourished, fleeing from the famine in Canaan; where also our Lord was preserved when He fled from the persecution set on foot by Herod; and [since] this interpretation of these Scriptures was made prior to our Lord's descent [to earth], and came into being before the Christians appeared — for our Lord was born about the forty-first year of the reign of Augustus; but Ptolemy was much earlier, under whom the Scriptures were interpreted; [since these things are so, I say,] truly these men are proved to be impudent and presumptuous, who would now show a desire to make different translations, when we refute them out of these Scriptures, and shut them up to a belief in the advent of the Son of God.[170]*

---

170 Ibid Book 3, Chapter 21, 3

The author makes clear that the scriptures were interpreted under Ptolemy, and translated into Greek. This is acknowledged to have been carried out by seventy-two elders in the reign Ptolemy II, when Egypt ruled Judea (circa 270 BCE).[171] It was during this period that knowledge and appreciation of the scriptures of both cultures became known and appreciated by each side. This in turn could explain how Ptolemy XIII became educated in both the Egyptian and Hebrew theosophies and how his son, born in Judea would have been able to reconcile what he had been told of both.

In relation to the Crucifixion of Jesus, Irenæus comments on one Gnostic heretic, Basilides, who taught from 117 to 138 CE. Basilides is believed to have written over two dozen books of commentary on the Christian Gospel (now all lost) entitled *Exegetica*, making him one of the earliest Gospel critics. Only fragments of his works are preserved that supplement the knowledge furnished by his opponents. The followers of Basilides, the Basilidians, formed a movement that persisted for at least two centuries after him. Interestingly, Irenaeus wrote that Basilides claimed that he inherited his teachings from Matthew. He quotes him as saying:

> *Wherefore he (Jesus) did not himself suffer death, but Simon, a certain man of Cyrene, being compelled, bore the cross in his stead; so that this latter being transfigured by him, that he might be thought to be Jesus, was crucified, through ignorance and error, while Jesus himself received the form of Simon, and, standing by, laughed at them.* [172]

Here we have a significant Gnostic philosopher of the time, who claimed to have obtained information directly from Matthew and who was preaching that the crucifixion was a fraud. If this claim had any validity, it would imply that all the elements

---

171 *The Antiquities of the Jews, Book XII* Flavius Josephus
172 Irenaeus; Against Heresies, Book I, Chapter XXIV, 4

of the gospels that spoke of Jesus death, entombment and rising were equally untrue. In fact, it would indicate that the gospels were a complete deception. Basilides does not question the existence of Jesus; he only questions those aspects of the Jesus story that would require Jesus to be divine (in the sense of incarnate and supernatural).

From the refutations by Irenaeus we can see that there were philosophers and intellectual groups who questioned basics tenants of the mainline Christian doctrine—in particular, the immaculate conception of a Jesus as a divine being and the Crucifixion, and (by implication) the resurrection of Jesus. They do not make claims regarding Jesus's heritage, albeit Basilides is quoted as saying that the men who were led out of Egypt also affirm that the barbarous name in which the Saviour ascended and descended is Caulacau (a name derived from Isaiah 28).

On balance, Irenaeus's *Against Heresies* does nothing to invalidate our central hypothesis. On the contrary, it presents second hand and circumstantial evidence validated by their refutation that supports the idea that Jesus was human and that the crucifixion and resurrection did not take place.

The Refutation of all Heresies—Hippolytus

Hippolytus is described as one of the first great Christian fathers (170—236 CE). He was based in Rome although he was Greek by birth and he was the disciple of Irenæus. His refutation is a comprehensive work, which identifies and details the prevailing philosophical ideas more clearly than did the work of his mentor. It includes a concise summary of each suggestion, ranging from the various belief systems of the Greeks and Druids to the arts of astrology and numerology. In this refutation, several passages might be relevant to an examination of our hypothesis.

The first section we have extracted is a discussion of the Naassene belief system regarding the location of God in the stars and how, whether as Osiris and/or Mercury, this god caused all things to exist. The Naassene were a Christian Gnostic sect from around 100 CE. They claimed to have been taught

203

their doctrines by Marianne, a disciple of James the Just who some claim is the brother of Jesus. They were among the first to be called simply Gnostics, as they alleged that they alone have plumbed the depths of knowledge:

> *Let us see how these (heretics), collecting together the secret and ineffable mysteries of all the Gentiles, are uttering falsehoods against Christ, and are making dupes of those who are not acquainted with these orgies of the Gentiles.*
>
> *The (Naassene) assert, that the Egyptians, who after the Phrygians, it is established, are of greater antiquity than all mankind, and who confessedly were the first to proclaim to all the rest of men the rites and orgies of, at the same time, all the gods, as well as the species and energies (of things), have the sacred and august, and for those who are not initiated, unspeakable mysteries of Isis. These, however, are not anything else than what by her of the seven dresses and sable robe was sought and snatched away, namely, the pudendum of Osiris. And they say that Osiris is water. But the seven-robed nature encircled and arrayed with seven mantles of ethereal texture—for so they call the planetary stars, allegorizing and denominating them ethereal robes, is as it were the changeable generation, and is exhibited as the creature transformed by the ineffable and unportrayable, and inconceivable and figureless one. And this, (the Naassene) says, is what is declared in Scripture, "The just will fall seven times, and rise again." For these falls, he says, are the changes of the stars, moved by Him who puts all things in motion.*
>
> *They affirm, then, concerning the substance of the seed which is a cause of all existent things, that it is none of these, but that it produces and forms all things that are made, expressing themselves thus: "I become what I wish, and I am what I am: on account of this I say, that what puts all things in motion is itself unmoved.*

For what exists remains forming all things and nought of existing things is made."He says that this (one) alone is good, and that what is spoken by the Saviour is declared concerning this (one): "Why do you say that I am good? One is good, my Father which is in the heavens, who causeth His sun to rise upon the just and unjust, and sendeth rain upon saints and sinners." But who the saintly ones are on whom He sends the rain, and the sinners on whom the same sends the rain, this likewise we shall afterwards declare with the rest. And this is the great and secret and unknown mystery of the universe, concealed and revealed among the Egyptians.

For Osiris, (the Naassene) says, is in temples in front of Isis; and his pudendum stands exposed, looking downwards, and crowned with all its own fruits of things that are made. And (he affirms) that such stands not only in the most hallowed temples chief of idols, but that also, for the information of all, it is as it were a light not set under a bushel, but upon a candlestick, proclaiming its message upon the housetops, in all byways, and all streets, and near the actual dwellings, placed in front as a certain appointed limit and termination of the dwelling, and that this is denominated the good (entity) by all. For they style this good-producing, not knowing what they say. And the Greeks, deriving this mystical (expression) from the Egyptians, preserve it until this day. For we behold, says (the Naassene), statues of Mercury, of such a figure honoured among them.[173]

The above excerpt shows clearly that the Egyptians had long believed that God was located in and around the seven main stars of Ursa Major. It also shows that the Egyptians belief system was persistent and continued to influence thinking regarding the mysteries that pertained to procreation. It tells nothing of the identity of Jesus Christ, nor does it help prove or

173 Hippolytus, The Eructation of All Heresies; Book V, Chapter 2

205

Greg Rigby

disprove our hypothesis. Its only contribution is to illustrate the background of ongoing Egyptian belief, out of which came the instigator of the Christian story.

The second quotation comes from Book IV of Hippolytus's *Refutation of All Heresies*, entitled *Recapitulation of Theologies and Cosmologies*:

> *Do not the Egyptians, however, who suppose themselves more ancient than all, speak of the power of the Deity? (This power they estimate by) calculating these intervals of the parts (of the zodiac; and, as if) by a most divine inspiration, they asserted that the Deity is an indivisible monad, both itself generating itself, and that out of this were formed all things. For this, say they, being unbegotten, produces the succeeding numbers; for instance, the monad, superadded into itself, generates the duad; and in like manner, when superadded (into duad, triad, and so forth), produces the triad and tetrad, up to the decade, which is the beginning and end of numbers. Wherefore it is that the first and tenth monad is generated, on account of the decade being equipollent, and being reckoned for a monad, and (because) this multiplied ten times will become a hundred, and again becomes a monad, and the hundred multiplied ten times will produce a thousand, and this will be a monad. In this manner, also the thousand multiplied ten times make up the full sum of a myriad; in like manner will it be a monad. But by a comparison of indivisible quantities, the kindred numbers of the monad comprehend 3, 5, 7 and 9.*[174]

Again, we see that the Egyptians believed that God was a logical concept and that he/it existed in a practical and calculable form. Again, it shows nothing of the identity of Jesus Christ, nor does it help prove or disprove our hypothesis. Its contribu-

---

174 Hippolytus, The Refutation of all Heresies, Book I, Chapter XLIII

tion is to reinforce our claim that the background of ongoing belief had emanated out of Egypt.

In condemning other belief systems as heresies, the early Christian theologians acknowledge that the theological construct from which all other systems grew was that of Egypt. In the case of Celsus, the self-righteous condemnation of his claims throws light onto Celsus's specific proposals regarding the birth and death of Jesus.

Many of the Heresies (particularly the Ebionites and Cerinthus) mentioned by Hippolytus refute the virgin birth and claim that Jesus was human. This (if anything) adds weight to that part of our hypothesis, which relates to Jesus being human and to his divinity being no more real than that claimed by the Pharaohs of Egypt over three millennia.

CHAPTER 15

Mary Magdalene

Extrapolations of the notion that Jesus fathered children have been famously speculated by a series of authors over the years. In more recent times, the Lincoln, Leigh and Bagient book, *The Holy Blood and the Holy Grail* prompted a BBC documentary which created a lot of public interest and the basic theme of the book was then exploited in a novel and a movie entitled *The DaVinci Code* by Dan Brown.

All of these various texts portray the wife of Jesus and therefore the mother of Jesus's children as Mary Magdalene. Thereafter, they have invited derision by focussing on a conspiracy of covert organisations that they say exist to protect the secret of Jesus's marriage and of any bloodline that has ensued. Indeed, and not surprisingly, critics of the propositions that Jesus was married and that there exists a lineage from Jesus Christ have been damning in their criticism.

If the hypothesis that we here propose has merit, then Jesus would have been aware of his importance in the perpetuation of the royal bloodline. Given the trouble that Ptolemy had gone to, it is not difficult to imagine that Jesus would have received strict instructions, regarding his duty of ensuring the maintenance and pedigree of the lineage.

If there is any validity to the claims that there was a bloodline from Jesus then it is not difficult to imagine that the mother of Jesus's children would have been chosen very carefully. This selection would have been extremely significant, since Jesus's own existence was central to the perpetuation of the bloodline of which he was a part. Here we will examine the evidence for and against Mary Magdalene being the wife of Jesus in the various documents that attributed to her or which discuss her as a subject to the story being told. The first of these is *The Gospel of Mary*, where it is generally agreed that the person named Mary is the person known as Mary Magdalene.

The Gospel of Mary

This document is found in the *Berlin Gnostic Codex*. It is a very important and well-preserved manuscript, which was apparently discovered in the late-nineteenth century somewhere near Akhmim in Upper Egypt. Importantly, the codex preserves the most complete surviving fragment of the *Gospel of Mary* and it gives us about half of the original text.

The story of this gospel is a simple one and involves a discussion between the Saviour and his disciples after the resurrection. After Jesus leaves the discussion (at the end of Chapter 4 of the Gospel of Mary), Mary consoles the group and gives them secret information. The text culminates in an argument between Mary and the other disciples concerning the nature of the information Mary has provided and of their mission.

We have extracted two verses that may be pertinent to our analysis. The first relates to Mary's status:

> *Peter said to Mary, "Sister we know that the Saviour loved you more than the rest of woman" (5:5).*

Here we have a statement of Peter, written about the subject of the text, which the author reproduces. If this reproduction is accurate and there is no aggrandisement by the author, then it is telling us that Mary was the closest female to Jesus. It does not state that they were married, but it is a reasonable place to start any examination. By implication, it also tells us (if the author was in fact Mary) that Mary was not reticent regarding her relationship with Jesus, quite the opposite in fact.

Our second extract refers to Jesus's instructions to the group, where he is reported to have said,

> *"Go then and preach the gospel of the Kingdom." (4:37)*

209

This instruction is strange in that it mentions a kingdom without stating which kingdom it refers to. In the Gospels Jesus variously mentions the Kingdom of God (Matt. 6:33, Luke 17:20), The Kingdom of Heaven (Matt. 13:52, 13:47, 13:44), and the Kingdom of the Son of Man (Matt. 16:28).

In chapter 5 verse 1 of the Gospel of Mary, immediately after Jesus's departure, the document states, "But they were grieved. They wept greatly, saying, 'How shall we go to the Gentiles and preach the gospel of the Kingdom of the Son of Man? If they did not spare Him, how will they spare us?'"

This may be an indication that 4:37 is talking about the kingdom of the Son of Man. However, this is speculation and the question therefore remains; why didn't the author, who claims to have been a confident of Jesus, specify the kingdom that Jesus referred to?

In the context of our hypothesis, there is a possibility that Jesus was referring to an earthly kingdom and that his teaching constituted the gospel of that kingdom. If this was the meaning of Jesus's reported words, then the only kingdom that would fit would be the Egyptian kingdom and the gospel being referred to would be the set of beliefs that were at the heart of the Egyptian theological tradition.

In chapter 5 of this gospel, the author makes an exposition of the private words of Jesus that she had been access to. She tells the group, "What is hidden from you I will proclaim to you." Mary then goes on in chapter 8, verses 13 through 18, to give an explanation that has all the hallmarks of extracts from the Gnostic beliefs that grew out of the Egyptian mysteries and which mirrors the outline of a selection of these mysteries by Hippolytus in The Refutation of All Heresies (see previous chapter):

> Again it came to the third power, which is called ignorance. The power questioned the soul, saying; where are you going? In wickedness are you bound. But you are bound; do not judge! And the soul said; why do you judge me, although I have not judged? I was bound,

though I have not bound. I was not recognized. But I have recognized that the All is being dissolved, both the earthly things and the heavenly. When the soul had overcome the third power, it went upwards and saw the fourth power, which took seven forms.

This exposition may be confirmation that the kingdom being referred to was the ancient kingdom of the Egyptians with all of its spiritual and theosophical implications. Certainly, the disciples in attendance were dumbfounded, as described in chapter 9 verse 1:

When Mary had said this, she was silent, since the Saviour had spoken thus far with her. But Andrew answered and said to the brethren; "Say what you think concerning what she said. For I do not believe that the Saviour said this. For certainly these teachings are of other ideas."
Peter also opposed her in regard to these matters and asked them about the Saviour. "Did he then speak secretly with a woman in preference to us, and not openly? Are we to turn back and all listen to her? Did he prefer her to us?"

These extracts from the Gospel of Mary point to two possibilities:

1. The first is that Mary was the confidante of Jesus who was closer to her than any other female, and she may have been his wife.
2. The second was that she was aware of Gnostic philosophy, which seemed to be similar to that inherent to ancient Egyptian religious belief. She and Jesus both wanted this gospel or set of beliefs to be evangelised.

If this Gospel of Mary is a valid document, and the Mary in the document is Mary Magdalene, it implies that the selection

Greg Rigby

of documents and truths incorporated into the Christian canon was biased to a particular end, in that it omitted beliefs espoused by the Gnostic movement to which Mary Magdalene and (by implication) Jesus were disposed.

The Lost Gospel

Recently, following a compendium of research, Simcha Jacobovici and Barrie Wilson published a book entitled *The Lost Gospel*, with the subheading *Decoding the Ancient Text that Reveals Jesus's Marriage to Mary the Magdalene*. They claim that Joseph and Aseneth is a Christian story—a Gospel if you will—about Jesus.

The book was described by at least one reviewer as tosh. Some like Ross Shepherd Kraemer and Rivka Nir however, believe that the work is Christian in origin, not Jewish and that it did refer to Jesus in allegorical terms. Kraemer is convinced that "this part of the story takes place in history and narrates the deeds of historical persons."[175] *The Lost Gospel* sets out to show that an ancient Syriac manuscript, which had been translated from its original Greek text, entitled *The Story of Joseph the Just and Aseneth his wife* was in fact the story of Jesus's meeting with and marriage with Mary Magdalene. It is compelling in its argument and it gives good reason to consider the possibility that the story is more than its title might lead one to believe.

In the Old Testament, Jacob (the grandson of Abraham) has four wives, one daughter and twelve sons (the fathers of the twelve tribes). Joseph and Benjamin are his sons from his marriage to Rachel. This family picture is duplicated in the Joseph and Aseneth story. The rest of the story is new in every respect. In summary, the story consists of the following elements:

- Joseph was in the service of the Egyptian Pharaoh as magistrate.
- One of the pharaoh's wealthy nobles was named Potiphar, the priest of On.

---

175 *When Aseneth Met Joseph,* Ross Shepard Kraemer

212

- Potiphar had a beautiful virgin daughter, Aseneth.
- Pharaoh's first-born son heard of her beauty and asked his father to give her to him; his father turned down his request.
- Pharaoh sent Joseph around the entire land of Egypt.
- During his journey and his supervision of the grain harvest, Joseph stayed at the home of Potiphar.
- Aseneth dresses up for the visit, and Potiphar tells her that he would like her to be betrothed to their royal visitor, who he describes as the savior.
- Aseneth has a tantrum and refuses saying that Joseph is "not one of my people" and he is "the son of a shepherd." She claims that she wants the "first born son of Pharaoh" because he is the "ruler and king of all Egypt."
- When Joseph arrives, Aseneth falls for him, recognising him as the son of God, telling herself that her foreign counsellors have deceived her. She observes Joseph from a tower.
- Joseph sees her, and on being told that she is a virgin and the daughter of Potiphar, he asks that she be brought to him.
- Joseph keeps her at bay and blesses her with a prayer.
- After he leaves, Aseneth goes into a lovesick tantrum that lasts seven days.
- On the eighth day, she prays and receives a visit from "a man from heaven—alike in respect to Joseph." He tells her that she will be married to Joseph.
- The man shares a honeycomb with her, and he blesses her seven virgin handmaids.
- Joseph's arrival is announced, and Aseneth dresses with a bridal veil as she had been instructed by the "man from heaven."
- On Joseph's arrival, there is an ecstatic meeting between the two.
- Potiphar suggests that there be a wedding.
- Joseph tells him that he needs to return to the Pharaoh, who will give her to him, and he leaves without "knowing his bride before the wedding."

213

- Joseph asks the Pharaoh's permission, and he summons Potiphar and Aseneth before him.
- Pharaoh blesses the union.
- The two get married and have two children, Manasseh and Aphraim.
- After seven years, Joseph's father Jacob comes to Egypt from Israel.
- Joseph and Aseneth visit, and there is a warm meeting.
- Levi, one of the brothers of Joseph, was a prophet who "knew the secrets of God."
- Aseneth was seen by the Pharaoh's first-born son from afar, and he desired Aseneth.
- The first-born son visits two brothers of Joseph to offer them gold for their allegiance in a plot to kill Joseph and take Aseneth for his wife.
- The two brothers reject the proposal.
- The first-born son then called on two of Aseneth's servants, and lies to them in order to persuade them to betray Joseph and Aseneth.
- The first-born son indicates that he intends to kill the Pharaoh in order to complete his intentions regarding Joseph and Aseneth.
- This pharaoh's son sends an army of two thousand men to help the two servants.
- There was a battle, and Aseneth's six hundred men defeated the two thousand.
- In their retreat, they confronted the pharaoh's son, but the boy Benjamin who was with Aseneth threw stones at the pharaoh's son and struck him on the temple. He then killed the remaining forty-eight men.
- The renegade servants of Aseneth confront her intending to kill her; they capitulate when she prays for them.
- Aseneth insists that they be spared.
- Pharaoh's son recovers and Levi, Joseph's brother, insists that he be spared.
- On the third day, the firstborn dies from the wound.

- Pharaoh dies and leaves the diadem to Joseph who rules Egypt forty-eight years.
- The diadem is passed to the grandson of Pharaoh who was a baby at the time the Pharaoh died.
- Joseph is like a father to the boy in Egypt for the rest of his life.

The following are the principal arguments used by the authors of the Lost Bible to convince us that this is an allegory relating to Jesus and Mary Magdalene:

- It was common to have coded texts at the time that did not call people in them by their real names.
- There is evidence in the gospels and other texts that Jesus had a wife and had brothers and that the Pauline Christian Cannon suppressed this.
- The story is confirmed by other Gnostic texts such as *The Thunder, Perfect Mind* in which the female author says about herself, "I am the first and the last . . . I am the honoured one and the scorned one. I am the whore and the holy one. I am the wife and the virgin."
- The story seems to confirm what we know as Gnostic Christianity, which originated with the followers of the Mara, the lady—Mary the Magdalene. For Gnostic Christians, especially Valentinians (Valentinus 100—160) it wasn't the last supper or the crucifixion that was the most significant episode in Jesus's life but his marriage to Mary Magdalene.
- A monk of the sixth century named Pseudo-Zacharias Rhetor published a manuscript entitled; *A Volume of Records of Events which have Shaped the World*, which lists *The Story of Joseph the Just and Aseneth His Wife* as one of the five titles in the anthology, which the authors of *The Lost Bible* conclude was an ancient Christian text.
- A sixth century letter from a monk involved in the translation of *The Story of Joseph the Just and Aseneth*

215

His Wife which he claimed has something to do with the word becoming flesh and is asked by an anonymous letter writer to explain its inner meaning.

- There is evidence that it was once a popular story inside the Christian community.
- Scholars who have examined the text have dated it to early Christian times.
- "Through typology, the New Christian movement created an ancient history for itself by retroactively usurping the Hebrew Bible for Christian purposes."
- Scholars who have examined the document have overlooked the context of Eastern Christianity in which it was written, and that community's fondness for typological analysis.
- Mary Magdalene and Aseneth's names are connected directly via the tower.
- Joseph is described as the Son of God.
- They link the honeycomb and bees mentioned in the text to Artemis/(Isis) and point out that if their proposition is correct, Mary Magdalene was seen by her followers as an incarnation of Artemis/(Isis), a direct connection with the royal bloodline.
- The marriage in the story was in fact the marriage and wedding feast at Cana described in John 2: 1-11.

Without realising the implications (in terms of our hypothesis), *The Lost Bible* states, "Because they were divine and human at the same time, their act of procreation was a metaphor for creation itself. In this sense therefore, Egyptian based Christian Gnosticism was drawing on millennia—we reiterate millennia—of Egyptian tradition. So it is not surprising that they viewed Jesus not merely as a prophet or messiah but, literally as a god." If the interpretation of *The Story of Joseph the Just and Aseneth his Wife* by the authors of The Lost Gospel is valid, then it fits well with the hypothesis we have proposed. In fact, it may be a more accurate interpretation of actual events than we could have hoped.

In this story, though the pharaoh is the king of Egypt, he is not a king in the ancient Egyptian tradition. Neither he nor his firstborn son is described as the Son of God. This means that they are NOT presented as being in the divine line that connects back to Osiris and Isis. Additionally, we can deduce from the story that they are not from the same family or bloodline as Joseph or his father Potiphar. Despite this, when the pharaoh dies, Joseph is delegated the role of Pharaoh, which he assumes for forty-eight years.

If the story is allegorical as proposed by Jacobovici and Wilson, then it is significant that the person they believe to represent Jesus becomes Pharaoh and that he is given the title in a similar way to Ptolemy I, who (we propose), may have been the ancestor of Jesus. Aseneth is described in the story as having ten bed chambers in her tower housing gold, jewels, exotic foods, replications of Egyptian gods and her seven virgin servants. Potiphar, Aseneth's father is described as having a 'manager of his home'. This means that Aseneth and her family were people of considerable substance.:

> *Potiphar said, "My Lord, the young woman you see in the tower is not a foreign woman but our daughter, a virgin who rejects all men and foreign husbands. No one has ever cleaved to her. No one has seen her except for you today. If you wish she may come to bow and greet your nobility, because our daughter is your sister." (7-8)*

There are several aspects of these verses that bear examination; not least, Potiphar's claim that no one had previously seen Aseneth contradicts the earlier claim in the narrative that news of her beauty spread throughout the land. (1:6)

In verse 8, Potiphar states that Aseneth is "your sister." The explanation for this in *The Lost Gospel* is that this was consistent with Gnostic Christian texts. A better explanation might be that it was tradition in Egypt that queens married their relatives. "A new sisterly title, sister-wife, reappears in Ptolemaic times, doubtless influenced by the brother-sister dynamic at the

217

Greg Rigby

time."[176] In 7:10, Joseph responds by calling her his kinswoman, and says that she is like a sister, indicating that he perceives an affinity with Aseneth other than that based on desire. In the period between Joseph's first visit and his return, Aseneth laments, and her prayers include some statements and claims that are worthy of mention:

> *"I Aseneth, daughter of Potiphar the priest, who, for some time, has been honoured as virgin and queen, proud and prosperous surpassing all women."*
>
> *"And therefore, Lord, stretch out your hands and lift me from the ground because behold, a wild animal, an old lion, persecutes me because he is father of the gods of Egypt."*
>
> *"For, behold, all the gifts of my father, Potiphar, given to me as an inheritance, are empty and transient; for a gift of your inheritance, Lord, is eternal and incorruptible."*
>
> *And to you Lord my God I have fled. But you save me, because in error I have sinned against you, I a virgin, a stray and a child, 9 who said evil empty things against my Lord Joseph because I did not know he was your son." (12:9-13:8)*

Here we see that Aseneth proclaims herself to be a queen, and she is conscious of her duty to God the Father, who in our hypothesis would be the Egyptian God Ra. She proclaims that the Lord's inheritance (the bloodline direct from Osiris) is eternal and incorruptible; she is therefore acknowledging that she is part of that inheritance. She then continues to voice her realisation that Joseph is of royal blood. In relation to our hypothesis, the most significant part of the text occurs immediately before Aseneth's marriage to Joseph:

> *Her Foster Father joined her again to tell her that everything had been made ready. But when he saw her*

---

176 *The Complete Royal Families of Ancient Egypt*, Aiden Dodson/Dyan Hilton

he was terrified and could not find his speech. He was afraid and fell before her feet. Then at last he said, "What is this appearance of virtue and marvellous beauty of the gods? The Lord God of Heaven truly chose you to be the bride of his firstborn son." (18:12-13)

Here we are told that Potiphar is not the father of Aseneth, which leads us to surmise who might be her true father. Who were her parents? Could she truly have been an inheritor of the sacred bloodline?

Most importantly, he describes Joseph as the firstborn son of the Lord God of Heaven. There can be no ambiguity here: Potiphar is proclaiming Joseph to be a direct descendent of God and therefore directly connected to Osiris, the Lord God of Heaven.

We do not know whether *The Story of Joseph the Just and Aseneth His Wife* is an allegory concerning Jesus and Mary Magdalene. If it is, it seems to indicate clearly that the perpetuation of the pharaonic bloodline is an important element in their union, and that Mary Magdalene was carefully chosen by Jesus to continue the mission he was given by his father.

The Canonical Gospels

Mary Magdalene is referred to by name fourteen times in the four canonical Gospels. She is not mentioned again in Acts or the rest of the New Testament. The first time Mary Magdalene is mentioned is in Luke 8:2:

After this, Jesus travelled about from one town and village to another, proclaiming the good news of the kingdom of God. The Twelve were with him, and also some women who had been cured of evil spirits and diseases: Mary (called Magdalene) from whom seven demons had come out; Joanna the wife of Cuza, the manager of Herod's household; Susanna; and many others. These women were helping to support them out of their own means.

219

In this extract, the author of the Luke Gospel tells us that Mary was among many people, including other women, who travelled with Jesus and his disciples. Apparently, she had been possessed by seven demons, which may indicate that she had been of somewhat fiery spirit and that during her time with Jesus, this spirit was calmed. In this verse from Luke, she is not described as Mary, the wife of Jesus. Rather, she is identified with Magdala her town of origin. This would seem to contradict the idea that she was married to Jesus. However, as we shall see from examination of other texts it is possible that her relationship with Jesus was deliberately played down and maybe even purposely avoided. The author of Luke indicates that these women contributed to the material needs of Jesus and his disciples. Because of this we can assume Mary was wealthy in her own right, which raises questions about where her inherited wealth might have come from.

There is no record of a first meeting between Jesus and Mary but there are times when we can infer that she might have been in Jesus's company even though she is not identified explicitly. One of these is in John 11, which describes the raising of Lazarus, an incident that we have already discussed. Towards the end of this chapter, we are told, "Therefore many of the Jews who came with/ to Mary, and saw what He had done, believed in Him."[177]

The other places where Mary is mentioned by name all occur in the verses describing the events of Jesus's crucifixion, his interment and his resurrection. Many scholars have argued that her close presence during these moments is an indication of her intimate relationship with Jesus and that because of this she must have been Jesus's wife.

Gnostic texts

One part of the Gospel of Philip mentions Mary Magdalene explicitly:

There were three who always walked with the Lord: Mary, his mother, and her sister, and Magdalene, the one

---

177 John 11: 45

who was called his companion. His sister and his mother and his companion were each a Mary.
As for the Wisdom who is called "the barren," she is the mother of the angels. And the companion of the (. . .) Mary Magdalene. (. . .) loved her more than all the disciples, and used to kiss her often on her (. . .). The rest of the disciples (. . .). They said to him "Why do you love her more than all of us?" The Saviour answered and said to them, "Why do I not love you like her? When a blind man and one who sees are both together in darkness, they are no different from one another. When the light comes, then he who sees will see the light, and he who is blind will remain in darkness."

Here we are told that Jesus kissed Mary Magdalene often and it is assumed that the word missing on the parchment that was discovered at Nag Hammadi was mouth or lips. This is not proof that they were man and wife but it is an indication that there was a special bond between them.

In **Pistis Sophia** ("Faith-Wisdom," a group of Gnostic writings from the late third and early fourth centuries), the risen Jesus appears to his closest followers who include Salome, Mary Magdalene, and Thomas. Jesus then invites questions, to which he gives extensive answers. Thirty-nine of the forty-six queries come from the Magdalene. And Jesus is reported as saying, *"Mary Magdalene and John, the virgin, will surpass all my disciples and all men who shall receive mysteries in the Ineffable; they will be on my right hand and on my left, and I am they and they are I . . . ."*
The Gnostic tradition is linked to the ancient Egyptian tradition via the Mother God. In this context, the Gnostics claimed to have knowledge of the link to the Mother God via Mary Magdalene: "One group of Gnostic sources claims to have received a secret tradition from Jesus through James and through Mary Magdalene [who the Gnostics revered as consort to Jesus]. Members of this group prayed to both the divine Father and

221

Greg Rigby

Mother: From thee, Father, and through thee, Mother, the two immortal names, parents of the divine being, and thou, dweller in heaven, humanity, of the mighty name . . . ."[178]

Summary

Mary Magdalene was an important member of Jesus's inner circle. She is Jesus's intimate confidant and companion, one who possesses significant insight into Jesus's teaching that she received directly from him. Some call her the first disciple. There is no direct evidence that she was the wife of Jesus. However, the circumstantial evidence does seem to point to an intimate relationship. Certainly, nothing in any of the texts contradicts that possibility or negates the hypothesis we propose. If the proposals of Jacobovici and Wilson relating to their analysis of the Joseph and Aseneth text are correct, then it would be the only document that directly supports the idea of Jesus being intrinsic to the perpetuation of the sacred pharaonic bloodline.

178 *The Gnostic Gospels*, Elaine Pagels

222

CHAPTER 16

The Offspring of Jesus

The beloved disciple

If Mary Magdalene was the wife of Jesus and they had children, it would not be surprising that these children would have accompanied them on their significant journeys though Palestine, Jordan, Cana (northern Egypt) and Israel. Any son of Jesus most likely would have been a close follower of his, and might well have been referred to in the Gospels.

The most obvious candidate for such a son is the person referred to in John as the beloved disciple and who may have been the one leaning on Jesus's breast at the last supper. The traditional view is that the beloved disciple was John, one of the sons of Zebedee. This view can be traced back to Irenaeus (circa 180 CE) and it was made part of the official Church history in the early fourth century.[179]

Arguments by some learned authors propose that the beloved disciple is John the Elder, and John the son of Zebedee is unlikely since he was a strong-willed and determined personality.

> *Jesus nicknamed him and his brother the sons of Thunder. (Mark 3:17):*
> *"They asked Jesus for permission to call down fire from heaven to consume a village that had not accepted their preaching" (Luke 9:54).* [180]

This proposition is refuted by the bulletin *The Disciple Jesus Loved* published by Andreas Kostenberger and Stephen

---

179 *Church History 6:25*, Eusebius
180 *Jesus and the Eyewitnesses*, Richard Bauckham

O. Stout, who conclude that "even though the reader cannot say with absolute certainty that the author of the Fourth Gospel is the apostle John, the son of Zebedee, because the author does not explicitly provide his name; he certainly leaves more than enough hints to narrow the list."

The beloved disciple is mentioned explicitly five times in John's gospels:

John 13:23-25: One of his disciples, whom Jesus loved, was lying close to the breast of Jesus; so Simon Peter beckoned to him and said, "Tell us who it is of whom he is speaking." So lying thus, close to the breast of Jesus, he said to him, "Lord, who is it?"

John 19:26-27: When Jesus saw his mother, and the disciple whom he loved standing near, he said to his mother, "Woman, behold, your son!" Then he said to the disciple, "Behold, your mother!" And from that hour the disciple took her to his own home.

John 20:2-8: So she [Mary Magdalene] ran, and went to Simon Peter and the other disciple, the one whom Jesus loved, and said to them, "They have taken the Lord out of the tomb, and we do not know where they have laid him." Peter then came out with the other disciple, and they went toward the tomb. They both ran, but the other disciple outran Peter and reached the tomb first; and stooping to look in he saw the linen cloths lying there, but he did not go in. Then Simon Peter came, following him, and went into the tomb. Then the other disciple, who reached the tomb first, also went in.

John 21:7: Therefore, that disciple whom Jesus loved said to Peter, "It is the Lord." So when Simon Peter heard that it was the Lord, he put his outer garment on (for he was stripped for work), and threw himself into the sea.

John 21:20: Peter, turning around, saw the disciple whom Jesus loved following them; the one who also had leaned back on His bosom at the supper and said, "Lord, who is the one who betrays You?"

Whilst he may have done so, it seems unlikely that the author of John's gospel would refer to himself in the third person this way. Additionally, it seems only sensible that if Jesus was going to ask someone to look after his mother, he would ask his eldest son, who would be her grandson.

Whilst the Jewish tradition requires children to honour their father and mother it makes no requirement to look after and/or care for grandparents. This may be the reason that Jesus tells the "disciple he loved" to "behold your mother" and thus induce the sense of obligation that would normally apply to children in relation to their parents.

There is only circumstantial evidence that the disciple whom Jesus loved was Jesus's son. If he was, then the other three Gospels must deliberately exclude him, which would confirm the early Christian pre-disposition towards hiding everything that might have led followers to question their proclamation that Jesus was God incarnate, Son of God Eternal. It might also mean that they had been guided by Jesus to protect his son's identity. Whatever the truth of it, the mentions of the beloved disciple create additional circumstantial evidence of the fact that there existed a bloodline from Jesus and do nothing to invalidate the hypothesis we propose here.

John/Mark

There are no other references in the Gospels to anyone who could be easily identified as Jesus's son or daughter. The only other mysterious young person that could be a contender for the role of Jesus's son is mentioned in the Acts of the Apostles. He is described in the text as John who was called Mark:

> *Acts 12:12, 25: And when he (Peter) realized this, he went to the house of Mary, the mother of John who was also called Mark, where many were gathered together and were praying. And Barnabas and Saul returned from Jerusalem when they had fulfilled their mission, taking along with them John, who was also called Mark.*

225

Greg Rigby

This person is mentioned again in Acts 15:

*Acts 15:**36-39**: After some days Paul said to Barnabas, "Let us return and visit the brethren in every city in which we proclaimed the word of the Lord, and see how they are." Barnabas wanted to take John, called Mark, along with them also. But Paul kept insisting that they should not take him along who had deserted them in Pamphylia and had not gone with them to the work. And there occurred such a sharp disagreement that they separated from one another, and Barnabas took Mark with him and sailed away to Cyprus.*

The verses from the Acts of the Apostles imply that John named Mark was young and needed guardianship.

We can only speculate why someone with one name, would be called another. The fact that this is admitted helps to nullify any reason that is based on keeping his true identity secret unless the author of the verses in Acts knew of the double names but did not know that John, the real name was not supposed to be used.

There has been much speculation concerning the identity of this person and some believe that he is same Mark the cousin of Barnabas mentioned by Paul (Col. 4:10) and (Tim. 4:11). The possibility that this John/Mark is John the beloved is mentioned above. Tradition tells us that Barnabas preached in Alexandria and Rome, and was stoned to death at Salamis about 61 AD. He is considered to have been the founder of the Cypriot Church. There is a Gnostic text entitled *The Acts of Barnabas - The Journeying and Martyrdom of St Barnabas the Apostle,* which purports to be written by John, whose name was changed to Mark. It starts with the following words:

I John, accompanying the holy apostles Barnabas and Paul, being formerly a servant of Cyrillus the high priest of Jupiter, but now having received the gift of the Holy Spirit through Paul and Barnabas and Silas, who

226

were worthy of the calling, and who baptized me in Iconium.

The author also tells us,

And Barnabas urged me also to accompany them, on account of my being their servant from the beginning, and on account of my having served them in all Cyprus until they came to Perga of Pamphylia.

The full text includes an explanation of the journey of Barnabas and John/Mark, describes the hanging of Barnabas by the Jews in Cyprus and culminates with John/Mark's escape to Alexandria where he "preached what he had been taught by the apostles of Christ." If this document is authentic and the words written by the author are true then John/Mark would not be the son of Jesus, neither was he the one who Jesus loved. Given what we are told in this document and in the Book of Acts, we can believe that John/Mark was one of the early evangelists in Alexandria and had significant impact on the formulation of Christian opinion there.

The Lost Gospel

In the allegory *The Story of Joseph the Just and Aseneth His wife*, Joseph and Aseneth in Genesis, the couple had two sons, Ephraim and Manasseh. If the story is meant to tell us about the Jesus and Mary Magdalene marriage, then it is telling us that they had two children. The names of these children were (presumably) changed to protect the document from condemnation, and because of that, it gives us no clue as to the names of any actual children if there were any.

There is no other direct reference to children or young persons identified as offspring of Jesus in the New Testament or in any other documents of that era that we are aware of.

This does not invalidate our hypothesis but it implies that if there were children of Jesus, their existence and their identities were not promoted and they were probably kept hidden. Unless

227

they had been sent away to be educated, it would not have been possible for them have been hidden from the entourage following Jesus. Because of that, if offspring did exist, there must have been a reason why they were not identified.

CHAPTER 17

The Ptolemies

Since our proposition is that Jesus descended from the Ptolemaic dynasty and that his father was Ptolemy XIII, it would be remiss to ignore anyone prominent who lived at the time of the early Christians who boasted Ptolemy as his/her family name. In this context, it my be significant that there were two very prominent individuals with this family name, Ptolemy the Gnostic and Claudius Ptolemy;

Ptolemy the Gnostic

We have no details of the life of this Ptolemy. We know that he was one of the oldest pupils of Valentinus who lived prior to 180 CE. It was through some of the pupils of this Ptolemy that Irenæus became acquainted with the ideas that were developed by the early Gnostics. Whether or not Ptolemy himself was alive when the Presbyter of Lyons wrote the opening chapters of his Refutation, somewhere about 185-195 CE, it is impossible to say.

Only two fragments of the writings of this Ptolemy have been preserved. One is an interpretation of the magnificent Poem of the Beginnings still extant in the Prologue to the fourth canonical Gospel and the other is a letter to a lady called Flora, quoted by Epiphanius.

Irenæus writes the following about Ptolemy: "I intend, then, to the best of my ability, with brevity and clearness to set forth the opinions of those who are now promulgating heresy. I refer especially to the disciples of Ptolemaeus, whose school may be described as a bud from that of Valentinus."

In *Against Heresies* (1.8.5.) he states,

Further, they teach that John, the disciple of the Lord, indicated the first Ogdoad, expressing themselves in these words: John, the disciple of the Lord, wishing to set forth the origin of all things, so as to explain how the Father produced the whole, lays down a certain principle—that, namely, which was first-begotten by God, which Being he has termed both the only-begotten Son and God, in whom the Father, after a seminal manner, brought forth all things. By him the Word was produced, and in him the whole substance of the Aeons, to which the Word himself afterwards imparted form. Since, therefore, he treats of the first origin of things, he rightly proceeds in his teaching from the beginning, that is, from God and the Word. And he expresses himself thus: "In the beginning was the Word, and the Word was with God, and the Word was God; the same was in the beginning with God." [John 1:1-2] Having first of all distinguished these three-Gods, the Beginning and the Word, he again unites them that he may exhibit the production of each of them, that is, of the Son and of the Word, and may at the same time show their union with one another, and with the Father. For "the beginning" is in the Father, and of the Father, while "the Word" is in the beginning, and of the beginning. Very properly, then, did he say, "In the beginning was the Word," for He was in the Son; "and the Word was with God," for He was the beginning; "and the Word was God," of course, for that which is begotten of God is God. "The same was in the beginning with God"—this clause discloses the order of production. "All things were made by Him, and without Him was nothing made," [John 1:3] for the Word was the author of form and beginning to all the Aeons that came into existence after Him. But "what was made in Him," says John, "is life." [John 1:3-4] Here again he indicated conjunction; for all things, he said, were made by Him, but in Him was life. This, then, which is in Him, is more closely connected with Him than those things which were simply made by Him, for it exists along with Him, and is developed by Him. When, again, he adds, "And the life was the light of men," while thus mentioning Anthropos, he indicated also Ecclesia by that one expression, in order that, by using only one name, he might disclose their fellowship with one another, in virtue of their conjunction. For Anthropos and Ecclesia spring from Logos and Zoe. Moreover, he styled life (Zoe) the light of men, because they are enlightened by her, that is, formed and made manifest. This also Paul declares in these words: "For whatsoever doth make manifest is light." [Eph. 5:13] Since, therefore, Zoe manifested and begat both Anthropos and Ecclesia, she is termed their light. Thus, then, did John by these words reveal both other things and the second Tetrad, Logos and Zoe, Anthropos and Ecclesia. And still further, he also indicated the first Tetrad. For, in discoursing of the Saviour and declaring that all things beyond the Pleroma received form from Him, he says that He is the fruit of the entire Pleroma. For He styles Him a "light which shineth in darkness, and which was not comprehended" [John 1:5] by it, inasmuch as, when He imparted form to all those things which had their origin from passion, He was not known by it. He also styles Him Son, and Aletheia, and Zoe, and the "Word made flesh, whose glory," he says, "we beheld; and His glory was as that of the Only-begotten (given to Him by the Father), full of grace and truth." [compare John 1:14] (But what John really does say is this: "And the Word was made flesh, and dwelt among us; and we beheld His glory, the glory as of the only-begotten of the Father, full of grace and truth.") Thus, then, does he [according to them] distinctly set forth the first Tetrad, when he speaks of the Father, and Charis, and Monogenes, and Aletheia. In this way, too, does John tell of the first Ogdoad, and that which is the mother of all the Aeons. For he mentions the Father,

231

and Charis, and Monogenes, and Aletheia, and Logos, and Zoe, and Anthropos, and Ecclesia. Such are the views of Ptolemaeus.

Here we can see that Ptolemy (as quoted) was interested in the relationship between Father and Son and their link to the originating Father in the heavens, thus specifying the divine inheritance. If this person believed that he was a near descendant of Jesus, had been told that he was pretender to the title Son of God (in the heavens) and that his status was to be a living God-king like his father and yet he found himself to be very human, this subject would have been very important. In this context, it is small wonder that attempted to find a rational link to 'God' and to explain this link in the framework of the education he had received and the traditional inheritance of which he believed himself to be a part. There is no proof of any relationship between Ptolemy the Gnostic and Jesus but in the context of our hypothesis, it is worth keeping an open mind.

Irenaeus refers to the views of Ptolemy regarding Jesus being the Son of Man in *Against Heresies 1.12.*

But the followers of Ptolemy say that he [Bythos] has two consorts, which they also name Diatheses (affections), viz., Ennoae and Thelesis. For, as they affirm, he first conceived the thought of producing something, and then willed to that effect. Wherefore, again, these two affections, or powers, Ennoea and Thelesis, having intercourse, as it were, between themselves, the production of Monogenes and Aletheia took place according to conjunction. These two came forth as types and images of the two affections of the Father—visible representations of those that were invisible—Nous (i.e., Monogenes) of Thelesis, and Aletheia of Ennoea, and accordingly the image resulting from Thelesis was masculine, while that from Ennoea was feminine. Thus, Thelesis (will) became, as it were, a faculty of Ennœa (thought). For Ennoea

232

continually yearned after offspring; but she could not of herself bring forth that which she desired. But when the power of Thelesis (the faculty of will) came upon her, then she brought forth that on which she had brooded.

These fancied beings (like the Jove of Homer, who is represented as passing an anxious sleepless night in devising plans for honouring Achilles and destroy-ing numbers of the Greeks) will not appear to you, my dear friend, to be possessed of greater knowledge than He who is the God of the universe. He, as soon as He thinks, also performs what He has willed; and as soon as He wills, also thinks that which He has willed; then thinking when He wills, and then willing when He thinks, since He is all thought, [all will, all mind, all light] 155 all eye, all ear, the one entire fountain of all good things.

Those of them, however, who are deemed more skilful than the persons who have just been mentioned, say that the first Ogdoad was not produced gradually, so that one Aeon was sent forth by another, but that all the Aeons were brought into existence at once by Propator and his Ennoea. He (Colorbasus) affirms this as confidently as if he had assisted at their birth. Accordingly, he and his followers maintain that Anthropos (Adamas) and Eccle-sia were not produced, as others hold, from Logos and Zoe; but, on the contrary, Logos and Zoe from Anthropos and Ecclesia. But they express this in another form, as follows: When the Propator conceived the thought of producing something; he received the name of Father. But because what he did produce was true, it was named Aletheia. Again, when he wished to reveal himself, this was termed Anthropos. Finally, when he produced those whom he had previously thought of, these were named Ecclesia. Anthropos, by speaking, formed Logos: this is the first-born son. But Zoe followed upon Logos; and thus the first Ogdoad was completed.

They have much contention also among themselves respecting the Saviour, for some maintain that he was

Greg Rigby

*formed out of all; wherefore also he was called Eudoce-
tos, because the whole Pleroma was well pleased through
him to glorify the Father. But others assert that he was
produced from those ten Aeons alone who sprung from
Logos and Zoe, and that on this account he was called
Logos and Zoe, thus preserving the ancestral names.
Others, again, affirm that he had his being from those
twelve Aeons who were the offspring of Anthropos and
Ecclesia; and on this account, he acknowledges himself
the Son of man, as being a descendant of Anthropos.
Others still, assert that he was produced by Christ and
the Holy Spirit, who were brought forth for the security
of the Pleroma; and that on this account he was called
Christ, thus preserving the appellation of the Father, by
whom he was produced. And there are yet others among
them who declare that the Propator of the whole, Pro-
arche, and Proanennoetos is called Anthropos; and that
this is the great and abstruse mystery, namely, that the
Power which is above all others, and contains all in his
embrace, is termed Anthropos; hence does the Saviour
style himself the "Son of man."*

Again, we see from third party references that Ptolemy the
Gnostic had been teaching 'gnosis' in relation to the connection
between Jesus and Creator God(s) in the heavens. Interestingly,
the phraseology indicates that the Egyptian belief had become
Hellenised and that it was these Hellenised beliefs that were at
the source of Ptolemy's Gnosticism.

The only direct link to Ptolemy the Gnostic is the letter
he wrote to Flora, which was preserved by Epiphanius in his
work *Against Heresies*, (33.3.1 - 33.7.10), which is duplicated
below.

The Law was ordained through Moses, my dear sister Flora, has not been understood by many persons, who
have accurate knowledge neither of him who ordained it
nor of its commandments. I think that this will be per-

fectly clear to you when you have learned the contradictory opinions about it.

Some say that it is legislation given by God the Father; others, taking the contrary course, maintain stubbornly that it was ordained by the opposite, the Devil who causes destruction, just as they attribute the fashioning of the world to him, saying that he is the Father and maker of this universe. Both are completely in error; they refute each other and neither has reached the truth of the matter.

For it is evident that the Law was not ordained by the perfect God the Father, for it is secondary, being imperfect and in need of completion by another, containing commandments alien to the nature and thought of such a God.

On the other hand, one cannot impute the Law to the injustice of the opposite, God, for it is opposed to injustice. Such persons do not comprehend what was said by the Saviour. *For a house or city divided against itself cannot stand* [Matt 12:25], declared our Saviour. Furthermore, the apostle says that creation of the world is due to him, for *everything was made through him and apart from him nothing was made.* [John 1:3] Thus, he takes away in advance the baseless wisdom of the false accusers, and shows that the creation is not due to a God who corrupts but to the one who is just and hates evil. Only unintelligent men have this idea, men who do not recognize the providence of the creator and have blinded not only the eye of the soul but also of the body.

From what has been said, it is evident that these persons entirely miss the truth; each of the two groups has experienced this, the first because they do not know the God of justice, the second because they do not know the Father of all, who alone was revealed by him who alone came. It reminds for us who have been counted worthy of the knowledge of both these to provide you with an accurate explanation of the nature of the Law and the legislator by whom it was ordained. We shall draw the proofs of what we say from the words of the Saviour, which alone can lead us without error to the comprehension of reality.

First, you must learn that the entire Law contained in the Pentateuch of Moses was not ordained by one legislator—I mean, not by God alone, some commandments are Moses's, and some were given by other men. The words of the Saviour teach us this triple division. The first part must be attributed to God alone, and his legislation; the second to Moses—not in the sense that God legislates through him, but in the sense that Moses gave some legislation under the influence of his own ideas; and the third to the elders of the people, who seem to have ordained some commandments of their own at the beginning. You will now learn how the truth of this theory is proved by the words of the Saviour.

In some discussion with those who dispute with the Saviour about divorce, which was permitted in the Law, he said; *Because of your hard-heartedness Moses permitted a man to divorce his wife; from the beginning it was not so; for God made this marriage, and what the Lord joined together, man must not separate.* [Matt. 19:8] In this way, he shows there is a Law of God, which prohibits the divorce of a wife from a husband, and another law, that of Moses, which permits the breaking of this yoke because of hard-heartedness. In fact, Moses lays down legislation contrary to that of God; for joining is contrary to not joining.

But if we examine the intention of Moses in giving this legislation, it will be seen that he did not give it arbitrarily or of his own accord, but by the necessity because of the weakness of those for whom the legislation was given. Since they were unable to keep the intention of God, according to which it was not lawful for them to reject their wives, with whom some of them disliked to live, and therefore were in the danger of turning to greater injustice and thence to destruction, Moses wanted to remove the cause of dislike, which was placing them in jeopardy of destruction. Therefore because of the critical circumstances, choosing a lesser evil in place of a greater, he ordained, on his own accord, a second law, that of divorce, so that if they could not observe the first, they might keep this and not turn to unjust and evil actions, through which complete destruction would be the result for them. This was his intention when he gave legislation contrary to that of God. Therefore it is indisputable that here the law of Moses is different from the Law of God, even if we have demonstrated the fact from only one example.

The Saviour also makes plain the fact that there are some traditions of the elders interwoven in the Law; *for God*, he says, *Said, Honour your father and your mother, that it may be well with you, But you*, he says addressing the elders, *have declared as a gift to God, that by which you have nullified the Law of God through the tradition of your elders.* Isaiah also proclaimed this, saying, *This people honours me with their lips, but their hearts are far from me, teaching precepts which are the commandments of men.*[Matt. 15:4-9].

Therefore it is obvious that the whole Law is divided into three parts; we find in it the legislation of Moses, of the elders, and of God himself. This division of the entire Law, as made by us, has brought to light what is true in it.

This part, the Law of God himself, is in turn divided into three parts: the pure legislation not mixed with evil, which properly called *Law, which the Saviour came not to destroy but to complete* [Matt. 5:17]—for what he completed was not alien to him but needed completion, for it did not possess perfection; next the legislation interwoven with the inferiority and injustice, which the Saviour destroyed because it was alien to his nature; and finally, the legislation which is allegorical and symbolic, an image of what is spiritual and transcendent, which the

Greg Rigby

Saviour transferred from the perceptible and phenomenal to the spiritual and invisible.

The Law of God, pure and not mixed with inferiority, is the Decalogue, those ten sayings engraved on two tables, forbidding things not to be done and enjoining things to be done. These contain pure but imperfect legislation and required the completion made by the Saviour.

There is also the law interwoven with injustice, laid down for vengeance and the requital of previous injuries, ordaining that an eye should be cut out for an eye, and a tooth for a tooth, and that a murder should be avenged by a murderer. The person who is the second one to be unjust is no less unjust than the first; he simply changes the order of events while performing the same action. Admittedly, this commandment was a just one and still is just, because of the weakness of those for whom the legislation was made so they would not transgress the pure law. But it is alien to the nature and goodness of the Father of all. No doubt it was appropriate to the circumstances, or even necessary; for he who does not want one murder committed, saying, *You shall not kill* and then commanded a murder to be repaid by another murder, has given a second law which enjoins two murders although he had forbidden one. This fact proves that he was unsuspectingly the victim of necessity.

This is why, when his son came, he destroyed this part of the law while admitting that it came from God. He counts this part of the law as in the old religion, not only in other passages but also where he said; *God said, He who curses father or mother shall surely die.*

Finally, there is the allegorical (exemplary) part, ordained in the image of the spiritual and transcendent matters, I mean the part dealing with offerings and circumcision and the Sabbath and fasting and Passover and unleavened bread and other similar matters.

Since all these things are images and symbols, when the truth was made manifest they were translated to another meaning. In their phenomenal appearance and their literal application they were destroyed, but in their spiritual meaning they were restored; the names remained the same but the content was changed. Thus the Saviour commanded us to make offerings not of irrational animals or of the incense of this worldly sort, but of spiritual praise and glorification and thanksgiving and of sharing and well-doing with our neighbours. He wanted us to be circumcised, not in regard to our physical foreskin but in regard to our spiritual heart; to keep the Sabbath, for he wishes us to be idle in regard to evil works; to fast, not in physical fasting but in spiritual, in which there is abstinence from everything evil.

Among us external fasting is also observed, since it can be advantageous to the soul if it is done reasonably, not for imitating others or from habit or because of a special day appointed for this purpose. It is also observed so that those who are not yet able to keep the true fast may have a reminder of it from the external fast. Similarly, Paul the apostle shows that the Passover and the unleavened bread are images when he says; *Christ our Passover has been sacrificed, in order that you may be unleavened bread, not containing leaven (by leaven he here means evil), but may be a new lump.* [1 Cor 5:7]

Thus the Law of God itself is obviously divided into three parts. The first was completed by the Saviour, for the commandment, *You shall not kill, You shall not commit adultery, you shall not swear falsely* are included in the forbidding of anger, desire and swearing. The second part was entirely destroyed, for *an eye for an eye and a tooth for a tooth* interwoven in with injustice, was destroyed by the Saviour through its opposite. Opposites cancel out, *For I say to you, do not resist the evil man, but if anyone strikes you, turn the other cheek to him.*

239

Finally, there is the part translated and changed from the literal to the spiritual, this symbolic legislation which is an image of transcendent things. For the images and symbols which represent other things were good as long as the Truth has not come; but since the Truth has come, we must perform the actions of the Truth, not those of the image. The disciples of the Saviour and the Apostle Paul showed that this theory is true, speaking of the part dealing with images, as we have already said, in mentioning *The Passover for us* and the *Unleavened bread*; for the law interwoven with injustice when he says that *the law of commandments in ordinances were destroyed* [Eph 2:15]; and of that not mixed with anything inferior when he says that *The law is holy, and the commandment is holy and just and good* [Rom 7:12]. I think I have shown you sufficiently, as well as one can in brief compass, the addition of human legislation in the Law and the triple division of the Law of God itself.

It remains for us to say who this God is who ordained the Law; but I think this too has been shown you in what we have already said, if you have listened to it attentively.

For if the Law was not ordained by the perfect God himself, as we have already thought you, nor by the devil, a statement one cannot possibly make, the legislator must be someone other than these two. In fact, He is the demiurge and maker of this universe and everything in it; and because he is essentially different from these two and is between them, he is rightly given the name, *intermediate*.

And if the perfect God is good by nature, in fact he is, for our Saviour declared that there is only a single good God, his Father whom he manifested; and if the one who is the opposite nature is evil and wicked, characterized by injustice; then the one situated between the two is neither good nor evil or unjust, but can properly be called just, since he is the arbitrator of the justice which is his.

On the one hand, this god will be inferior to the perfect God and the lower than his justice, since he is generated and not un-generated—there is only one un-generated Father, from whom are all things [1 Cor 8:6], since all things depend on him in their own ways. On the other hand, he will be greater and more powerful than the adversary, by nature, since he has a substance of either of them. The substance of the adversary is corruption and darkness, for he is material and complex, while the substance of the un-generated Father of all is in corruption and self-existent light, simple and homogeneous. The substance of the latter produced a double power, while the Saviour is an image of the greater one.

And now, do not let this trouble you for the present in your desire to learn how from one first principle of all, simple, and acknowledged by us and believed by us, un-generated and incorruptible and good, were constituted these natures of corruption and the Middle, which are different substances, although it is characteristic of the good to generate and produce things which are like itself and have the same substance.

For, if God permit, you will later learn about their origin and generation, when you are judged worthy of the apostolic tradition which we too have received by succession. We too are able to prove all our points by the teaching of the Saviour.

In making these brief statements to you, my sister Flora, I have not grown weary; and while I have treated the subject with brevity, I have also discussed it sufficiency. These points will be of great benefit to you in the future, if like fair and good ground you have received fertile seeds and go on to show forth their fruit.

Whilst we know that Irenaeus obtained information from disciples of Ptolemy the Gnostic and that this fact dates Ptolemy to be earlier that 180 CE and probably nearer 150 CE, this letter to Flora indicates clearly that Ptolemy the Gnostic was not alive at the time of Jesus since he quotes the Gospels and the Epistles by chapter and verse. His letter must therefore have been written at a time when such references had become known and standard in the Christian world. In the letter to Flora, he shows that family, in the sense of husband, wife and offspring are important to him, and he justifies Jesus's authority to pronounce on law in the sense of social regulation.

At best, Ptolemy the Gnostic was a descendant of Jesus, (in relation to the hypothesis we propose) at worst he was a follower of the Gnostics that existed alongside but separate from the Pauline Christian movement.

There are several significant (but circumstantial) elements to these works, which perhaps can assist us in our quest to establish a lineage from Jesus:

1. The fact that Irenaeus quotes Ptolemy as he does indicates that Ptolemy was a respected figure in the Christian world, and his teaching carried weight. Irenaeus even tells us that Ptolemy had followers or disciples.
2. The Gnostic teachings of Ptolemy the Gnostic seem to mirror those in the Gospel of Mary Magdalene.
3. In the letter to Ruth, Ptolemy claims that he had received the apostolic tradition by succession. This may refer to his being appointed as a bishop and that the hands-on ceremony involved was interpreted as passing the apostolic tradition by succession. Alternatively, it could relate to Ptolemy claiming a genealogical succession.

We cannot claim that a bloodline from Jesus existed or that it included Ptolemy the Gnostic. The only thing that we can say, based on the minimum evidence available, is that it is possible.

Claudius Ptolemy

Claudius Ptolemy (c. 85-165 CE) was a Greco-Egyptian writer known as a mathematician, astronomer, geographer and astrologer. He lived in the city of Alexandria in the Roman province of Egypt, where he wrote in Greek, but held Roman citizenship. Beyond that, few reliable details of his life are known. His birthplace has been given as *Ptolemais Hermiou* in the Thebaid (the South of Egypt stretching from Abydos to Aswan) in an uncorroborated statement by the fourteenth century astronomer Theodore Meliteniotes. One of his teachers is believed to have been Theon of Smyrna.

The ninth-century Persian astronomer Abu Ma'shar assumed Ptolemy to be a member of Egypt's royal lineage, stating that the ten kings of Egypt who followed Alexander were wise "and included Ptolemy the Wise, who composed the book of the *Almagest*." Ptolemy's several great works are discussed below.

The Almagest

This document is a critical source of information on ancient Greek astronomy and is one of the most influential scientific works in history. It has also been valuable to students of mathematics because it documents the ancient Greek mathematician Hipparchus's work, which has been lost. Hipparchus wrote about trigonometry, but because his works no longer exist, mathematicians use Ptolemy's book as their source for Hipparchus's work and ancient Greek trigonometry in general. Ptolemy increased the number of stars mapped from Hipparchus's 850 to 1022. This probably means that he had access to records maintained in secret by astronomer-priests brought up in the Egyptian tradition. In this work, he includes the following poem.

I know that I am mortal by nature, and ephemeral;
but when I trace at my pleasure the windings to and fro
of the heavenly bodies, I no longer touch the earth with
my feet: I stand in the presence of Zeus himself and take
my fill of ambrosia.

In the text, Ptolemy states that the kind of science that seeks after Him (God) is the theological, for such an act can only be thought of as high above the loftiest things of the universe and is absolutely apart from sensible things. But the kind of science that traces through the material and ever moving quality, and has to do with the white, the hot, the sweet, the soft, and such things, would be called physical; and such an essence since it is only generally what it is, is to be found in corruptible things and below the lunar sphere. And the kind of science that shows up quality with respect to forms and local motions, seeking figure, number, and magnitude, and also place, time, and similar things, would be defined as mathematical. Betraying how his beliefs are akin to the ancient Egyptian tradition, he says in chapter two,

> *"Whatever is beyond this is fixed and immovable, and the professors of our orthodox faith affirm it to be the empyrean heaven which GOD inhabits with the elect."*

To have written the *Almagest*, Ptolemy would need to have been immersed in learning from an early age. His tutors would have been astronomer priests and since he lived and worked in Alexandria, we can assume that they would have been Egyptian. This would fit well with the idea that a son of Jesus would have been sent away to be educated, at an early age.

The Geography
This is a treatise on cartography and a compilation of what was known about the world's geography in the Roman Empire of the second century. Ptolemy relied mainly on the work of an earlier geographer, Marinos of Tyre, and on gazetteers of the Roman and ancient Persian Empires. As with the model of the solar system in the *Almagest*, Ptolemy put all this information into a grand scheme. He assigned latitude and longitude coordinates to all the places and geographic features he knew, in a grid that spanned the globe. Latitude was measured from the equator, as it is today, but Ptolemy preferred to express it as the length of the longest day rather than degrees of arc (the length of the Midsummer Day increases from twelve hours to twenty-four as one goes from the equator to the polar circle). He put the meridian of zero longitude at the westernmost land he knew, El Hierro—one

of the Canary Islands. He illustrated the Earth to be spherical, albeit that this view did not become the established view until many centuries later. His work was probably the foundation of cartography as we know it today.

However, nothing obvious in this work alludes to links with Jesus or indicates Ptolemy's belief system.

The Apotelesmatika or Tetrabiblos

This work, written in four parts, is his third work. It is an astrological treatise in which he attempted to adapt horoscopy to the Aristotelian natural philosophy of his day. He quotes the signs of the zodiac as used by Egyptians and Chaldeans, and makes claims for the benefit of astrology. His summary states:

> *In somewhat summary fashion, it has been shown how prognostication by astronomical means is possible, and that it can go no further than what happens in the ambient and the consequences to man from such causes—that is, it concerns the original endowments of faculties and activities of soul and body, their occasional diseases, their endurance for a long or a short time, and, besides, all external circumstances that have a directive and natural connection with the original gifts of nature, such as property and marriage in the case of the body and honour and dignities in that of the soul, and finally what befalls them from time to time. The remaining part of our project would be to inquire briefly as to its usefulness, first distinguishing how and with what end in view we shall take the meaning of the word usefulness. For if we look to the goods of the soul, what could be more conducive to well-being, pleasure, and in general satisfaction than this kind of forecast, by which we gain full view of things human and divine? And if we look to bodily goods, such knowledge, better than anything else, would perceive what is fitting and expedient for the capabilities of each temperament. But if it does not aid in the acquisition of riches, fame, and the like, we shall be able to say the same of all*

philosophy, for it does not provide any of these things as far as its own powers are concerned. We should not, however, for that reason be justified in condemning either philosophy or this art, disregarding its greater advantages.

Nothing in this work throws any light on the hypothesis we are investigating or on the possibility that Claudius Ptolemy was a descendant of Jesus.

Optics

This work only survives in a poor Arabic translation and in about twenty manuscripts of a Latin version of the Arabic, which was translated by Eugene of Palermo (c. 1154). In it Ptolemy writes about the properties of light, including reflection, refraction, and colour.

The work is a significant part of the early history of optics and influenced the more famous eleventh century *Optics* by Alhazen (Ibn al-Haytham). It contains the earliest surviving table of refraction from air to water, for which the values (with the exception of the 60° angle of incidence), although historically praised as experimentally derived, appear to have been obtained from an arithmetic progression. It is the work of someone dedicated to learning the workings of this important aspect of the human body and indicates the prodigious self-imposed variety of subjects that Ptolemy studied and wrote about. It throws no light on Ptolemy's family tree.

Ptolemy's Harmonics

This was an influential work on music theory and the mathematics of music. In it, he showed how musical notes could be translated into mathematical equations and vice versa. This is called Pythagorean tuning because it was first discovered by Pythagoras. However, Pythagoras believed that the mathematics of music should be based on the specific ratio of 3:2, whereas Ptolemy merely believed that it should just generally involve tetra chords and octaves. He presented his own divisions of the tetra chord and the octave, which he derived with the help of a monochord. Ptolemy's astronomical interests also appeared in a discussion of the music of the spheres wherein he defined his diatonic scale.

This prolific philosopher was born in the first century and attempted to provide answers to everything affecting the human spirit. His work espoused a unique view of reality and an appreciation of all things complex and mysterious. In the rhyme, which he includes in *Almagest*, he talks of someone human who studies the heavens and its movements and who finds himself elevated into the presence of God.

If Jesus did have children, it is not difficult to imagine that he would have had them educated in the way that he himself had been educated.

Within the overall hypothesis that we propose, Ptolemy XIII would have ensured that Jesus spent time studying the overlapping Hellenic and Egyptian religious as well as Pharaonic traditions and the links to the stars in the heavens. This area of learning, which had been at the centre of the Egyptian religious tradition for millennia, was at the core of all contemporary belief systems. Ptolemy's predisposition to a body of Egyptian knowledge is confirmed in Chapter 3, Book 1 of the Tetrabiblos:

> *"Of this, the Ægyptians seem to have been well aware; their discoveries of the great faculties of this science have exceeded those of other nations, and they have in all cases combined the medical art with astronomical prognostication."*

We can assume that the children and grandchildren of Jesus would have developed an in-depth appreciation and interest in all the subjects addressed by Claudius Ptolemy. If he was Jesus's son, he would not have been able to his true identity or his relationship to the Ptolemaic genealogical tree but that did not stop him from studying the meaning of these things.

It is easy to imagine that any progeny of the Jesus (and therefore Ptolemaic) bloodline had been informed by their parents that they were in the divine line and even that they were in fact gods on earth, with links back to Osiris. At the same time, there would have been nothing godlike in their everyday existence other than their philosophical imaginings as they asked themselves fundamental questions about the earth, the stars and science (mathematics), and as they attempted to rationalise the messages they had received from parents with the conflicting scientific evidence. There is nothing, other than his name, to link Claudius Ptolemy to Ptolemy XIII. What can be said of him is that his work and publications created a meaningful and lasting legacy in the field of science and betrayed a philosopher as eminent as any that succeeded him.

There is no direct evidence Claudius Ptolemy was a descendent of Jesus. Strangely, however, given that we have here two very prominent individuals, there is no evidence of any kind about family or progeny of him or of Ptolemy the Gnostic. The fact that they were both known by the name Ptolemy is the only link available to us.

All we can say is that there is a possibility (given our general hypothesis) that these men were descended from Jesus and that there is no information available to tell us that this is not possible.

There were other less famous people with the name Ptolemy in the early Christian era. The information we have regarding these individuals is detailed below.

Ptolemy (Acts of Peter)

This a character mentioned in the Acts of Peter, who was a rich man trying to marry the daughter of Peter. The Acts of Peter tells us,

> *Ptolemaeus, unable to win the maiden by fair means, comes and carries her off. Peter hears of it and prays to God to protect her. His prayer is heard. She is struck with palsy on one side of her body. (Then the text resumes.) "The servants of Ptolemaeus brought the maiden and laid her down before the door of the house and departed.*

*But when I perceived it, I and her mother, we went
down and found the maiden, that one whole side of her
body from her toes even to her head was palsied and
withered: and we bore her away, praising the Lord which
had preserved his handmaid from defilement and shame
and (corruption?). This is the cause of the matter, why
the maiden continueth so unto this day.*

*Now, then, it is fitting for you to know the end of
Ptolemaeus. He went home and sorrowed night and day
over that which had befallen him, and by reason of the
many tears which he shed, he became blind. And when
he had resolved to rise up and hang himself, lo, about
the ninth hour of the day, he saw a great light which
enlightened the whole house, and heard a voice saying
unto him: Ptolemaeus, God hath not given thee the ves-
sels for corruption and shame, and yet more doth it not
become thee which hast believed in me to defile my virgin, whom thou shalt know as thy sister, even as if I were
unto you both one spirit (sic). But rise up and go quickly
unto the house of the apostle Peter, and thou shalt see my
glory; he shall make known unto thee what thou must do.*

*But Ptolemaeus was not negligent, and bade his ser-
vants show him the way and bring him unto me.*

*And when they were come to me, he told me all that
had befallen him by the power of our Lord Jesus Christ.
Then did he (Ptolemaeus) see with the eyes of his flesh,
and with the eyes of his soul, and many people believed
(hoped) in Christ: and he/it did them good and (it)
gave them the gift of God. Thereafter Ptolemaeus died,
departing out of this life, and (he) went unto his Lord.*

Earlier in the paragraph, this Ptolemy is described as wealthy,
but any son of Mary Magdalene and Jesus would probably have
inherited Mary Magdalene's wealth and could therefore have
been described thus. However, if Peter had believed this person
to be the Son of Jesus he would surely have said that he went
unto the Lord or our Lord as he does in the previous sentence.

249

Greg Rigby

This is perhaps semantics but there is little in the short reference to this Ptolemy that provides any clue about his parentage. It is unlikely that this person was related to Jesus.

Ptolemaeus Chennus (Hephaestion)

This Ptolemy from the second century CE was a grammarian who lived in the Greek culture of Roman Egypt. He wrote a series of imaginative but fictional stories based on the classical Greek personalities and heroes in ways that are "free of things impossible to believe, which offer knowledge above the ordinary, but which is not unpleasing."

Nothing in these stories in any way links the author to our hypothesis.

Ptolemaeus and Lucius

These two individuals were Christian martyrs. We know little about this Ptolemy, but in the Second Apology of St Justin Martyr, we are told the following:

> *And her quondam husband, since he was now no longer able to prosecute her, directed his assaults against a man, Ptolemæus, whom Urbicus punished, and who had been her teacher in the Christian doctrines. And this he did in the following way. He persuaded a centurion—who had cast Ptolemæus into prison, and who was friendly to himself—to take Ptolemæus and interrogate him on this sole point: whether he were a Christian? And Ptolemæus, being a lover of truth, and not of a deceitful or false disposition, when he confessed himself to be a Christian, was bound by the centurion, and for a long time punished in the prison. And, at last, when the man came to Urbicus, he was asked this one question only: whether he was a Christian. And again, being conscious of his duty, and the nobility of it through the teaching of Christ, he confessed his discipleship in the divine virtue.[181]*

---

181 *New Advent* article, Kevin Knight

250

Nothing here or elsewhere connects this person to Jesus other than the fact that he was a Christian.

Having examined all of the above references to persons names Ptolemy, we are confident that any family connection to Jesus via the name Ptolemy cannot be authenticated. Despite that, the fact that we have no knowledge of any family connections to the various Ptolemies in the early Christian era does not mean that a link can be ruled out.

At the same time, since it is our contention that the bloodline is important, one would expect any direct descendant of Jesus to be married and to produce children. There is no mention of wives or children in any historical literature covering the Ptolemies listed above.

To find direct evidence of a bloodline without someone making a statement that proposes or supports this notion is impossible. The best than can be found is weak circumstantial evidence from a time when any such evidence would be suppressed at worst and downplayed at best. In that context, the best that can be said about the information we have about the Ptolemies in the early Christian period is that it does not eliminate the possibility of one or more of them being pretenders to the Ptolemaic crown but that there is no positive evidence to support it.

CHAPTER 18

The Bloodline

Without DNA from someone close to Ptolemy XIII and matching DNA from someone living more recently, it would be difficult to prove a connection back to Ptolemy XIII. Even if such a link could be found, it would be impossible to place Jesus in the chain unless some of his remains could be authenticated and placed in the same line. For this reason, we can only rely on circumstantial evidence to support our hypothesis.

In 1972 and 1974, the BBC broadcast a series of programmes hosted by Henry Lincoln that focussed on the village of Rênnes-le-Chateau in the South of France and the antics of its curé Bérenger Saunière, the resident parish priest from 1885 until January 1917. In 1891, this priest is said to have carried out some refurbishment of the church and found coded documents hidden in the altar, which he then took to learned people locally and in Paris. These documents were difficult to interpret but they referred to Dagobert II, a Merovingian king who was assassinated in 679 CE. In the years following his discovery, Saunière spent the equivalent of several million pounds, which some believe was part of a hidden Templar treasure. Anyone visiting this small hilltop village today will still find a stream of treasure seekers wandering around with their metal detectors, looking for the same hidden treasure.

Following the TV broadcasts, Henry Lincoln was inundated with information from a variety of sources, some of which added a new and enthralling dimension to the Rênnes-le-Chateau story. Based on this information, Henry Lincoln joined forces with Michael Bagient and Richard Leigh, and together they investigated the additional information they had received and the places and the people they were pointed towards. In particular, they were directed towards a file named *Dossiers Secret*s in the Bibliotèque Nationale in Paris and an elusive figure named Pierre Plantard. This file alluded to an organisation called the *Prieuré de Sion* whose purpose was to reinstate descendants of the Merovingian bloodline onto the French throne. The results of their research was published in 1982 in a book entitled *The Holy Blood and The Holy Grail* and it listed as the Grand Masters of the *Prieuré de Sion* from 1133 which included such well-known names as Leonardo DaVinci, Robert Boyle, Isaac Newton, Victor Hugo, Claude Debussy and Jean Cocteau. The book exposes secret claims that the Merovingian bloodline came from Jesus and Mary Magdalene and that the *Prieuré de Sion* existed to protect the bloodline. In 2012, a novel was published by Dan Brown entitled *The DaVinci Code,* which was subsequently turned into a successful movie. The story was concocted around many of the ingredients published in *The Holy Blood and The Holy Grail*—i.e. that there is a secret bloodline from Jesus and Mary Magdalene.

Early in 2015, Henry Lincoln was interviewed for a television documentary, and during the programme, he stated that Pierre Plantard had admitted to him before he died that the documents in the *Bibliotech Nationale* were a hoax. This may well be true, but it is thought by some that this retraction of his former assertion may itself have been misleading, and that it may have been made in order to take all the now baying bloodhounds off the scent of the real truth. Certain things we do know: a Merovingian bloodline started with Merovée or Merovech in the fifth century CE. This Frankish king's routes are shrouded in mystery. Gregory of Tours (538-594 CE) is the famous historian of the period, and we are told of his writings:

> Gregory's ambiguous sentence giving Merovech as "of the race of Clodio, according to some" has been much discussed. Many admit today that this formulation finds its explanation in a legend reported by Fredegar:

Greg Rigby

Merovech would not be the son of Clodio but of a mari-
time monster that had relations with his mother, Clodio's
wife. In this case, one can obviously accept the filiation
between Merovech and Clodio.[182]

In this account, Clodio (c 392-448 CE) is presented as
someone similar to Joseph the Carpenter in that his wife is
impregnated by a mysterious supernatural being. He was a king
of the Salien Franks and was known as the Long-Haired King.
He is believed to have lived in Thuringian territory, at the castle
of Duisberg. His father is said to have been another mysterious
and legendary figure, named Pharamond. Some modern scholars claim that he in turn was the son of Marcomer who is also
known as Marcomir VI, a descendent of King Priam Podarces
of Troy by Priam's son Helenus from whom the Kings of Cim-
merian Bosporus descend.[183]

Nothing in historical records links the Merovingian dynasty
to Jesus. In *The Holy Blood and the Holy Grail*, the authors
suggest that the Holy Grail could be linked in some way to
the mystery. Specifically, they tell us, "In many of the earlier
manuscripts, the Grail is called Sangraal, and even in later versions by Malory, it is called Sangreal. It is likely that some such
form—Sangraal or Sangreal—was in fact the original one. It
is also likely that the one word was subsequently broken in the
wrong place. In other words, Sangraal or Sangreal may not have
been intended to divide into San Graal or San Greal—but into
Sang Raal or Sang Real—or, to employ the modern spelling,
Sang Royal, or Royal Blood."

In Chapter 15, they go on to say, "If our hypothesis is correct, the Holy Grail would have been two things simultaneously.
On the one hand it would have been Jesus's bloodline and
descendants—the Sang Raal, the Real or Royal blood of which
the Templers, created by the Prieuré de Sion, were appointed
guardians. At the same time, the Holy Grail would have been
quite literally the receptacle or vessel that received and con-

---

182 *Clovis*, Godefroy Kurth
183 *The Franks*, Edward James

254

tained Jesus's blood. In other words, it would have been the womb of Magdalene—and by extension the Magdalene herself."

Since we have no factual evidence to go on, we are forced to resort to an analysis of myths and legends, and there is good reason to believe that the Holy Grail is a good subject for such examination. In our previous work,[184] we showed a conclusive link between the Egyptian Mysteries, the Grail legends, The Tarot (which is thought to have originated in Egypt) and the Book of Revelation. The grail is normally presented as an elusive cup or vessel that was used by Jesus at the Last Supper and has never been found. This characterization has been transmitted through history and stood the test of time. The phrase Holy Grail by consequence has come to mean the secret revelation, the answer, the pot of gold at the end of some hidden rainbow.

The first Grail story, *Le Conte de Graal* was written by Chrétien de Troyes between 1170 and 1190 AD. It was written following visits to Jerusalem by the founders of the Knights Templar. Perhaps significantly, there is strong circumstantial evidence indicating that during their early expeditions to the Holy Land these same French nobles came upon a cache of information, which was the source of the power and their subsequent downfall. The same persons assisted in the foundation of the Cistercian order of Christian monks who over the following century built more than 300 abbeys and monasteries and propelled the commencement of the construction of the many Gothic cathedrals that still exist today.

Seven variations of Grail stories were written by other authors between 1190 and 1220 AD. Fifteen years after the emergence of the unfinished *Conte du Graal,* Wolfram von Eschenbach published *Parzival.* In the epilogue, he claimed that Chrétien had failed to do justice to a tale that already existed. By way of explanation, he claimed that the original legend came from an Arabic manuscript discovered by a "master," Kyot in Toledo, Spain. Kyot in turn spoke of Flegetanis—a "king of old time" who "could read the heavens high":

---

184 *The God Secret*, Greg Rigby

"He read the stars and strange secrets he saw, and he spake again low with bated breath and fearful, of the thing that is called the Grail. In a cluster of stars was it written, the name nor their lore shall fail."

Key symbols in the grail romances are the grail itself, whether cup or dish, the lance, the sword and the stone. These same symbols are the four suits of the tarot cards: cup, wand or lance, sword and pentacle. The ace of each of these suits in the enigmatic Smith-Rider-Waite tarot deck duplicates the star pattern around the Ursa Major constellation at one of the equinoxes or the solstices. The Book of Revelation, which contains the phrase "the mystery of the seven stars," also features a cup/bowl/vessel, a tree/spear, a stone and a sword, forging a connection between the grail romances, the tarot and the Book of Revelation, which is the constellation of Ursa Major. This final book of the New Testament talks about "a throne set in heaven, and around the throne four living creatures before and behind. And the living creature the first like (to) a lion, and the second living creature like (to) a calf, and the third living creature having the face as of a man, and the fourth living creature like (to) an eagle flying."

The Gematria (numerical value) of this phrase is 25920, which is the length of the precessional circle of the poles in terms of the number of earth years it takes to be completed. The Ursa Major constellation becomes oriented to create each of the pictures mentioned in the above verse—the lion, the calf, the face of a man and an eagle flying—at the summer solstice position on each of the four quarters of this 25,920-year precessional circle (Fig. 19). In so doing, the Ursa Major constellation and its appearance in the Heavens becomes the link between the Ancient Egyptian home of its god(s) and the one sitting on the throne in the enigmatic Book of Revelation.

Ursa Major was the home of Osiris in all his aspects and was the place where all the god-kings would return when the departed their lives on earth. This place was Heaven and consisted of the imperishable stars in Ursa Major that rotated around the northern pole position without setting.

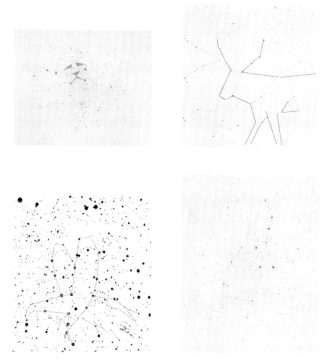

**Fig 19 The lion, the calf, the face of a man
and the eagle in Ursa Major**

The bloodline that the Egyptian Kings shared was their direct link to Osiris and it was that that gave them the claim to the title Son of God. Because of that, if Jesus was in fact the son of Ptolemy XIII and, more importantly, was directly (through his mother) in this lineage, he would have been educated by his father to do all that he could to protect that bloodline. He would then have ensured that the importance of its protection was passed on to his children.

The Egyptians believed their pharaoh to be a god-king who was the mediator between the gods and the world of men. He was named Son of God. After death, the pharaoh became truly divine by joining with Osiris, the father of Horus and God of the dead. At his passing, he passed on his sacred powers and position to the new pharaoh, his son. As a divine ruler, the pha-raoh was the preserver of the god-given order, called Ma'at. We

257

cannot be sure what the Pharaohs believed of themselves and of the authenticity of their connection with the gods. They must have known that they were human but the indoctrination they received might well have convinced them of their divine status and that they would rise to be with Osiris in Heaven.

It is entirely possible that Jesus and his kin were educated in such a way (by their parents and priests who had been approved by their parents) that they too believed they were divine and would return to heaven to join God the Father. They most likely considered themselves superior and privileged, and felt condescension toward the rest of humanity. That being the case, any descendants of Jesus would either have believed in their status but kept it to themselves or would have asserted themselves and their beliefs in ways they felt to be appropriate. At the same time, they would have needed to balance the danger of their identity becoming known against the loss of credibility brought on by servility and/or anonymity.

If a descendant of Jesus was a low profile individual, he probably would have been judged as weird by his contemporaries and would of necessity lived in a detached manner. This is an unlikely scenario, since this person would have realised that to teach his own children of their inherited dominion would have been almost impossible if they could not witness it in their father.

The second of these two options, that they have asserted themselves, seems to be the more likely. This does not mean that they had to be kings or prominent historical figures, but it does imply that they had a prestigious role within their own community. They would have been educated to a higher standard than most, thus feeling free to be judgmental. They may even have felt it appropriate to encourage a body of supporters or a movement that would be obliged to keep their identity secret (if they knew it) but that would support and protect them. This approach mirror's the approach of Jesus himself.

If Jesus did have children and he was the legitimate heir to the throne of the Egyptian line of god-kings, there does appear to be a contradiction to his approach. The Egyptian tradition was that the king's offspring took the throne. In Jesus's case, he delegated the leadership of the movement he had started to one of his disciples. His children, if there were any, were kept hidden and were not involved. This is perhaps understandable given Ptolemy XIII's history of being pursued and persecuted, and of the reactions that Jesus provoked from Roman and Hebrew authorities to his own limited attempts to make known his identity.

However, it is difficult to believe that Jesus taught any children to be anonymous in the long term, and he perhaps hoped that the movement he had started would engender a culture under whose protection his descendants could re-assert their divine authority. He would not have anticipated that the early development of the Church would have been affected by the interloper Paul in the manner it was and that the Church would become a body that would never be able to admit Jesus's identity without destroying itself in the process.

The Jewish, Christian and later Muslim theologies successfully replaced the religious traditions and beliefs of the Egyptians, the Greeks and eventually the Romans. The Christians became invincible by basing their movement on the fact that their founder had been the incarnate and eternal Son of God who had taken human form. At the same time, they had removed the home of God the Father from a physical location in the heavens to a mysterious, wonderful and unseen place called heaven. The appearance of someone claiming to be the Son of God based on a bloodline from Osiris (via Jesus) would have immediately demolished the philosophical structure upon which the Church had been constructed.

If there was a protected bloodline and a series of generations in which young offspring were taught of their divine inheritance, then one can only surmise that some amongst them might well have made moves towards the long-term re-establishment of themselves and their own descendants in the role of god-king. With each generation, this would have been more difficult as the advance of science made their claims seem less and less credible. There would of course have been cause for optimism created by their observations that human beings never cease to be gullible and that in one form or another, we cling to a variety of religious concepts and occultist ideas to give us answers to the unknown.

For that reason, any success they achieved would have been in a role that encouraged ritual affirmation to a core set of beliefs.

The most obvious role in which Jesus's descendants might have asserted themselves would be to get control of the monarchy of the country or countries where they had influence. In such circumstances, they would have been monarchs who imposed a strong religious ethos as part of their reign. There have been many instances of religious leaders also being kings/rulers during the last two thousand years:

- Certain leaders of Muslim countries have been imams, or have ruled with the leading religious person of the country concerned as their appointee.
- For millennia, the pope effectively controlled the appointment of monarchs in many of the Christian nations of Europe.
- Several popes such as the Borgia have ruled Italy or parts of Italy.
- A succession of kings and queens of England became the self-appointed heads of the Church of England.

It may be, for instance, that the Christian King Merovée, the founder of the Merovingian dynasty in the fifth century CE, was of the royal bloodline. There is no evidence for this, and there are many other rulers of countries in Europe and the Middle East into which Jesus's family might have emigrated and who had historical kings who could just as easily have been the god-king we are looking for.

At the same time, European history is swamped with stories of battles between conflicting pretenders to the throne as prominent individuals strove to introduce, impose or retain a ruling Christian dynasty. These have largely been eliminated by the emergence of democracy and by nations separating the inter-relationship between church and state.

Since the eighth century, Islam has continued to expand its influence into many countries under the guidance of a large number of local imams. If the movement were being directed centrally, we may have been tempted to ask if it was being orchestrated in favour of an objective of the person in control. As it is not, then it can be eliminated as a place from whence descendants of Jesus might be operating.

Other movements that emerged and had influence in the second millennium include the very powerful Knights Templar, established following the discovery of a secret cache of information by a small band of French Nobles during the first the first crusade (1096—1099 CE) and on a subsequent visit in 1104 CE. The Order of the Knights Templar was dissolved by Pope Clement V in 1312 CE and was prosecuted out of existence in France where many of its most prominent members were executed. The Order of Freemasonry appeared in the wake of the Templars' elimination. It was probably created by Templar officials who left France to escape persecution.

Freemasonry is still thriving in those countries whose institutions were established by European invaders and colonists. Grand Lodges and Grand Orients are independent and sovereign bodies that govern Freemasonry in an individual country or geographic area. No ruling body presides over the independent Grand Lodges, albeit the United States has more members than any other Grand Lodge.

The Freemasonry movement is an obvious candidate as one that protects an ancient Egyptian tradition as it has a secret agenda and openly uses ceremonies and monograms that stem directly from that tradition:

- The five-pointed star from its resting place in the cup of Ursa Major
- The eye which replicates the eye of Ra
- Seven stars
- Gods in the sun and the moon
- The columns that are the portals to the temple

The only symbol or item that is common to the Freemasons and the grail quest is the elusive five-pointed star, referred to in Parzival as the stone.

Fourteen US Presidents have openly declared themselves Masons, including Harry Truman and Gerald Ford. Others (such as George W Bush and G W Bush) are accused of being members without any direct evidence. Additionally, it is acknowledged that there are a large number of Freemasons in all levels of the US administration and of the governments of most other Western democracies. This membership is supplemented by influencers in all the other key elements of each country's infrastructure and includes bankers, judges and law enforcement officials.

It is difficult to know what influence these Masons (as a body) have on the people of the free world. One would suspect that any government official who comes from a selected elite and who separates him or herself from ordinary citizens is more likely to be attuned to this group than are incumbents who arrive from a more plebeian background. It is for this reason that a series of conspiracy theories have grown up related to the Free-masons' interests and objectives, especially in relation to them wanting to establish a New World Order.

Jim Shaw gives us a glimpse into the mindset of those involved in Freemasonry. He was awarded the thirty-third degree of Freemasonry and later left the movement. He states that whenever he was asked, "Of what religion are you?" he had always answered, "I believe the Ancient Mysteries, the Old Religion, and I believe in reincarnation." When he decided to leave the Freemasons, he thought *I will never return*. With each step, his thoughts repeated, *I will never return. I will never return.* He describes the moment he made the decision to leave: "The decision was made, the die was cast. From that night onward, I would serve the true and living God, not the Great Architect of the Universe. I would exalt and learn of Him, not Osiris, Krishna or Demeter. I would seek and follow Jesus, not the will-of-the-wisp of hidden wisdom."

This brief glimpse shows clearly that the beliefs underpinning Freemasonry, which Jim Shaw rejected in favour of conventional Christianity, appear to be closely associated with an ancient Egyptian philosophy. From that perspective, Freemasonry would seem to be an ideal candidate for a movement designed to protect ancient Egyptian philosophy and maybe, if it exists, the sacred pharaonic bloodline.

Perhaps the question that should be asked is this: if Freemasonry does not exist to maintain and protect the Ancient Egyptian beliefs and philosophy, what is its underlying purpose? An association designed to promote or protect the interests of its members would never have needed to refer to Ancient Egyptian paraphernalia to achieve their objectives. Since the organisation was itself born in the fourteenth century CE the rituals and ceremonies that exist today must have been incorporated at that time and it is the maintenance of these rituals that has brought them through undamaged for six centuries. It is known that the Knights Templar were accused of and condemned for practising strange rituals and it is perhaps reasonable to assume that the artefacts and rituals of Freemasonry came directly from the traditions that had been constructed by the Knights Templar, out of their discoveries in the Middle East.

Why were those rituals established? What was it that was discovered by the Knights Templar and subsequently passed to the Freemasons?

Since the sixteenth century, Roman Catholics have been banned from becoming Freemasons and this prohibition has continued until the present time. In 1985, the US Catholic Conference Bishops' Committee on Pastoral Research and Practices concluded in its letter to American bishops concerning Masonry that "the principles and basic rituals of Freemasonry embody a naturalistic religion, active participation in which is incompatible with Christian faith and practice." On September 15, 2000, the Reverend Thomas Anslow, Judicial Vicar of the Roman Catholic Archdiocese of Los Angeles, wrote a letter to David Patterson, Executive Secretary of the Masonic Service Bureau of Los Angeles. In reply to the question of whether a practicing Catholic may join a Masonic Lodge, Father Anslow said, "At least for Catholics in the United States, I believe the answer is probably yes." This letter was publicly retracted by Father Anslow on February 12, 2002, with the explanation that his analysis was faulty. He said that Freemasonry fostered a "supra-confessional humanitarian" conception of the divine "that neutralizes or replaces the faith dimension of our (Roman Catholic) relationship with God."

On March 1, 2007, Archbishop Ginafranco Girotti, the regent of the Apostolic Penitentiary, made a statement that membership in Masonic organisations "remains forbidden" to Catholics, and he called on priests who had declared themselves to be Freemasons to be disciplined by their direct superiors. This was in reaction to the declaration that the eighty-five-year-old Italian priest Rosario Francesco Esposito had declared himself a Freemason, even though he was once commissioned by the Church to study the Church's teaching on masonry.

The Catholic Church believes that the route to God is through the Church and through Jesus. The Freemasonry concept that there is a direct route to God eliminates the Church's raison d'être, and because of this, it is small wonder that Freemasonry has been condemned. If other more fundamental questions are at the heart of the conflict, we are not aware of them. However, the ongoing alienation of Freemasonry does imply that the Roman Catholic Church fears this organisation and its impact.

Whatever the truth of it, we cannot know if the Freemasonry movement exists to protect a royal bloodline and/or to promote its public re-emergence in any more formal way than may exist at present. All we can say is that if there is such a movement, Freemasonry is the most likely mainstream candidate for the organisation to guard and protect its secret existence.

The fact that we do not know of and cannot specify the location of descendants of Jesus does not invalidate our general hypothesis. During two millennia, there are a myriad of possibilities. However, given the importance of the bloodline, we would expect that it was administered carefully and protected to ensure its continuance.

CHAPTER 19

The Covenant

Whilst the examinations made here do not confirm the general hypothesis that Jesus was the son of Ptolemy XIII, we have presented strong circumstantial evidence pointing towards the hypothesis being valid and none that proves it fallacious.

Three of the gospels do report that Jesus made a pronouncement regarding his blood at the last supper with his disciples. Using the conventional translation from the Ancient Greek, Luke tells us,

> *"And in the same way He took the cup after they had eaten, saying, "This cup which is poured out for you is the new covenant in My blood." (Luke 22:20)*

Even with amendment, it is easy to see that this statement indicates a covenant *in* my blood and prompts us to ask what the author was trying to say.

In John 16:26, it is reported that Jesus tells us that he speaks figuratively. This being the case, we must ask ourselves if the extract from Luke (above) is also meant to be figurative. In addition, it is probably worth mentioning that the Greek words in which the original document was written have alternative meanings in English:

- The word for cup can be translated divine appointment or lot.
- The word for covenant could be read as will or arrangement.
- The word for blood could be read as seat of life or essence.

- Poured out could equally be read bestowed.
- For can be translated as over, above, or on behalf of.

Using the alternative words and meanings, we could have a translation that reads as follows:

> *And after this he supped the cup in like manner saying, "This, the divine appointment, the arrangement by (means of) the blood of me, this lot/covenant is bestowed on/over you."*

Here, Jesus was saying that his divinity was an outcome of his inherited blood or the bloodline of which he was a part. For the first time we have direct evidence of a link between the divine status claimed by Jesus and his blood. His divine status and his title Son of God are only claimed by Jesus because of his blood. He is acknowledging his place in the pharaonic bloodline that started with the first god-king Osiris.

In this Luke version of the Last Supper, Jesus is also being magnanimous, in that he is saying that this arrangement by the blood is bestowed on his listeners. By implication, there is a command here that the arrangement by blood should be honoured and protected.

Matthew's version of the same events contains some additional words:

> *"And when He had taken a cup and given thanks, He gave it to them, saying, "Drink from it, all of you for this is the blood of me, of the covenant, which is poured out for many for forgiveness of sins." (Matt. 26:27-28)*

Matthew claims that the blood is bestowed/poured out for the forgiveness of sins or wanderings from the path of honour. Such an addendum is not included in the Gospels of Mark or Luke, and because of that, we must either assume that it is embellishment by the author of Matthew or that there is a deeper meaning.

Greg Rigby

The words "the blood bestowed/distributed for many for for-giveness of sins" can be translated from the Greek as "the blood bestowed for many unto/for wanderings from the path of hon-our/violations of the divine law." This implies that the many are expected to maintain the path of honour, which, in the context of the hypothesis we proclaim means that the speaker believes there is an imperative to maintain the path of honour, which is part of some kind of central belief system. More importantly, he says that the blood is bestowed to stimulate reconciliation to this system. In contrast, the translation made by the Church is one that justifies the story that Jesus's blood was spilled and that he died in recompense for the sins of humanity.

Over and above the dialogue, there are certain intriguing elements to the reports concerning the organisation of the Last Supper:

- Though Matthew tells us that the twelve disciples were present, commentary about the events at the last supper is not included in John's gospel. This is a significant omission, and it provokes one to speculate whether John's commentary of the event was edited from the Gospel, or if the Gospel of John was written after the event by an author who was someone other than John.
- Matthew tells us in verse 18 that Jesus said, *"Go into the city to a certain man, and say to him, 'The Teacher says, "My time is near; I am to keep the Passover at your house with my disciples."'* Who is this certain man whose name is so carefully omitted?
- Mark's account of this certain person is even more intriguing: *"And He sent two of His disciples and said to them, 'Go into the city, and a man will meet you carrying a pitcher of water; follow him; and wherever he enters, say to the owner of the house, "The Teacher says, 'Where is My guest room in which I may eat the Passover with My disciples?'"' And he himself will show you a large upper room furnished and ready; prepare for us there."* (Mark 14:13-15)

Here we have an unnamed person who is wealthy enough to own a large house, who is not known to the disciples, but who is sufficiently well known to Jesus that he is prepared to give over his large guest room. One can only wonder at the relationship between the two and the ways that relationship was established.

How could Jesus know a wealthy man in Jerusalem unbeknown to his disciples? In what circumstances had they previously met when none of the disciples were not in attendance? Does this relationship imply a group of people or an organisation separate from the disciples?

Over and above that, there would appear to have been some kind of understanding or arrangement previously made. Had this been made by Jesus and the owner of the house directly, or had there been an intermediary? If the latter, the only obvious intermediary who was a confidante of Jesus and not one of the twelve would have been Mary Magdalene.

We showed earlier that there was a possibility that the events surrounding the crucifixion and the resurrection were planned and quite possibly contrived. The above passages indicate conclusively that a lot of organisation was incorporated into the measures taken immediately preceding those events. It seems that nothing had been unforeseen.

The fact that the disciples were not part of these detailed plans points to the possibility that there was some hidden agenda. The circumstances provoke speculation that the apostles were encouraged to believe in the crucifixion and resurrection in order that they would have the zeal to prosecute Jesus's message. Strangely, the apostles were, for the most part, absent from the death and the subsequent resurrection of Jesus, and because of that, the stage was left available for the implementation of any planned subterfuge.

Hidden confidantes of Jesus and Mary Magdalene might have included Joseph of Arimathea, the wealthy member of the council who interceded to have Jesus's body taken down from the cross. According to Mark, only he, Mary Magdalene and Mary the mother of Jesus "saw where Jesus was laid," and they were most likely to have been parties to any deception. The field was certainly wide open for Jesus's death and resurrection to have been contrived. The fact that Jesus appears in the flesh to the disciples and shows himself to be a mortal human being after his reported death and so-called resurrection would seem to add credence to this possibility.

If Jesus did not die, he had created the opportunity to disappear along with Mary Magdalene and maybe accompanied by or with the help of Joseph of Arimathea. In this scenario, we have the beginnings of an organisation to protect Jesus and his children and to keep all of their identities hidden.

The people of the Egyptian empire had been defeated and overcome by the Jews, the Greeks and the Romans. They had moved away from the path of righteousness. Only the blood of the pharaonic line could bring back honour and truth and forgiveness for this horrendous wrong.

Conclusion

W e have not proved that Jesus was the son of Ptolemy XIII. However, this analysis finds no facts or obstacles that would disprove such a hypothesis. On balance, we believe that it is a real possibility. More than that, if there is to be a rational explanation of the Jesus story that does not call on mysticism and divine intervention to explain it, it is probably the only credible explanation. It would explain Jesus's conception and life as portrayed in the gospels and perhaps more importantly, Jesus's belief that he was of divine heritage and that this heritage was based on blood.

As to the maintenance and perpetuation of the lineage, we have no information that points directly to any person or organisation that might be involved with such a well-planned and covert operation. The only organisation that fits the obvious profile of protector of the Pharaonic sacred beliefs and maybe protector of the sacred bloodline is Freemasonry—why else do Freemasons do what they do?

If there is a person alive who is the descendant of Jesus, he or she is not making it obvious, and to that extent, it could be argued that if the Freemasons are members of an organisation that has been created to hide the truth, they have done a remarkably good job. The order of Freemasons is known to be a society/ organisation with secrets. If one puts these words *freemasons, secrets* into the Google search engine, it offers an alternative sub-heading: *freemason's secrets revealed*. This is nonsense, of course, since a secret is something that isn't revealed. Anything that is revealed is no longer a secret.

No one will ever know the truth. It is for this reason that the mantra of "it's a matter of faith" will be a convincing argument for devout Christians. Whatever the truth of it, the followers of

Jesus Christ were extremely successful in building an organisation to promote their belief that Jesus was the divine Son of God incarnate who took human form and then was crucified to atone for the sins of humankind. Though fantastic in any sense of the word, this reading of the Jesus story and the message that Jesus's disciples proselytised down the ages is unlikely but it may be true and valid.

In this analysis, we have presented an alternative explanation: Jesus was the son of the Egyptian Pharaoh Ptolemy XIII and by Egyptian tradition held the title Son of God. He was born to perpetuate the royal and divine bloodline from Osiris and to consolidate an imperial dynasty. He may even have believed, based on what he had been told that he was divine. In this scenario, those helping to protect and secretly ensure the perpetuation of this bloodline believed that they would be rewarded when they died and they joined God in heaven. Those who proselytise Jesus and his teachings have kept his identity hidden. It is possible that they were never told the truth but in their portrayal of Jesus's conversations, they betrayed much of what he had been taught of his role and of its implications. Jesus even admitted that to understand him, one needed to read between the lines.

Jesus's ministry was consolidated by the contrivance of his death and resurrection, which was executed in a manner that it fooled many of those close to him. So convinced were they that they felt energised to preach the message that they sincerely believed they had been given, whilst the truth was hidden and suppressed.

The alternative is that the disciples of Jesus knew and understood his real identity, and they deliberately connived to promote the divine attributes he was deemed to possess as god-king in the pharaonic bloodline that linked directly to Osiris.

It is impossible to prove which if any of these scenarios was the true one. Devout Christian believers are blinded by their faith from consideration of any logical alternative. In many cases, their world would collapse if they were persuaded to believe that Jesus is not the living Son of God who through congregation exists to protect them, forgive them and give them solace.

Others, who may be interested to consider alternative explanations, have little real evidence to help them. All we can offer here is a possibility that seems to fit the facts as they have been recorded.

When we look back at the ancient Egyptians, we see people who we judge to have been deluded in their adoration of what seems to have been a fanciful portrayal of God in his/her many aspects. However, it is important to remember that the people of that time were as sincere in their beliefs as Christians are today.

Over the five thousand years that have passed since Egyptian records were made, scientists have shown that the stars and the patterns they make are not gods, and that the astronomical deductions that were made in the earliest of times led priest-astronomers to reach ill-founded conclusions.

In the future, quantum physicists will help us find information about reality and our perceptions of it that may change our view regarding the infinite controlling intelligence that we know as God. From our position of relative ignorance, we can only guess what their history of the twenty-first century and its religious beliefs will be.

APPENDIX 1

Gematria Isopsephia

The practice of giving each letter of the alphabet a numerical value was initiated in the wider Mesopotamian area. Each letter had a value, and therefore the value of each word was the sum of the values of the letters in the word. At that time, all the gods had numbers, which Simo Parpola has shown to be numerically related by the Assyrian Tree of Life. For example, Sargon (d. 705 BCE) states that the perimeter of his palace at Khorsabad (16,283 cubits) was equal to his name.

This practice was in common use in Babylon in the eighth century BCE and was further developed in Greece under the influence of Pythagoras (circa 500 BC) where it was known as Isopsephia (equal (to) the calculation/count). So, for example, Zeus is the Geometric Mean of Hermes and Apollo. This common use is an indication that the science was developed earlier than this and may have been a key to the development of alphabets in the Middle East.

The Hebrew Gematria came from the Greeks. It is claimed that textual specialists, Soferim (counters), were specialists in Gematria and that they used their skill to ensure that the scriptures and Torah were replicated without error.

Number	Greek	Hebrew
1	α	א
2	β	ב
3	γ	ג
4	δ	ד
5	ε	ה

7	ζ	ז
8	η	ח
9	θ	ט
10	ι	י
20	κ	כ
30	λ	ל
40	μ	מ
50	ν	נ
60	ξ	ס
70	ο	ע
80	π	פ
100	ϱ	ק
200	ς	ר
200	σ	
300	τ	שׁ
400	υ	ת
500	φ	ך
600	χ	ם
700	ψ	ן
800	ω	ץ

The Egyptian Pharaohs

Name	Date	Known as
Ptah/Hephaestus		Craftsmen and Creation
Ra		Sun
Shu		Air
Geb/Cronus		Earth
Osiris		Afterlife
Set/Typhon		Chaos, war
Horus/Orus		War, Sky
Thoth		Knowledge
Ma'at		Order
Second dynasty of gods	1255 years	Dynasty of half-gods
Three Achu Dynasties	1790 years	Thirty kings from Memphis
Dynasty of disciples of Horus	350 years	Ten kings from Thinnis
Hsekiu		
Khayu		
Tiu		
Thesh		
Neheb		
Wazner	c. 3100	
Mekh		
(destroyed)		
Double Falcon		
Scorpion 1	c. 3150	
Iry Hor	c. 3150	
Ka	c. 3100	
King scorpion	c. 3150	

1st Dynasty		
Narmer (Menes)	c. 3150	He who ensures
Hor-Aha		Horus the fighter
Djer		The ruler has come (defender of Horus)
Djet		Serpent of Horus
Merneith		Beloved of Neith
Den		King of Upper and lower Egypt, the one of the two deserts
Anedjib		He with the bold heart; beloved founder of the brazen throne
Semerkhet		King of Upper and lower Egypt, he of the two ladies; companion of the divine community
Qa'a		King of Upper and lower Egypt, he of the two ladies, he is kissed by them (he from the north)
Sneferka	c. 2900	His Ka (soul) is completed/perfect
Horus Bird		
2nd Dynasty		
Hotepsekhemwy	c. 2890	King of Upper and Lower Egypt, he of the two ladies, the satisfied; Sehotep-Nebty (He who pacifies the two ladies)
Raneb		King of Upper and Lower Egypt; he of the two ladies, Nebra
Nynetjer		Godlike one of the two ladies
Weneg		Weneg-Nebty, Uneg (King of Upper and Lower Egypt, he of the two ladies, Weneg)

Senedj	Sethenes,
Seth-Peribsen	King of Upper and Lower Egypt, he of the two ladies, Peribsen; he who comes forth by will of Seth
Sekhemib-Perenmaat	King of Upper and Lower Egypt, he with powerful force of will, he of the two ladies, who comes forth for the Ma'at
Khasekhem	Horus, he whose two powers appear
3rd Dynasty	
Djoser c. 2686	Tosorthos, Sesorthos, King of Upper and Lower Egypt, he of two ladies, with a divine body; golden one of Ra
Sekhemkhet	Djoser-tety, Tyreis, powerful body of Horus; the two ladies are pleased with his name
Sanakhte, Nebka, Nakht-Sa,	Horus Sa; Horus, the victorius protector
Khaba	Hor-Khaba (the soul of Horus appears); Hudjefa II (the soul of Horus appears)
Huni	Ny-Suteh, Nisut-Hu, Hu-en-Nisut, Qahadjet, Kerpheris, Aches
4th Dynasty	
Sneferu c. 2613	Soris (he who makes things perfect)
Khufu	Cheops, Suphis, Sofe, Saurid, Salhuk, Chnoubos (I am protected); he who crushes the enemies for Horus
Djedefre, Radjedef, Ratoises, Rhampsinit, Rhausis,	The son of Ra; he endures like Ra

278

Name	Date	Description
Khafra, Suphis II, Saophis,		Son of Ra; he appears like Ra; strong heart of Horus
Menkaura		Mykerinos, Menkheres (His Kas will stay like Ra; bull of the divine company)
Shepseskaf		Severkeris (his Ka is noble); Horus, noble of body
Djedefptah		Thamphthis

5th Dynasty

Name	Date	Description
Userkaf	c. 2498	Usercheres (his ka is powerful)
Sahure		Sephres (he who is close to Ra); Horus, Lord of apparitions
Neferirkare Kakai		Beautiful is the soul of Ra, Sekhemunebu, Khaiemnebty (he who is the perfect form and Ka of Ra)
Shepseskare Isi		
Neferefre		Isi, Raneferef (beautiful is Ra)
Nyuserre ini		Rathoris (ossessed of Ra's power)
Menkauhor Kaiu		Menkeris (eternal are the souls of Horus)
Djedkare Isesi		The soul of Ra endureth
Unas	2375–2345	Oenas, Unis, Wenis,

6th Dynasty

Name	Date	Description
Teti	c. 2345	Othoes; Horus, who satisfies the two lands
Userkare	c. 2333	The soul of Ra is strong
Meryre Pepi I	2332 - 2283	Beloved of Ra; Neferdjahor, Phiops; Horus; He of the perfect protection
Merenre Nemtyemsaf 1	2283 - 2278	Nemty is his protection; Beloved of Ra

Neferkare Pepi II	2278 - 2247	Perfect is the soul of Ra; Phiops; Divine of apparitions
Neferka	2200 - 2199	
Nefer	2197 - 2193	
Aba	2193 - 2176	
Merenre Nemtyemsaf II	2184 -	The Lord of strength is Ra
Neitiqerty Siptah		
7th and 8th Dynasties		
Netjerkare	c. 2181	Divine is the Ka of Ra
Menkare		Stable is the Ka of Ra
Neferkare II		Perfect is the Ka of Ra
Neferkare III Neby		Perfect is the Ka of Ra, the protector
Djedkare Shemai		The Ka of Ra endures; a wanderer
Neferkare IV Khendu		Perfect is the Ka of Ra; he who treads
Merenhor		Beloved by Horus
Neferkamin		Sneferka (perfect is the Ka of Min)
Nikare		He belongs to the Ka of Ra
Neferkare V Tereru		Perfect is the Ka of Ra
Neferkahor		Perfect is the Ka of Horus
Neferkare VI Pepiseneb	2278– 2184	Neferkare Khered Seneb (perfect is the Ka of Ra), Pepi (the child) is healthy
Neferkamin Anu		Sneferka Anu, Nefer, Nufe
Qakare Ibi	c. 2170	Aba Iby, Kakere, Kakaure, Qaikare (mighty is the soul of Ra)
Neferkaure	c. 2160	Khabau (perfect are the Kas of Ra)

Neferkauhor Khuwihapi		Chuwihapi (perfect are the Kas of Ra)
Neferirkare II		Demegjibtawy (he who unifies the heart of two lands; what the Ka of Ra does is perfect)
9th Dynasty		
Merybre Khety (Acthoes I)	c. 2160	Kheti, Akhtoy, Achtoes, Merybtawy
Unkown		
Nebkaure Khey (Acthoes II)		Kheti, Akhtoy
Senenh		Setut
Unknown		
Mery -		
Shed -		
10th Dynasty		
Meryhathor	c. 2130	Neferkare-Meryibre (beloved of Hathor by the heart of Ra)
Neferkare VIII		Beautiful is the Ka of Ra
Wahkare Khety (Acthoes III)		The Ka of Ra is purified; the divine ruler
11th Dynasty		
Iry-pat	2134 -	Intef son of Iku
Mentuhotep I Mentuhotepa Marysatetnebetabu		Father of the Gods (Mentuhotep the great) (Beloved son of Satet, lady of Abu); Hor Tepia (the ancestor)
Sehertawy (Intef I)		Antaf, Inyotef, Anjotef, Enyotef, Horus Sehertawy (Son of Ra); (maker of peace in the two lands)
Wahankh (Intef II)	2112 - 2063	(Enduring of life) Inyotef II, Antef II, (Son of Ra) (Strong in life)

Greg Rigby

Nakhtnebtepnefer (Intef III)		Nakht-neb-Tepnefer (King of Upper and Lower Egypt, Son of Ra, Intef, fashioner of beauty, living like Ra) (Son of Ra)
Nebhetepre (Mentuhotep II)	2060 - 2010	Horus; he who invigorates the heart of the two lands; the divine one the white crown; the Lord of the Rudder is Ra; the son of Hathor, the lady of Dendera; Mentuhotep
Sankhare (MentuhotepIII)	2010 - 1998	He who embellishes the soul of Ra; He who invigorates the two lands
Nebtawyre (Mentuhotep IV)	1998 - 1991	Lord of the two lands of Ra; the God Montu is content
12th Dynasty		
Sehetepibre Amenemhet I	1991 - 1962	The son of Ra; Wehemmesu (Rebirth; He who makes the heart of Ra satisfied; Amen is the foremost
Kheperkare Senusret I (Sesostris I)	1971 - 1926	The Ka (soul) of Ra is created; the man of Useret
Nubkaure Amenemhet II		Golden are the souls of Ra; Amen is at the head
Khakheperre Senusret II (Sesostris II)	1897 - 1878	The Ka of Ra comes into being; the man of Useret
Khakaure Senusret III (Sesostris III)	1878 - 1839	Appearing like the souls of Ra; the man of Useret
Nimaatre Amenemhet III Lamares, Ammenemes	1860 - 1814	Belonging to the justice of Ra; the king of Lower and Upper Egypt; Amen is the foremost
Maakherure Amenemhat IV		True of voice; justified is Ra; the son of Ra
Sobekkare Sobekneferu	1806 - 1802	Nefrusobek

13th Dynasty		
Sekhemre Khutawy Sobekhotep (Wegaf)	1802 - 1800	Mighty Ra, who protects the two lands; Sobek is pleased
Sonbef	1800 - 1796	Amenemhat Senbef
Nerikare	1796	Sobek
Sekhemkare Amenemhat V		Powerful of soul, Ra; the son of Ra; Amen is foremost
Ameny Qemau	1793 - 1791	Aminikimau, Ameny-Amu, Amen's son Qemau
Hotepibre Qemau Siharnedjheritef	1791 - 1788	Law of Ra; Qemau's son; Horus he who seizes power
Iufni		Jewefni, Afni; He belongs to me
Seankhibre Amenemhet VI	1788 - 1785	He who causes the heart of Ra to live; Amen is his father; Amen is the foremost
Seankhibre Nebnuni		Nebennu; Lord of the foreign countries; Nu is my lord
Sehetebibre Sewesekhtawy	1783 - 1781	The king of Upper and Lower Egypt; he who satisfies the heart of Ra
Sewadjkare		He whom the Ka of Ra causes to flourish
Nedkemibre		Ra; he who pleasures the heart
Khaankhre Sobekhotep	1780 - 1777	Son of Ra; pleasing to the God Sobek; living as the apparition of Ra; powerful like Ra
Renseneb	1777	My name is healthy
Awybre Hor I	1777 - 1775	Hor; the friend of Ra; Horus
Sekhemrekhutawy Khabaw	1775 - 1772	Mighty Ra; he who protects the two lands; permanent renewal

Greg Rigby

Djedheperew	1772 - 1770	Ka of Ra; enduring of manifestations; enduring of births
Sebkay		
Sedjefakare		Amenemhat VII (Amen is the foremost); the Ka of Ra is flourishing
Khutawyre Wegaf	1794 - 1757	Ra protects the two lands; the power of the Gods
Khendjer		Userkare (the soul of Ra is powerful); Boar
Imyremeshaw		Mermeshau (Vigorous is the Ka of Ra); overseer of troops
Sehetepkare Intef	1759 - 1749	The one who appeases the soul of Ra; His father brought him
Seth Meribre		He who is beloved of the heart of Ra
Sekhemresewadj-tawy Sobekhotep III		Pleasing to the god Sobek; powerful is Ra; he makes to flourish the two lands
Khasekhemre Neferhotep I	1742 - 1730	Beautiful and pleasing; the might of Ra appears
Medwadjre Sihathor		Ra, the son of Hathor; Ra, he whose prosperity is lasting
Khaneferre Sobenhotep IV		Pleasing to the god Sobek; the perfect apparition of Ra
Merhotepre Sobenhotep V		Pleasing to the god Sobek; beloved satisfaction of Ra
Khahotepre Sobenhotep VI		Pleasing to the god Sobek; the satisfaction of Ra appears
Wahibre Ibiau		Constant is the heart of Ra; he whose heart is pure
Merneferre Ay I	1701 - 1677	He who loves the perfection of Ra
Merhotepre Ini	1677 - 1675	Ana, Inai, In(j); beloved satisfaction of Ra

284

Sankhenre Sewadjtu	1675 - 1672	The one who Ra has brought to life; he who is caused to flourish
Mersekhemre ined		Neferhotep II (beautiful and pleasing); he who loves the power of Ra
Sewadjkare Hori	1669 - 1664	He who causes the Ka of Ra to flourish
Merkawre Sobenhotep VII	1664 - 1663	Pleasing to the god Sobek; he who loves the Kas of Ra
Seven kings unknown		
Merkheperre	1663 - 1649	Beloved manifestation of Ra
Merkare	1663 - 1649	Beloved Ka of Ra
Sewadjare Mentuhotep V	c. 1655	The God Montu is content
Four kings unknown		
Seheqenre Sankhptahi		He whom Ka causes to rule; he whom Ptah causes to live
Two kings unknown		
Dedumose I	c. 1654	The peace of Ra is stable; a god has fashioned him
Dedumose II		Enduring and perfect is Ra; a god has fashioned him
Sewahenre Senebmiu		
Snaaib	c. 1649	Established are the apparitions of Ra; he who causes the two lands to flourish
14th Dynasty (Coincident with 13th Dynasty based in Itjtawy)		
Yakbim Sekhaenre	1805 - 1780	He who appears through Ra— Semetic ruler of the Delta
Ya'ammu Nubwoserre		Ra is the golden ruler; Yammu

285

Greg Rigby

Qareh Khawoserre	1770 - 1760	Ra is the mighty apparition; the bald one
Ammu Ahotepre		Ra is greatly pleased
Shesh	c. 1630	Maaibre Sheshi; Manetho; Beon; seeing is the heart of Ra
Nehesy		The Hall of the Council of Ra is pleased; the Nubian
Khakherewre		
Nebefawre		
Sehebre		Wazad, Sheneh (he whom Ra causes to be festive)
Merdjefare		
Sewadjkare III		
Neddjefare		
Webenre		
Unknown		
Djefare		
Webenre	c. 1690	
Sekheperenre		He who Ra causes to come into being
Anati Djedkare		
Bebnum		The Ka of Ra
Apep		
Wazad		The good god Wazad given life
Sheneh		
Shenshek		The rescuer
Khamure		
Yakareb		
Yaqub Har	c. 1650	The son of Ra; strong is the love of Ra
15th Dynasty		
Semqen	1649 -	Ruler of the foreign lands

Aper Anat		Ruler of the foreign lands; dust of Anat
Sakir Har		Ruler of the foreign lands; he who subdues the bow people
Khyan		
Apepi		Ra is the lord of strength; great is the power of Ra; Seheteptawy; he who pacifies the two lands
Khamudi	1555 - 1544	The last Hyksos ruler
Abydos Dynasty		
Sekhemraneferkhau Wepwawetemsaf		King of Abydos; Apuatemsaf; mighty Ra; he whose apparitions are perfect Wepwawet is his protection
Sekhemrekhutawy Panyjeny		He of Thinnis; mighty Ra; he who protects the two lands
Menkhaure Snaaib		Established are the apparitions of Ra; he who causes the lands to flourish
Woseribre Senebkay	c. 1650	
16th Dynasty		
Djehuti Sekhem-resemantawy	1650 -	King of Upper Egypt
Sobenhotep VIII Sek-hemresemantawy		Djehuty; Dhout; pleasing to the god Sobek; powerful is Ra; he makes to flourish the two lands
Neferhotep III Sek-hemresemantawy		Beautiful and pleasing; powerful is Ra; he makes to flourish the two lands
Mentuhotep VII Seankhenre	1628 - 1627	The god Mentu is content
Nebiryraw I Sewadjenre	1627 - 1601	

Greg Rigby

Nebiriau II		
Semenre		He who is established by Ra
Bebiankh Seuserenre	1603 - 1588	
Dedumose I Djedhotepre		Tutimaos; the peace of Ra is stable; a god has fashioned him
Dedumose II Djedneferre		Enduring and perfect is Ra; a god has fashioned him
Montuemsaf Djedankkhre		Enduring of life like Ra; Mentu is his protection
Merankhre mentuhotep VI		He whose life is beloved by Ra
Senusret IV Seneferibre	-1580	Man of Goddess Wesret; he who delights the heart of Ra; Sankhtawy; he who nourishes the two lands; Neferkhaw; beautiful of apparitions
17th Dynasty		
Sekhemrewahkhaw Rahotep	c. 1650 -	Mighty is Ra; enduring of apparitions; Ra is satisfied
Sekhemre wadjkhaw Sobekemsaf I		Sobek is his protection; Powerful Ra, whose apparitions are flourishing
Sekhemre Shedtawy Sobekhemsaf		Mighty Ra, saviour of the two lands; Sobek protects him
Sekhemre-Wepmaat Intef		Mighty like Ra; he who judges righteously; his father brought him; the great
Nobkheperre Intef		The golden apparition of Ra; his father brought him
Sekhemre-Heruhirmaat intef		Mighty like Ra is the one who satisfies Maat
Senakhtenre Ahmose		Perpetuated like Ra; Iah bore him; beloved of Maat

Seqenenre Tao		He who Ra makes brave; Thoth is great
Kamose	1555 - 1550	Flourishing is the manifestation of Ra; he who is born of the bull; he who appears on his throne
18th Dynasty		
Nebpehtire Ahmose I	1550 - 1525	The Lord of strength is Ra; son of Iah; perfect of birth
Djeserkare Amenhotep I		Holy is the soul of Ra; Amun is satisfied; he who inspires great fear
Aakheperkare Thutmose I		Great is the manifestation of the soul of Ra; son of Thoth
Aakheperenre Thutmose II		Great is the form of Ra; son of Thoth
Maatkare Hatshepsut		Truth is the soul of Ra; joined with Amun; flourishing of years
Menkheperre thutmose III	1466 - 1412	Established is the form of Ra; son of Thoth; enduring in kingship like Ra in heaven
Aakheperrure Amenhotep II	1414 - 1388	Great are the forms of Ra; Amun is satisfied
Menkheperure Thutmose IV	1388 - 1378	Established of forms is Ra; son of Thoth
Nebmaatre Amenhotep III	1378 - 1339	Lord of truth of Ra; Amun is satisfied; one establishing laws; pacifying the two lands
NeferKheperure-waenre Amenhotep IV/Akhenaten	1339 - 1322	Beautiful are the manifestations of Ra; dearest of Ra; Amun is satisfied; glare of the sun
Ankhkheperure Smenkhkare	1324 - 1321	Living are the manifestations of Ra; vigorous is the soul of Ra; holy of forms
Nebkheperure Totankhateen/ Tutenkhamun	1321 - 1311	Lord of manifestations of Ra; living image of Amun

289

Greg Rigby

Kheperkheperure Irimaat Ay	1311 - 1307	Everlasting are the manifestations of Ra, who does what is right; God's father Ay
Djeserkheperure-setpenre Horemheb	1320 - 1307	Holy are the manifestations of Ra; the chosen one of Ra; Horus is in jubilation;
Djeserkheperure-setpenre Horemheb	1320 - 1307	Holy are the manifestations of Ra; the chosen one of Ra; Horus is in jubilation;
Meriamun	-1292	Beloved (son) of Amun; he who is great of miracles in Ipetsut
19th Dynasty		
Menpehtire Ramesses I	c. 1292/3-1291/0	Eternal is the strength of Ra; son of Ra He who appears as a king like Atum
Menmaatre Seti I		Eternal is the strength of Ra; he of the God Seth, beloved of Ptah
Usermaatre-setpenre Ramesses II	c. 1279/90	Ramesses meryamun; the justice of Ra is powerful; chosen of Ra; son of Ra; beloved of Amum; protector of Egypt who curbs foreign lands
Banenre Merenptah		Son of Ra; the soul of Ra; beloved of the gods; beloved (son) of Ptah; joyous is truth
Menmire-setpenre Amenmesse		Son of Ra; eternal like Ra; the chosen one of Ra; fashioned by Amun; the ruler of Waset
Userkheperure Seti II		Powerful are the manifestations of Ra; the chosen one of Ra; Seth; beloved of Ptah

Sekhaenre/Akhenre Merenptah		Siptah; Akh spirit of Ra; the chosen one of Ra; Ra fashioned him; son of Ptah
Satre-merenamun Tausret	1191 - 1190	Daughter of Ra; beloved of Amun; mighty lady chosen of Mut
20th Dynasty		
Userkhaure Sethnakht Mereramonra	1190 - 1186	Powerful are the manifestations of Ra; chosen of Ra; Set is victorious; beloved (son) of Amon-Ra
Usermaatre-mayamun Ramesses III	1186 - 1155	Powerful is the justice of Ra; beloved (son) of Amun; son of Ra
User/Heqamaatre-setpenamun Ramesses IV	1155 - 1149	Ruler of justice like Ra; son of Ra; beloved (son) of Amun; the protector of Egypt
User maatre-sekheperenre Ramesses V	1149 - 1145	Powerful is the justice of Ra; shaped/formed by Ra; son of Ra
Nebmaatre-meryamun Ramesses VI	1145 - 1137	The lord of truth like Ra; beloved (son) of Amun; son of Ra; he whose blow is powerful
Usermaatre-setpenre-meryamun Ramesses VII	1137 - 1130	Powerful in justice like Ra; chosen of Ra; beloved (son) of Amun; son of Ra
Usermaatre-akhenamun Ramesses VIII	1130 - 1129	Powerful in justice like Ra; chosen of Ra; life of Amun; son of Ra
Neferkare-setpenre Ramesses IX	1129 - 1111	Beautiful is the soul of Ra; chosen of Ra; son of God; he whose bow is powerful invigorates the two lands
Khepermaatre-setpenptah alKhem Ramesses X	1111 - 1107	The justice of Ra abides; chosen of Ptah; son of Ra

Greg Rigby

Menmaatre-setpenptah Ramesses XI	1107 - 1077	Eternal is the justice of Ra; chosen of Ptah; son of Ra
21st Dynasty		
Hedjkheperre-setpenre Nesbanebdjed Smedes I	1077 - 1051	Radiant manifestations of Ra; he of the Ba ram; Lord of Mendes; beloved of Amun; mighty of power
Neferkare Heqawaset Amenemnisu	1051 - 1047	Perfect is the Ka of Ra; Amun is king
Aakheperre Pasebakhennuit Meriamun I Psusennes I		Great is the manifestation of Ra; the chosen (son) of Amun
Usermaatre Amenemope Meriamun		Powerful is the Maat of Ra; the chosen of Ra; beloved (son) of Amun
Aakheperre Setepenre Osorkon	992 - 986	Great is the manifestation of Ra; the chosen (one) of Ra
Netjerikheperre-setpenamun Siamun-meryamun		Divine is the manifestation of Ra; beloved (son) of Amun
Titheperure Setepenre, Pasebakhennuit II Mariamun, Psusennes II	967 - 943	Image of the transformations of Ra; the chosen one of Ra; Horus, the star who appears in the city; beloved son of Amun
22nd Dynasty		
Hedjkheperre-setepenre Shoshenq I Meriamun	943 - 922	Radiant is the manifestation of Ra; the chosen one of Ra; Sheshenq, beloved (son) of Amun
Sekhemkheperre Osorkon I Meriamun		Powerful are the manifestations of Ra; the chosen one of Ra; Osorkon, beloved (son) of Amun

Heqakheperre Shoshenq II Meriamun		The manifestation of Ra rules; the chosen one of Ra; Shoshenq, beloved (son) of Amun
Hedjkheperre Setepenre Takelot I Meriamun	885 - 872	Radiant manifestation of Ra; the chosen one of Ra; Takelot, beloved (son) of Amun
Hedjkheperre Setepenanum Harsiese Merianum		Radiant manifestation of Ra; the chosen one of Amun; Horus, son of Isis, beloved (son) of Amun
Usermaatre-setepenanmum Osorkon II Merianum	872 - 837	Rich in Maat is Ra, the chosen one of Amun; Osorkon, beloved (son) of Amun
Usermaatre-setepenre Shoshenq III Meeriamun	837 - 798	Powerful is the Maat of Ra, the chosen one of Ra; Shoshenq, beloved (son) of Amun
Shoshenq IV Maryamun Sabast Netjerheqaiunu	798 - 785	Radiant is the manifestation of Ra; the chosen one of Ra; Shoshenq, beloved (son) of Amun
User maatre-setepenre Pami		Powerful is the Maat of Ra; chosen one of Ra (Amun); Pami, beloved (son) of Amun; son of Bast; divine ruler of Iunu
Aakheperre Shoshenq V	778 - 740	Great is the soul of Ra
Aakheperre-setepenamun Osorkon IV Meriamun	740 - 720	Great is the manifestation of Ra; chosen by Amun; Oskoron, beloved (son) of Amun
23rd Dynasty		
Hedjkheperre-setpenre Takelot II-siese-meramun	837 - 813	Radiant is the manifestation of Ra; the chosen one of Ra; Takelot, son of Isis, beloved (son) of Amun

Usermaatre-setepenanum Meriamun-Pedubast		Powerful is the justice of Ra; the chosen one of Amun; beloved (son) of Amun; the gift of Bastet
Usermaatre-setepenanum Iuput I	812 - 811	Rich in Maat is Ra; the chosen one of Amun; Iuput, beloved (son) of Amun
Usermaatre Maryamun, Shoshenq VI Meryamun	801 - 795	Powerful is the Maat of Ra; beloved (son) of Amun; Shoshenq, beloved (son) of Amun
Usermaatre-setepenanum Osorkon III Maryamun Saiset	795 - 767	Rich in Maat is Ra; the chosen one of Amun; Oskoron, beloved (son) of Amun, son of Isis
Usermaatre-setepenanum Takelot III Meriamun Siese	773 - 765	Powerful is the Maat of Ra; the chosen one of Amun; Takelot, beloved (son) of Amun, son of Isis
Usermaatre-setpenanum Meriamun Rudamun	765 - 762	Powerful is the Maat of Ra; the chosen one of Amun; beloved (son) of Amun; Amon is strong
Menkheperre Ini	c. 740	Enduring is the apparition of Ra; son of Ra
24th Dynasty		
Shepsesre Tefnakhte	732 - 725	Noble like Ra; son of Khet
Wahkare Bakenrenef (Bocchoris)	725 - 720	Constant is the heart of Ra
25th Dynasty		
Usermaatre Piye	752 - 721	Usimare Sneferre
Neferkare Shabaka	721 - 707	Beautiful is the soul of Ra
Djedkaure Shebitku	707 - 690	Enduring is the soul of Ra

Khuinefertemre Taharqa	690 - 664	Nefertum is his protector
Bakare Tantamani	664 - 653	
26th Dynasty		
Menkheperre Nekau I (Necho I)	672 - 664	Lasting is the manifestation of Ra
Wahibre Psamtik I (Psammetichus I)		Aaib, Neba
Wehemibre Nech II (Necho II)	610 - 595	Maaib, Maakheru
Neferibre Psamtik II (Psammetichus II)	595 - 589	
Haaibre Wahibre (Apries)	589 - 570	Jubilant is the heart of Ra forever Constant is the heart of Ra
Khnemibre Ahmose II (Amasis II)	570 - 526	He who embraces the heart of Ra forever The moon is born; son of Iah
Ankhkaenre Psamtik III (Psammetichus III)	526 - 525	
27th Dynasty	525 - 404	Egypt conquered by Persia; the Achaemenid Shahs were acknowledged as Pharaohs in the period
28th Dynasty		
Amytaeus Amenirdisu	404 - 398	Directly related to the kings of the 26th dynasty (Amen causes him to be given)
29th Dynasty		
Baenre Nepherites I, Nefaarud I Psamtik I	398 - 393	Soul of Ra, beloved of the gods; the great ones prosper; of great mind

Psammuthes Userre setpenptah	393	Powerful is Ra, chosen of Ptah; child of Mut
Khenemmaatre Hakor (Achoris)	393 - 380	Justice is the heart of Ra; great of intellect who loves the two lands
Nefaarud II Nepherites II	c. 380	
30th Dynasty		
Kheperkare Nekhtnebef (Nectanebo I)	380 - 362	The manifestation of the Ka of Ra; the strong one of his lord
Irimaatenre Djedher (Teos)	362 - 360	Carrying out the justice of Ra
Senedjemibre Nakhthorhebyt (Nectanebo II)	360 - 342	Pleasing is the heart of Ra; chosen of Onuris; one who contents the hearts of the gods
31st Dynasty	343 - 332	Egypt again came under Persian rule
Argead Dynasty		
Setepenre-meryamun Alexander III		Chosen of Ra; beloved (son) of Amun who was pronounced the Son of Amun at the Oracle of Siwa Oasis; calls Zeus-Ammon his true father; legend that Nectanebo II was Alexander's real father.
Meryamun Setepenre Philip III Arrhidaeus		Beloved (son) of Amun; chosen of Ra; brother of Alexander III
Alexandre IV Haaibre Setepenamun	317 - 305	Jubilant is the heart of Ra; chosen of Amun; son of Alexander III

Ptolemaic Dynasty		
Setepenre Meryamun Ptolemy I Soter I (Lagides)	305 - 285	Chosen of Ra; beloved (son) of Amun; son of Lagus (myth that he was brother of Alexander)
Berenice I	? - 285	Wife of Ptolemy I
Weserkare-meryamun Ptolemy II Philadelphos	288 - 246	Powerful is the soul of Ra; beloved (son) of Amun; son of Ptolemy I and Berenice I
Arsinoe I	284 - 274	Wife of Ptolemy II
Arsinoe II	277 - 270	Daughter of Ptolemy I and Berenice I
Ptolemy III Euergetes I— Iwaennetjerwy-senwy Sekhemank-hre Setepanum	246 - 222	Heir of the twin gods; chosen of Amun; benefactor; son of Ptolemy II and Arsinoe I
Berenice II	244 - 222	Wife of Ptolemy III
Ptolemy IV Philo-pater Setepptah Userkare Sekhemankhamun	222 - 204	Father-loving; heir of the twin gods; chosen of Amun; son of Ptolemy III and Berenice II
Arsinoe III Philopater	220 - 204	Queen; beloved of the father (child of God); daughter of Ptolemy III and Berenice II
Hugronaphor horwennefer	205 - 199	Ruler of Upper Egypt; the one on high forever
Ankhmakis - Chaonnophris or Ankhwennefer	199 - 185	Ruler of Upper Egypt; key of life; close to god; Osiris still lives; everlasting; key of life forever
Ptolemy V Epiphanes	204 - 180	Illustrious one; son of Ptolemy IV
Cleopatra I (Thea Epiphanes)	193 - 176	Wife of Ptolemy V; illustrious goddess
Ptolemy VI Philometor	180 - 164	Mother-loving; son of Ptolemy V and Cleopatra I

Cleopatra II	175 - 164	Daughter of Ptolemy V and Cleopatra I
Ptolemy VIII Euergetes II (Physcon)	171 - 163	Father was Ptolemy V mother Cleopatra I Syra
Ptolemy VI Philometor	163 - 145	Restored
Cleopatra II	163 - 127	Daughter of Ptolemy V and Cleopatra I
Ptolemy VII Neos Philopater	145 - 144	New beloved of the father (new son of God); son of Ptolemy VI and Cleopatra II
Ptolemy VIII Euergetes II	145 - 131	Restored
Cleopatra III Euergetes— (benefactor) Cleopatra Philometor Soyeira	142 - 131	Queen of Egypt 142 - 101 Second wife of Ptolemy VIII; benefactor; Mother-loving saviour
Ptolemy Memphitis	131	
Ptolemy VIII Physcon Euergetes II	127 - 116	Restored - Father was Ptolemy V; mother was Cleopatra I Syra (meaning sausage or potbelly)
Cleopatra III— Cleopatra Kokke	127 - 107	The scarlet one; restored with Ptolemy VIII; coregent with Ptolemy IX and X
Cleopatra II	124 - 116	Restored; daughter of Ptolemy V and Cleopatra I; married both her brothers
Ptolemy IX Soter II - Lathyros	116 - 81	Son of Cleopatra III and Ptolemy VIII
Cleopatra IV	116 - 115	Daughter of Ptolemy VIII and Cleopatra III; married her brother Ptolemy IX
Ptolemy X Alexander I	110 - 109	Son of Ptolemy VIII and Cleopatra III

Berenice III	81 - 80	Daughter of Ptolemy IX and Cleopatra Selene I
Ptolemy XI Alexander II	80	Son of Ptolemy X
Ptolemy XII Neos Dionysos (Auletes)	First reign 80 - 58	The new Dionysus; son of Ptolemy IX
Cleopatra V Tryphaena	79 - 68	Daughter of Ptolemy IX
Cleopatra VI Tryphaena	58 - 57	Daughter of Ptolemy VIII
Berenice IV	58 - 55	Bearer of victory; daughter of Ptolemy XII
Ptolemy XII Neos Dionysus Theos Philopater Auletes	Restored 55 - 51	New Dionysus; God; beloved (son) of the father; son of Ptolemy IX
Cleopatra VII Philopater	51 - 30	Beloved (child) of the father; Horus name—the great one; sacred image of her father
Ptolemy XIII Theos Philopater	51 - 47	Beloved (son) of the father God; son of Ptolemy XII; married to co-ruler, his sister Cleopatra VII
Arsinoe IV	48 - 47	Youngest daughter of Ptolemy XII
Ptolemy XIV - Theos Philopater II	47 - 44	Beloved (son) of the father God; younger son of Ptolemy XIII; brother of Cleopatra with whom he co-ruled
Ptolemy XV Philopater Caesarion	44 - 30	Son of Cleopatra and Caesar

Review Requested:
If you loved this book, would you please provide a
review at Amazon.com?

Lightning Source UK Ltd.
Milton Keynes UK
UKOW02f1042030416

271405UK00001B/42/P